POPE JOHN XXIII
Model and Mentor for Leaders

Pope John XXIII

Model and Mentor for Leaders

May 22, 2003

To Marsha
*May this tale of Pope John
inspire you in your
continuing leadership in
interfaith work.*

W Bonnot

Rev. Bob (Bernard R.) Bonnot, Ph.D.

ST PAULS

Alba
House

Library of Congress Cataloging-in-Publication Data

Bonnot, Bernard R. (Bob).
    Pope John XXIII: Model and mentor for leaders / Bob (Bernard R.) Bonnot.
        p. cm.
    Includes bibliographical references and index.
    ISBN 0-8189-0916-1 (alk. paper)
    1. John XXIII, Pope, 1881-1963. 2. Christian leadership. 3. Leadership.
4. Management.   I. Title.

BX1378.2 .B63 2002
280'.092—dc21

                                                            2002018565

Produced and designed in the United States of America by the
Fathers and Brothers of the Society of St. Paul,
2187 Victory Boulevard, Staten Island, New York 10314-6603,
as part of their communications apostolate.

ISBN: 0-8189-0916-1

Printing Information:

Current Printing - first digit   1   2   3   4   5   6   7   8   9   10

Year of Current Printing - first year shown

2003   2004   2005   2006   2007   2008   2009   2010   2011   2012

Dedication

To

Bishop James W. Malone

Model, Mentor, and Leader
in the pattern of
Blessed Pope John XXIII

Table of Contents

Part II: Getting the Job Done

Conclusion

Preface

Pope John XXIII was one of humankind's notably successful leaders during the 20th century, unexpectedly so. He didn't get the job because he was recognized as a great leader. To the contrary. Nonetheless, he emerged as a great leader and got the job done. He managed a revolution in one of the most conservative of human institutions. How Pope John did that provides a model for anyone who cares to learn from him.

This book is set up as a manual with case-study for leaders and managers. Each chapter briefly states an essential principle of successful managerial leadership, then studies John's record as an exemplification of that principle, concluding with questions to help each reader apply the principle and John's modeling of it to their own situation. Thus can John become a mentor to all who will accept him.

I hope this book will lead its readers and others to look at John also as the patron saint of leadership, specifically of the managerial kind. His fame rests on what he did in four and a half short years as CEO — Chief Everything Officer — of the Roman Catholic Church. Pope John Paul II declared him "blessed" in September, 2000. That is just one step short of being formally declared a "saint." Whether and when the final step is taken, this book documents how Pope John XXIII stands as a model and mentor for leaders at all levels in all sorts of organizations, from pastors to presidents, and that he merits standing as their patron saint.

I thank Sr. Angela Ann Zukowski, MHSH, of the University of Dayton, past president of Unda-World, a global

Catholic organization for communicators, for urging me to refresh my work on Pope John in conjunction with his being declared "blessed." Fr. Edmund Lane, Editor-in-Chief of Alba House, readily undertook publishing a reworked version of my 1979 Alba House volume on Pope John XXIII. Cardinal Roger Mahony and Moderator of the Curia Msgr. Terrance Fleming of the Archdiocese of Los Angeles together with Fr. Robert Milbauer, pastor of St. John Baptist de la Salle Parish in Granada Hills, CA, have provided hospitality and support during its writing. I thank my current bishop, Thomas J. Tobin of Youngstown, OH, for his graciousness in continuing my assignment to national communications work.

Most especially, I thank Bishop James W. Malone, former bishop of Youngstown, now deceased. Throughout his episcopacy he admirably modeled what he learned from Pope John during the Second Vatican Council's first session in 1962, providing inspiring leadership for me and my brother priests in Youngstown as well as many others throughout the world. As my bishop, he afforded me the opportunity to do the doctoral studies in administration that enabled me to grasp Pope John's surprising success and write about it. Finally, I thank my parents for bringing me into this world and God for sustaining me through completion of this essay — and I hope beyond.

I dedicate this work to Bishop Malone, in homage to Pope John XXIII. I offer it as a gift to administrators, managers and leaders of all sorts. In the end, administrative and managerial leadership is ministry — service to God and God's people. May all who lead as servants be blessed.

Fr. Bob (Bernard R.) Bonnot
Los Angeles, CA, October 11, 2002
40th Anniversary of the
Opening Session of Vatican II

Starting Point: Getting the Job

Whatever the Reason You Got the Job,
Seize the Opportunity and Do Something With It
Whoever You Are, Be Yourself, Drawing on Your Strengths
Respect History, Your Own and the Organization's
Play the Hand you are Dealt (Status of the Organization)

How we wind up with our current job is often a mystery. The job itself and the organization in which it is embedded may be mysteries too. We may have sought the position; the position may have sought us. We may have "fallen into it"; it may have "fallen on us." Whatever the case, once you are entrusted with managerial responsibilities, which is to say leadership, at any level, you've got a job to do. You have to do it starting from where you are (your background and status) and from where your organization is now (its background and status). And you must play the particular hand you are dealt at the specific point in time that you assume your role as the leader (the job's history and status). That includes how you got the job.

Pope John's story embodies some wisdom about starting points that may help you deal with yours. This chapter tells you enough about how he got his job (rather unexpectedly), the history of the organization he was asked to lead (the Catholic Church worldwide), its specific situation when he was put in charge (at the end of the long "reign" of Pope Pius XII in a Church ready for change in a world recovering from real war but locked in a cold one), the status of his role (strongly stamped by Pius XII's style) and the status of the bureaucracy that surrounded him (decayed and dysfunctional), the dynamics of his career (a functionary of the Roman bureaucracy yet distant from it), and who he was as he took it on (himself: a peasant and a pastor). Knowing something about all that may give you insight into your own starting point and what you might do now that "you've got the job."

How John XXIII Got His Job[1]

The Catholic Church's universal pastor and chief executive officer is elected. The story of how that happened in John XXIII's case is intriguing. He was elected by at least 35 of 51 votes (2/3 plus one) cast by a group of mostly old men, the cardinals of the Roman Catholic Church able to get to the consistory in 1958. No one knows for sure what happened because all 51 involved were sworn to secrecy and the archives won't be opened until about 2040. All 53 of the cardinals then alive were in some sense candidates, including József Mindszenty from Hungary and Alojzije Stepinac from Yugoslavia. They could not get to Rome from behind the Iron Curtain and so could not vote. Only five of the 53 were considered serious candidates. Angelo Cardinal Roncalli, Patriarch of Venice, was one of them, but not the favorite. He was the dark horse. If we do not know exactly how he got the job, we do have some idea as to why.

Five factions can be discerned among those who elected John XXIII and among the five viable candidates. Identifying and analyzing those factions will shed initial light on the situation John XXIII faced. Geographical and ideological factors were at play. The geographic factors can be reduced to a divide between the Italians and the non-Italians. The Italians meant primarily the Romans, i.e. those in or closely associated with the Vatican bureaucracy, then dominated by Italians. The non-Italians were those from beyond the Alps who wanted a more international perspective in the papacy, perhaps even a non-Italian. The French represented this approach most strongly. In many respects this tension reflected the standard organizational dilemma of whether to promote an insider or bring in an outsider. John fit both profiles. He was an Italian whose career had been largely in the Vatican bureaucracy, but that very career had kept him outside Italy (in Bulgaria, Turkey, Greece, and France) or distant from the Vatican (in Venice). That experience left him with the mindset of an outsider.

Five Factions

Analysts have discerned five ideological factions in the 1958 conclave that elected John XXIII.

The first and seemingly most powerful group was rooted in the bureaucracy which runs the Church from the Vatican, the Curia. Thirteen cardinals worked there, most of them decidedly conservative.[2] They had an apprehensive approach to Church affairs, especially theology. This curial bloc tended to see any change as a threat to the eternal values they felt bound to defend. As a result they clung to the past and resisted all development in theological thinking and Church teaching. They stood for the integrity of the Catholic heritage and so were called "integralists."

A second group consisted of a minority of cardinals who worked in the Vatican.[3] They too were conservative, but less fearful and more open to new developments. Reportedly, some even favored the election of a non-Italian. To be effective, this group would have to ally itself with other groups of cardinals coming to the conclave from outside Rome.

A third group consisted of a few cardinals from northern

Italy.[4] Though small, this group was open and progressive in its thinking and constituted a potential ally for those with reservations about candidates put forward by the "integralist" faction. Roncalli, then Cardinal Patriarch of Venice in northeast Italy, was well known to them.

A fourth group consisted of the French cardinals. They held a position that strongly contrasted with the dominant curial position. After World War II, the Church in France had seeded new developments in both theology and pastoral practice. Postwar French theologians such as Henri de Lubac, Jean Danielou, M.-D. Chenu and Yves Congar had generated what came to be called the "new theology." Such French hierarchs as the great Emmanuel Cardinal Suhard of Paris had faced the fact that their country was dechristianizing. They explored revolutionary approaches to the problem, such as the worker-priest program that sent ordained clergy into factories. Their innovative approaches to both theology and mission challenged the traditional concepts and structures favored by the Roman Curia. Pope Pius XII's response was the doctrinal encyclical of 1950, *Humani generis*, which chastised the new theology, followed in 1954 by a disciplinary decision that severely restricted the worker-priests. As a result the French came to the conclave of 1958 wanting leadership that would respect their energies and initiatives and adopt a more open approach. They looked to the few cardinals from other lands who were addressing pastoral problems with fresh initiatives for support in the conclave.

The fifth and last group consisted of mostly non-Italian cardinals who were not strongly identified with either conservative or progressive positions. They constituted a swing group. Customarily they followed Rome's lead, but many were willing to make important decisions with open minds.

These five groups — Curial Conservatives, Progressive Frenchmen, Minority Members of the Curia, Northern-Italian liberals, and Others — determined the outcome of the papal conclave of 1958.

Five Candidates

The above five factions of cardinals gathered in Rome thinking about the presumed *papabili* or "popables." These too were five. A very young (52) and conservative Guiseppe Cardinal Siri from Genoa was the integralist candidate. The colorful and innovative Giacomo Cardinal Lercaro from Bologna was the progressive candidate. An Armenian, Pietro Cardinal Agagianian, a bland and careful veteran of the Curia, was the centrist candidate. The likely compromise candidate was the moderately conservative Aloisi Cardinal Masella, Italian and curialist but one with service abroad. The cardinals had chosen him to run the Church during the interregnum. The fifth *papabile* and other potential compromise candidate was Angelo Cardinal Roncalli, Patriarch of Venice.

Roncalli stood center-left on the spectrum sketched above. A holy, expansive, and pastoral man, he was enormously popular in his own diocese. His Venetian background gave him special prestige as one of only two Patriarchs in the West (the other being from Lisbon). A previous Patriarch of Venice, Giuseppe Sarto, had become Pope Pius X in 1903. Roncalli had served for nine years as nuncio to France, the center of progressive Catholic thought. For many years before that, he was the Vatican's representative to Bulgaria, Greece and Turkey, predominantly Orthodox and/or Muslim countries. He was pious, devout and pleasant. He had no profile as a leader of thought nor did he identify sharply with any particular faction. Being from northern Italy, he had some association with the progressive faction there — Archbishop Giovanni Battista Montini of Milan and Cardinal Lercaro of Bologna. Roncalli was just a week shy of 77 but still vigorous.

Who John Was When He Got the Job

Before the conclave, Angelo Giuseppe Roncalli enjoyed a reputation as a good and holy man, a devoted churchman, a veteran papal diplomat, and a beloved pastor. He was not particularly esteemed as an administrator, organizer, planner, manager, or leader. Indeed, there was serious question at the time whether Roncalli was adequately prepared to lead the Church. Even years later, Léon-Joseph Cardinal Suenens of Belgium, one of his strong supporters, shook his head when asked about Pope John's abilities. Administrative leadership was something about which John knew very little, he said. Was Suenens right?

The answer depends on how one defines leadership. John himself did not claim administrative expertise or outstanding leadership ability. He felt that Archbishop Montini of Milan was better qualified than he to be pope and that Montini, had he been a cardinal, would have been elected. John knew his own strengths and openly stated them in his coronation speech. He did not claim administrative or managerial skills. He presented himself simply as a pastoral leader. Some, he said,

> expect the Pope to be a statesman, a diplomat, a scientist, a social organizer, or one who is willing to accept all the forms of progress shown in modern life, without any exception.[5]

"After the vicissitudes of his life," his own ideal was to be

> like the son of Jacob, who, meeting his brothers in distress, reveals to them the tenderness of his heart and, bursting into tears, says "I am Joseph, your brother" (Gn 45:4). The new Pope, let us repeat, first of all expresses in himself that shining image of the Good Shepherd.... We wish to make this clear, that we cherish as dearest to our heart our task of shepherd of the whole fold. The other human qualities — learning, intelligence, diplomatic tact and organizing skill, may serve as an adornment and completion of papal rule, but can never be substitutes.[6]

He asked the world to pray that he would embody two qualities: gentleness and humility.

John obviously had formed views of the role he was assuming. He did not disclaim "the other human qualities." He simply did not claim them. But he possessed them, particularly an "organizing skill" that would have much to do with his success as pope. The sources of that particular skill were deep.

Born on November 25, 1881, Angelo Giuseppe Roncalli was the fourth child and firstborn son of landless peasant farmers in Northern Italy. He grew up in Sotto il Monte where he was born, a little village of one thousand inhabitants in the foothills of the Alps. His parents and early environment endowed him with a robust constitution, a shrewd native intelligence, a strong sense of human community, a simple but firm faith, and a traditional religious piety. They had little else to offer. That was enough.

In 1892, at the age of eleven, Angelo entered the seminary for the diocese of Bergamo. There certain qualities ripened that the future pope himself summarized as seriousness, wisdom, discipline, dignity, decisiveness, strength of character, firmness of convictions when tested, solid piety which makes God the center of life, order and tranquillity based on trust in providence, and a disposition for religiously inspired social action.[7]

As a student Roncalli started slowly but learned quickly. In 1901, he received a scholarship to study theology in Rome and was ordained there in 1904. During his studies he took special interest in the history of the Church, especially the papacy. He came to know the Vatican establishment of his day, the problems it faced and the contrasting currents moving within it. Most importantly, he became acquainted with Monsignor Giacomo Maria Radini Tedeschi, a Vatican prelate, who became bishop of Bergamo in 1905. Radini Tedeschi chose Roncalli, then a graduate student in canon law, to be his secretary.

Roncalli spent ten years with Radini Tedeschi in Bergamo as his chief assistant, his confidante, friend, and eventual biographer.[8] Radini Tedeschi was a progressive and energetic leader in the Italian Church at the turn of the century and Bergamo was a progressive diocese. Radini Tedeschi led with a strong sense of purpose and a planned program that he persistently pursued yet flexibly managed. His program had short-range and long-range dimensions that led eventually to a reorganization of the diocese and a major legislative assembly or "synod" to update its laws and practices. He addressed public concerns in the region regularly and also helped direct the regional, national, and international activities of the Church.

Angelo Roncalli was at Radini Tedeschi's side through all this. Among his many roles, Roncalli served as secretary of the organizing commission for the diocesan synod, was principal author of a document issued by the regional bishops, traveled with Radini Tedeschi, and met many prominent churchmen from around Italy and Europe. He also suffered with Radini Tedeschi. Rome suspected both of being sympathetic to Modernism, a contemporary strain of theology considered heretical. In short, Radini Tedeschi gave Roncalli a thorough initiation into the dynamics of Church administration and leadership.

Roncalli learned his lessons well as evidenced by his journal comments on the leadership of Radini Tedeschi's successor, Bishop Luigi Marelli:

> it always hurts me to see the bishop having nothing to say except good things about the past and bad things about the present, when he ought to be the strongest proponent of every movement which is intended to benefit Christian people. All initiatives, in whatever sector you mention, are immediately seen from the side of the dangers or defects which they might present instead of in terms of the advantages which they in fact offer. He gives me the impression of a holy and upright man, but he is absolutely negative and does not have a well-thought out program.[9]

Roncalli argued the necessity of a well defined pastoral program:

The poor bishop hesitates, then makes up his mind all of a sudden and then he turns back.... He really is a very lovable man, but as far as his vision of the modern questions and needs or the force of his ideas and program goes, he is really sad, poor — very poor. Certain situations elude his comprehension. Certain activities which would in fact bring him great honor, he does not have the courage to undertake. He gets lost and pulls back.... He impresses me as a man of great goodness and integrity, and a man greatly preoccupied about anything which is for the good of his diocese, but along with it there is a diffidence and a fear of everything that is new. He is more preoccupied with avoiding inconvenient matters and resolving one at a time the single questions which come up daily than he is with defining a clear program and throwing his energy behind it.[10]

As pope, Roncalli would combine lovableness with a clear program, courage, optimism and a willingness to try something new. Roncalli's insights into the dynamics of leadership were gained early.

During World War I, Roncalli served as a military chaplain. After the war he organized many groups and activities within his diocese, including a student hostel, a new idea at the time, and he energized several other organizational efforts.

In 1920, the Congregation for the Propagation of the Faith in Rome was looking for a "capable person, one possessed of such a spirit and initiative and of such evident organizational gifts that he can provide the spirit necessary to launch a new movement and breathe life into the Mission Works of Italy"[11] as Director. Roncalli got the job and went to Rome early in 1921. His task was to launch a national Italian organization and to integrate it with other national groups to form one international effort.

Roncalli undertook the challenge energetically and systematically. He traveled extensively to acquaint himself with the people involved, manifested considerable persuasive skills, used the press to stimulate public opinion, wrote extensively, and sought to involve the energies of as many groups as he could. He enjoyed marked success over four years, increasing income by 400 percent. More importantly he laid an organizational foundation which served the effort well for years to come. He demonstrated diplomatic skills as well as organizational abilities in dealing with delicate national sensitivities. That led Pope Pius XI to tap Roncalli in 1925 for service in the Vatican's diplomatic corps. There he would serve for the next 28 years. These many experiences in organizational leadership equipped him with skills that served him well throughout his life, especially when he became pope.

From 1925 to 1935 Roncalli served in Bulgaria, from 1935 to 1944 in Greece and Turkey, and from 1944 to 1953 in France. The first two posts were obscure, the last the most prestigious assignment in the Vatican foreign service. Roncalli's record as a diplomat was adequate but not brilliant. His assignment to Paris was the personal choice of Pius XII, against the counsel of Msgr. Domenico Tardini, his chief assistant in the Secretariat of State. Tardini would later become John's Secretary of State.

Whatever the reasons for his assignments, Roncalli accepted them. His first love was being a pastor, not a diplomat. His lengthy diplomatic assignments brought disappointment and anguish, especially his assignment to Bulgaria, an obscure outpost of the Roman Catholic world. His posting there was supposed to be brief, but it lasted for ten years during which he was passed over for promotion at least twice. His reports and recommendations were often neglected. He felt exiled but stuck with it. He plunged into the largely Orthodox and Muslim world about him. He learned to appreciate other churches and religions and to feel at home with them. He grew in self-knowledge and came to terms with his own inner struggles.

At the same time, as a diplomat Roncalli experienced large scale social and organizational change. While in Turkey he observed first hand Ataturk's national modernization process. He helped organize international relief efforts for both Turkey and Greece during World War II. He experienced directly the reorganization of the French government after the War and participated in the founding and development of UNESCO. While in France he found himself in the midst of vigorous new theological thought and pastoral experimentation. In short, he lived with large scale social change for many years in various situations. Efforts to take big and new directions did not frighten him.

In 1953 Pius XII made Angelo Roncalli a cardinal and appointed him Patriarch of Venice. It was his first assignment as a pastor, a fitting and welcome conclusion to his career. Following the pattern he had learned under Radini Tedeschi, he pursued a vigorous program of pastoral visitation and leadership in Venice, culminating in a diocesan synod in 1957. Like his mentor Radini Tedeschi, Roncalli played an active public role and sought to form public opinion. As Patriarch he was responsible for the regional leadership of the Church. In all of this Roncalli proved himself popular and competent.

This background formed Angelo Roncalli into who he was when he became Pope John XXIII in October of 1958. He was a pastor at heart, an historian by scholarly preference, an organizer and diplomat by experience. His past acquainted him with the demands of leadership, both within and outside the Church. He had definite ideas about the requirements of leadership, such as the need for a firm program and a clear purpose. He had definite skills, including an ability to use the media to influence public opinion. His core attitudes included flexibility and a willingness to collaborate with others. He was ready to serve as pope and to do the job well.

The State of the Organization and the Office in 1958

Why did the five factions sketched above come together to choose John rather than another one of the five candidates at hand? What did the organization need that turned the electors to him? The state of the Catholic Church in 1958 and the state of the papacy after Pius XII's long reign help explain their choice.

The office of the Pope in the Roman Catholic Church has evolved over nearly two thousand years. Using two criteria, (1) the position of the Church within society and culture generally, and (2) the position of the papacy within the Church, one can trace that evolution through three epochs: Ancient, Medieval, and Modern.

During the Ancient epoch, Christianity was a modest religio-social movement, not a major element of the social power structure. The Church played a predominantly religious role in society and the pope was primarily the bishop or leader of the Christian community. This period is symbolized by the Church of St. Clement in Rome, originally a private home near the Colosseum. There the early Christians met; it is named after St. Clement, the third Pope.

The Medieval epoch started when Christianity was established as the official religion of the Roman Empire. At that point the Church added a major political role to its religious one. The pope gained significant temporal power, especially after the Empire collapsed. This Medieval epoch can be symbolized by the Church of St. John Lateran in Rome (a gift from Constantine) and by the papal palaces in Avignon. It was personalized in such figures as Pope St. Leo the Great (440-461) who saved Rome from the barbarians, Pope St. Leo III (795-816) who crowned Charlemagne, and two politically powerful popes of the 13th century, Innocent III (1198-1216) and Boniface VIII (1294-1303). During this period the Church claimed the right to oversee secular powers and sought to dominate the state.

During the Modern epoch the Church lost temporal dominance and retreated again to a predominantly religious role in society, but with a difference. During this period the papacy suffered grievous humiliations in the political realm (for example, Napoleon imprisoned the Pope early in the 1800's and Garibaldi seized the Papal States in 1870), but strengthened its position within the Church to nearly absolute control. This was symbolized in the First Vatican Council's declaration of Papal infallibility and universal jurisdiction in 1870, the same year the Papal States collapsed. A series of strong popes stretching from Pius IX (elected in 1846) to Pius XII (died in 1958) resurrected a position for the Church in society and Western culture as a moral and spiritual force but with greatly reduced temporal prerogatives and pretenses. The Vatican continued to exist as a city-state with international recognition, but the pope ceased being a temporal ruler in any significant sense. Still, he was more than simply the Bishop of Rome. He was the monarch-like "ruler" of the universal Church. His decisions came to be invested with finality and an aura of infallibility. Lacking the strength to govern the world, the popes isolated themselves in the Vatican and looked out on the world with pessimistic sadness. They believed the world had gone astray and spoke authoritatively to those who governed it, trying to direct them. They considered it their divine duty and right to do so. This period is symbolized by the Church of St. Peter's within the Vatican complex and is personalized in such pontiffs as Pius IX (1846-1878) and Pius XII (1939-1958).

When in 1958 Angelo Roncalli was elected the 262nd pope,[12] the papacy seemed to be at the height of its influence in the third epoch. Few expected him to initiate a fourth epoch, yet some today suspect that he may have done so: a Post-modern, Pastoral epoch.

The Era of John's Predecessor, Pope Pius XII (1939-1958)[13]

Within each epoch several eras can be discerned, each marked by the lengthy and/or forceful rule of a given pope. Pope

Pius XII marked an era on both counts. He held the office for 19 years during which humankind experienced tumultuous events. He made the office a tent pole around which the Roman Catholic Church centered herself and through which she set herself apart from the world. Yet he attempted on her behalf to act as spiritual and moral tutor of modern people and nations.[14]

Eugenio Pacelli was admirably suited to the task which faced the Church and the papacy when the cardinals gathered in 1939 to elect a successor to Pius XI. Descended from an old family long active in Vatican affairs, Eugenio had entered the Vatican's diplomatic service in 1901 as a priest attached to the Secretariat of State. He was given important jobs and he did them well, so he rose rapidly. In 1917 he was sent to Bavaria as papal nuncio and in 1925 to Prussia. In both places he negotiated concordats, special agreements made by the Vatican with civil governments. In 1929 he became papal Secretary of State, a post he held until elected pope in 1939. He was so well prepared for the papacy that he had no rival. He was elected on the first ballot.

Pacelli had the right background to guide the Church in a world about to go to war and he had outstanding personal qualities. He was exceptionally bright, a master linguist and a hard worker. He was ascetic and intensely "spiritual" in an otherworldly sense of the term, so much so that he seemed "superhuman," "separated," "cut off," "on another plane," "with us but not like us."[15] This served him well in a role conceived as that of a religious and spiritual leader with divine guidance that enabled him to infallibly direct the Church's life and authoritatively speak to a confused human community.

Pius XII conducted a brilliant pontificate. He strengthened the internal life of the Church; issued revolutionary encyclicals on biblical studies, liturgy and the nature of the Church; reformed seminary studies, revised religious life and introduced new structures for living dedicated lives of service to the Church and humankind. He introduced major reforms into the celebration of the Church's liturgy, making it easier for people to receive the sacraments and attend Mass; he updated the Church's official thinking on practically every important modern concern. Pius XII left 20 volumes of highly technical and polished discourses and messages. He played a significant (today disputed) diplomatic role during the Second World War. He made both papacy and Church bastions of Western anti-communism in the early years of the Cold War. He received huge numbers of people from all walks of life and of many religious faiths. He was a unique phenomenon, a celebrity. With him the prestige of the papacy and of the Church rose to unprecedented heights. When he died the Church was flourishing by practically every measure, and the papacy with it. Pius XII's manner of being pope seemed right for the times.

But Pacelli's strengths had a dark side. Brilliant, capable, and "not like us," Pius pushed these talents to such an extreme that they became liabilities. He came to disdain the capacities of others and so left key offices unfilled. He did the required work himself or simply left others to do what they could in an undermanned situation. He made cardinals only twice during his 19 years. As a result only 55 of the authorized 70 held office when he died and only 13 of the standard 30 served in Vatican offices. Most of the 55 were quite old. Two of them died before the conclave to elect his successor began. Pius became a kind of theocrat, surrounding both his person and office with an aura of divinity, isolating himself except for a few trusted aides.

The results were predictable. The central administration of the Church fell into decay. Power became concentrated in the hands of a few curial officials. High-handedness ensued, a style which disturbed bishops running dioceses throughout the world. They could not stand the Curia, but they could not reach the Pope. They had no redress. The problem became acute during the last four years of Pius XII's reign (1954-1958) as the effects of a stroke aggravated his faults.

Finally, though Pius' brilliance was respected by the world, his teaching went unheeded. His words were reported, but his message was little followed. It was too abstract, too remote even for those within the Church. Thus a splendid pontificate "ended in a kind of precise Byzantinism, formality for formality's sake, generously touched with intrigue and decay."[16] Pius perfected the Modern style of papal leadership but by exaggerating certain aspects of it he provoked problems which threatened its well-being.

The Need for a Change

When Pius died, both bureaucrats in Rome and local bishops all over the world knew that an era had ended and that a change was needed. What they wanted was a change of style, a change away from isolated autocracy and divine-like mysticism. Few if any wanted a substantial change in the fundamental model of papal leadership or of the role the Church was playing in culture and society. The enterprise as a whole was doing well enough. But the working style of its head needed revision.

The cardinals who gathered in 1958 to elect a new pope, regardless of outlook, recognized this need for a change. Practically all had experienced individual difficulties in getting to see Pope Pius XII and in dealing with or working in the Curia. Once they gathered and compared notes, the need became even more apparent. Their group was advanced in age and missing such leading churchmen as Montini of Milan, a brilliant aide to Pius XII for many years but still only an Archbishop. The understaffing of the Curia resulted in a few cardinals holding several major positions. Two cardinals present, Thomas Tien Chen Sin who was exiled from China and Stefan Wyszynski of Poland, represented Catholics living under Communist regimes. The absence of two others from Communist nations, Mindszenty of Hungary and Stepinac of Yugoslavia, suggested the need to do more for those churches than Pius XII's rigid anti-communism had.

Their feeling that a change of tone was needed found official voice in the traditional *De eligendo pontifice* ("As Regards Electing the Pope") speech delivered to the assembled cardinals. Msgr. Antonio Bacci of the Curia[17] delivered this speech after consultation with many leading cardinals. He articulated the emerging consensus of the 1958 College of Cardinals as a whole. Bacci praised Pius XII's great virtues, noting that he had won for himself such admiration that "it seemed he should live forever." But then Bacci sketched the characteristics most needed in the new pontiff: that he be able to build peace among peoples and make the Christian religion flourish in both private and public morals; that he be a man of courage penetrated with the most intense charity especially toward the churches suffering persecution; that he be a strong teacher who could address the rampant errors of modern society and destroy them; that he be an especially effective pastor, a man who would strive to be a "Good Shepherd" (*pastor* in Latin), willing to lay down his life for his sheep. In particular, the new pope would need to

> freely receive and welcome the bishops whom "the Holy Spirit has chosen… to rule the Church of God" (Acts 20:28). He will be ready to give them counsel in their doubts, to listen to and comfort their anxieties, and to encourage their plans.[18]

This last quality had been notably missing in Pius XII. Finally, Bacci insisted that the new pope had to be a true "pontifex," a bridge-builder and himself a bridge, a good example of priestly qualities and holy life.

In short, Bacci's speech called for a good and holy man who would carry on the basic functions of the papacy — to teach, govern, and embrace with pastoral love — while letting others play their legitimate role in the leadership of the Church. It called for a change of style, not a change of direction.

How John Grasped His Starting Point

The conclave that chose John did not elect him merely to hold the fort. Things needed attention. On the other hand, he was old and a compromise choice. It took four days to elect him (compared to the 20 hours needed to choose Pius XII in 1939 or the two days spent selecting Paul VI, John's successor, in 1963). On August 10, 1961, Roncalli himself wrote in his spiritual journal that he had been elected to be a "provisional and transitional pope."[19]

Still he was given a mandate to *restore* Vatican affairs to normality after the neglect and decay occasioned by Pius XII's decline. That was the challenge facing Angelo Roncalli when the cardinals elected him in October of 1958. "Provisional and transitional" he might be, but he had to refurbish the central ecclesiastical bodies that assisted the pope and restore the papacy and Church to a richer contact with the day-to-day life of the world. That at least is how Angelo Roncalli grasped his starting point.

On October 17, eight days before the conclave, he wrote a letter to the rector of the seminary in Venice asking for prayer that the next pope "not represent a solution of continuity." He felt the need for a change, at least of style.[20] On the 24th he wrote to Bishop Giuseppe Piazzi of Bergamo:

> A word about my entry into conclave. It's like an invocation I make by the voice of the bishop to all that which is dearest to my heart as a good Bergamasco. Reflecting on the many venerated and beloved images of Mary found in our diocese and remembering all of our patron saints, our bishops, our holy and outstanding priests, and our religious men and women of special virtue, my soul is conflicted with confidence in the new Pentecost which will be given to the Church through the renewal of its head, the reconstruction of the ecclesiastical organism, and a new vigor in pursuing the victory of truth, of good-

ness and of peace. It matters little whether the new
pope be a Bergamasco or not. Our common prayers
should be that we get a leader [*uomo di governo*] who
is wise and meek, who is holy and who makes others
holy. Your Excellency, you know what I mean.[21]

This quickly jotted paragraph manifests that Roncalli had synthesized the needs of the Church all were talking about and had
outlined a program which would meet those needs. He did this
using a religious intuition which would soon make him famous
and beloved. The phraseology of his private letter to Bishop
Piazzi would soon become common vocabulary for the world's
Catholics: new Pentecost, renewal, reconstruction (i.e. restoration or renewal), truth-goodness-peace, new vigor (youthfulness), gentle wisdom, contagious holiness. In Roncalli's view,
these words expressed the mandate the conclave would give its
electee. And clearly he knew he was in the running.

Another letter written that same day, October 24, confirms
that Roncalli recognized the possibility and indeed the probabil-
ity that he would be elected. He was getting ready to take the
job. Writing to Giuseppe Battaglia, an old friend, then Bishop
of Faenza, Roncalli admits that he is anxious and preoccupied.
He invites his friend to pray with him Psalms 77 and 86 in
which, "you will find the emotions my spirit is experiencing."
Both are prayers in times of distress. The psalmist cries out for
help, asking whether God has abandoned him. But then he finds
comfort in recalling the way of the Lord and the great wonders
God has done for his people in the past. He remembers that it
is God himself who leads his flock. He asks God, "Teach me
your way that I may walk in your truth: direct my heart that it
may fear your name." The psalmist ends his prayer confident
that God will indeed help and comfort him.

Those were precisely Roncalli's sentiments. On Monday
evening, October 27th, the day before he was elected, Roncalli
wrote in his journal a passage that later became famous:

Who is it that rules the Church? Is it you or the Holy
Ghost? Well, then, Angelo, go to sleep.... I feel as if
I were an empty bag that the Holy Spirit unexpect-
edly fills with strength.[22]

The next morning Roncalli's anticipations were confirmed when
Maurilio Cardinal Fossati of Turin told him, "if God wants you
to become pope, it is obvious that he will give you all the gifts
and strength necessary to overcome all difficulties."[23] Already
by then John had scribbled out a list of 22 previous popes who
had taken "John" as their name. By the afternoon he had
scratched out additional notes about why he would take John
as his papal name. He took these scraps of paper to the last balloting of the conclave. A few minutes after the cardinal in charge
announced the conclusive count, he asked Roncalli what name
he chose. At that point Roncalli said, "I will be called John!"
pulled out his scraps of paper, and made the first statement of
what his pontificate would mean. It would change the Church
profoundly. Roncalli had been a dark horse, but once elected
he led the Church in ways no one could have predicted, probably not even himself.

What John Had to Manage and Lead

John's "starting point", like every leader's, was heavily con-
ditioned by how the papacy was organized when he took over.
One expects an organization two thousand years old to be complex and the Vatican certainly is. In 1958, it consisted of four
main components: the Papal Office, the College of Cardinals,
the Curia, and the Court. All except the Court, which Pope John
significantly reduced and/or eliminated during his term of office,
are important for grasping his pastoral strategy.

The complexity of the papacy is suggested simply by list-
ing the pope's titles: the Vicar of Jesus Christ, Successor of the
Prince of the Apostles, Supreme Pontiff of the Universal Church,

Patriarch of the West, Primate of Italy, Archbishop and Metropolitan of the Roman Province and Sovereign of the Vatican State. Titles from other epochs include "Rector of the World upon Earth" and "Father of Princes and Kings." In the early Church he was simply the Bishop of Rome. Today the preferred title is "Servant of the Servants of God." Yet all those titles generate expectations for the office.

The word "pope" reflects the growth of the papacy. It is derived from either the Greek (*pappas*) for "father" or the Latin (*pater patrum*) for "father of fathers." Originally it referred to the great patriarchs of the East and to senior bishops in the Latin Church. In 1073, Pope Gregory VII forbade its use for anyone except the Bishop of Rome, at least in the Western Church. The title is still used for others in some Eastern Churches.

The general impression all these titles make is that the papacy enjoys supreme authority within the Roman Catholic Church. That is in fact the case. The issue was conclusively settled in 1870 when the First Vatican Council defined the primacy of the pope. That decree stated, among other things, that the pope held "the full plenitude of the supreme power" of jurisdiction. Even after the discussion of Vatican II which sought to balance the power of the pope with the power of bishops, the supremacy of the pope is explicit:

> in virtue of his office, that is, as Vicar of Christ and pastor of the whole Church, the Roman Pontiff has full, supreme, and universal power over the Church. And he can always exercise this power freely.[24]

In short, the pope is the chief legislator, administrator, teacher, and judge in the Church. Nothing in the life of the Church is beyond his competence.

However, the pope shares this power with a bureaucracy consisting of two main branches, the College of Cardinals and the Curia. The College of Cardinals is a body of individuals (all male clerics) appointed by the pope with a twofold task: to elect a new pope when the current one dies and to serve as advisors to him during his reign. As the scope of the Church and of papal power waxed and waned through time, the size and composition of the college has varied. In 1958 it was authorized to have a maximum of 70 members. Today it is authorized to have significantly more than that. A major distinction sets those cardinals in charge of dioceses, caring directly for people, apart from those who are in charge of major Vatican offices, working full-time in the Curia directly with the pope. Thirty of the seventy cardinals were normally *in curia,* the vast majority of them Italians. Pius XII started to internationalize the College by naming more heads of non-Italian dioceses cardinals and also by appointing a few non-Italians to major Vatican offices.

A mutual relationship exists between the pope and the College of Cardinals. The College elects the pope and the pope constitutes the College by his appointments. The pope remains absolute. The College is in no sense a legislature or board. Its only real power is that of electing the pope. As individuals, however, the curial cardinals hold considerable power by virtue of their proximity to the pope and their positions in the Curia.

The Curia is a bureaucratic structure that assists the pope in governing and administering the Church. In 1958 it consisted of twelve congregations (equivalent to cabinet level departments in the U.S.), three tribunals (courts) and six executive offices. Its basic structure developed after the Council of Trent (c. 1586) but was reorganized in 1910 by Pius X (1903-1914). His structure was written into the Code of Canon Law in 1917 under the brilliant supervision of Eugenio Pacelli, who became Pius XII. Further revisions were implemented after Vatican II by Paul VI in 1967. Pope John Paul II approved a new Code of Canon Law in 1983.

The 1910/1917 reorganization of the Curia made the Congregation of the Holy Office and the Secretariat of State (one of the six executive offices) particularly prominent in the workings of the papacy.

The Holy Office was called "supreme" because it enjoyed

doctrinal, legislative, administrative and judicial power. Its competence was not limited by any other congregation. Its preeminence reflected the doctrinal preoccupations of the Roman Church at that time.

The Secretariat of State is the office on which the pope relies most heavily in his administration of the Vatican's extensive diplomatic network and of the Curia as well. Under Pius XII it became a miniature double of the curial structure, facilitating his autocratic centralization of power. It became quite large yet retained a flexibility and immediacy that could not be matched by any other office. When Pius XII died, about 1200 persons worked in the Curia, one hundred plus of them in the Secretariat of State.

Given this capsule description of the Curia one can begin to see the papacy as a highly centralized bureaucratic organization in which the pope holds all the power. He is assisted in his supreme responsibilities by a series of committees (the congregations) whose task it is to elucidate and interpret the laws of the Church (i.e. the Code of Canon Law) and to supervise their proper application. The instructions and decrees they issue and the decisions they formulate constitute a commentary on the Code and have the weight of law. Significant new understandings of the law cannot be adopted without the consent of the pope. The tribunals give further help by adjudicating specific cases. However, they cannot legislate new points of law. The offices provide predominantly administrative help. A series of ad hoc committees (commissions) and auxiliary offices fill out the organization.

The Curia works according to committee-centered procedures. The process is such that the pope controls all curial operations and any significant developments that might occur there, but the Curia itself maintains enormous control of the day-to-day operations of local dioceses scattered throughout the world. The Curia can determine whether something goes forward or is stopped; whether new ideas and directions rise to the attention of the pope or not. This is especially true if the pope cuts himself off from non-curial channels of communication, as did Pius XII. The top man in each congregation (called either Prefect or Secretary) and the second man (called either Secretary or Assessor) thus hold considerable power. They decide what goes to the pope.

When Pius XII died the Curia was afflicted with intrigue and decay. The decay set in as a result of Pius' failure to make appointments to the College of Cardinals. This left many offices vacant and only a handful of elderly men to do the necessary work. No one, for example, held the office responsible for taking charge when Pius died. When he expired, confusion reigned.

During Pius' reign, "interlocking directorates" developed. A few cardinals held many positions and controlled many decisions. When Pius XII stopped meeting regularly with the heads of congregations following his stroke in 1954, these cardinals ran things on their own, some of them in a highhanded fashion. If the bishops of dioceses objected to their decisions, they had no recourse. It was practically impossible to get to the pope himself.

In themselves "interlocking directorates" are an asset to a committee form of government. It makes good sense to create linkages between committees by appointing the same person to two or more groups. However, when too few persons do too much of the linking, the benefit becomes a defect. A small group can then control the key positions on practically all important committees, thereby monopolizing power. This happened under Pius XII.

Five cardinals in particular — Nicola Canali, Giuseppe Pizzardo, Clemente Micara, Alfredo Ottaviani, and Adeodato Piazza — held numerous positions. One observer dubbed them collectively the "Vatican Pentagon."[25] Canali and Pizzardo (84 and 81 respectively) had influence over Vatican finances. These two together with the younger Ottaviani (68) were especially powerful. Ottaviani served as their chief ideologist and spokesman.

The important dimension of this particular interlocking directorate was not the individuals involved or the positions and power they held but the mentality they represented. Their outlook stemmed from the concerns of the Church at the turn of the 20th century. Pope Leo XIII (1878-1903) had attempted to relate to modern developments more positively than had the negative Pius IX (1846-1878). Unfortunately Leo's efforts to update Catholic thinking in the fields of philosophy, theology, scripture and history led to a severe reaction known as the Modernist Crisis during the reign of Pope Pius X (1903-14). This stance took the form of a systematic pursuit and elimination of anyone suspected of any of a set of errors collectively called "Modernism." This concern about the errors attending some contemporary thinking caused Rome to be cautious about anything new and adamantly attached to the past. Anything which introduced change, anything which looked or sounded new, was suspect. A clandestine spy network was established throughout the Catholic world. Vigilante committees were established to protect the Church from the threatening dangers. This mechanism, with multiple ties to the Curia, persisted well into the 1950's.

The resulting Church mentality was called "Integralism." Neither conservative nor progressive as such, Integralism is "concerned merely with eternal values, [and is]... prone to see these threatened by any change of their temporal embodiment.... The integralist thinks to preserve only by ossification."[26] Integralists attached themselves to form, alienating themselves from the changing world. In large part, that was the stance of the Curia in 1958 — rooted in the past, estranged from the present and determined to maintain their position in the future while combating "modern errors."

Many of the men who held high positions in Rome in 1958 started their Vatican careers during the anti-Modernistic period. Their mentality had been set at that time and since Integralism suspects change, they grew little over the years. Furthermore, because Rome controls appointments to the hierarchy around the world, by 1958 many of the Church's bishops reflected the same closed mindedness. Priests who became bishops often studied in Rome, many at the Lateran University where Integralism reigned. Many Lateran graduates staffed Vatican offices.

Integralists were content with Pius XII during most of his reign. His doctrinal purity and otherworldly spirit made him a perfect symbol of the integralist understanding of Catholicism. On the other hand, Pius' willingness to allow new developments in scripture, theology and liturgy were unsettling. When Pius died the integralists were clearly in control. They knew what they wanted in the new pope: someone less aloof, less autocratic, even less impressively capable than Pius XII. They wanted a peacemaker capable of making Christian values prevail in both private and public morals, a teacher to correct the errors of the day, a good shepherd who would allow others to play their legitimate role in the Church. They wanted a friend to the poor and oppressed (as opposed to Pius' aristocratic style) and a holy man. They wanted a change in style but not in substance. They wanted someone who would share authority, appoint new cardinals and rebuild the Curia. All of this was intimated in Msgr. Bacci's oration as the cardinals entered the conclave of 1958. It was also intimated in the letters and notes of Angelo Giuseppe Cardinal Roncalli as he prepared for the conclave.

But there was something in Roncalli that the integralists did not want: he was not afraid of change. He signaled that in the first words he uttered upon being elected pope. "I will be called John," a name not used by Roman pontiffs for centuries.

Questions for You from John's Model

1. Do you understand your starting point?
2. Why do you think you got the job? What evidence supports your view?
3. What is the history of your organization?
4. What is the history of the job you have?
5. What was the pattern of your predecessor?
6. What are your strengths overall?
7. What are your strengths in terms of organizational ability?
8. What elements of your biography and career have prepared you for this role?
9. What are your basic convictions about how to lead an organization and manage? What are your instincts?
10. Do you feel ready to do the job?
11. Have you come to terms with your inner struggles? Do you know yourself?
12. Are you willing to try something new with optimism and courage?
13. Can you be personable and caring while pursuing a clear and dynamic program of action?
14. How do you see yourself as related to those you will manage and lead: As friend? brother/sister? a "Good Shepherd"? or simply as boss?
15. Do you intend to embody gentleness and humility in your leadership style?
16. Whatever the reason you got the job, what do you plan to do with it?

Part I
GETTING SET

CHAPTER 1

Setting a Tone

The "first hundred days" of any administration have become mythic in terms of leadership expectations and management theory. There is a reason for that. During the first days of anyone's administration, from manager of a small department to president of the United States, one sets a tone that largely will determine the way people perceive leadership throughout its term. The first days cast a die: what is not set then is difficult to introduce later.

During his first one hundred days in office — from early November 1958 through the end of January 1959 — John XXIII set a tone to which he held firmly during his last 1600 days. This chapter traces some of the things John did to establish the tone of his papacy during his first hundred days. It might help you set and/or review your tone.

The First Hundred Days

Names have symbolic value. A pope's name, freely chosen by him, suggests the tradition out of which the new pope wishes to operate. It signals the concerns closest to his heart. Roncalli could have taken a name like Pius, Benedict, Charles, or Francis, but he chose John.[1] No pope since the Middle Ages had been called John. To be exact, a John XXIII had reigned from 1410-

1415, but since he was an "anti-pope" (there were three claimants at the time!), he was not included in the official list of popes.

Roncalli explained why he chose the name John immediately. It was his father's name, the name of his parish church, the name of many cathedrals, and the name of the two men closest to the Lord. Furthermore, it was historically the most frequently used papal name, allowing him to "hide the smallness" of his name behind the long list. Moreover, the terms of office of all the popes John were brief, as his own would likely be since he was a week shy of 77. What Roncalli said indicated his concern with humble people, parish life, and the diocesan church. But it also suggested his intent to be a reformer (like John the Baptist) and a promoter of love (like John the Evangelist). Roncalli's first speech signaled what he intended to do now that he had the job.

He wasted no time. The next day he addressed a radio message to the world. He greeted all those now under his care, expressing special concern for the poor and disadvantaged. He touched on two themes that would dominate the next four and a half years: unity and peace, relating them in a special way to the leaders of other churches and of nations. He repeated this theme in his first Christmas message on December 23, 1958 summing up the teachings of Pius XII's nineteen Christmas messages in two words: unity and peace. Their attainment, he said, depends on people's good will. One role of the Church is to develop good will and to promote unity and peace in both the spiritual and social orders.

In his Christmas sermon John used two other themes that would become typical: Pentecost and youthfulness. He projected security in his new job and an intention to pursue his goals vigorously. Above all, these early speeches show that John possessed a sweeping vision of being a brother and pastor to his fellow human beings. He was anxious to make his vision real, and he asked others to help him. The response to his appeal grew with each year of his leadership.

The ritual that installed John as pope (then called "coronation") occurred on November 4, the feast of St. Charles Borromeo, one of Roncalli's favorite saints. Borromeo had helped bring the 16th century Council of Trent to a successful conclusion. Then by implementing its decrees in his own diocese of Milan, he had become a model bishop and pastor. John recalled this, commenting that "in the course of time the Church of God has sometimes lost its vigor and at others has pulled together new energies." The new pope reviewed the various models people were proposing for his papacy — diplomat, scholar, ruler. He claimed only the two he felt to be most important: to be a brother to others and to be a Good Shepherd. According to the Gospel, such a shepherd reaches out to others "not of his fold" so they might become one with the flock; and he is meek and humble in the way he leads.

The verbal imagery John used for his coronation contrasted sharply with the image of "supreme authority" projected by the papacy since the First Vatican Council (1870). In effect John announced his intention to reform without saying it. By holding up the image of Charles Borromeo, Pope John proposed reform as a model not just for the pope but for all bishops, indeed for the whole Church.

Certainly John had reform in mind from early in his pontificate. When an aide helping prepare his coronation speech objected that he was not using proper papal language according to Palazzi's Italian dictionary (the standard under Pius XII), John replied, "if necessary we shall reform even Palazzi."[2] Over a year later John wrote in his spiritual journal:

> the experience of this first year gives me light and strength in my efforts to straighten, to reform, and tactfully and patiently to make improvements in everything.[3]

Everything! Imagine, at 77. One condition John was mandated to correct was the depleted state of the Curia and College of Cardinals. Appointments came quickly. He named Domenico

Tardini Secretary of State and Aloisi Masella Camerlengo within days. On November 17, he announced a list of 23 new cardinals. Eleven of these were assigned to the Curia, immediately easing the work load and beginning the process of breaking up the interlocking directorates that controlled so much. John's new cardinals also signaled reform. With 23 new cardinals added to 53 old ones, the traditional limit of 70 was broken. John saw little sense in the arbitrary limit when more were needed. Acting pragmatically, he set no new limit — he simply abolished the old by exceeding it. John improved another aspect of curial operations when he restored regularly scheduled meetings with heads of congregations and other offices. Pius XII had suspended them in the latter years of his reign.

John selected the new cardinals for various reasons: some to reward for long years of service, others to recognize for work they were doing. He appointed outstanding churchmen from around the world, including Richard Cushing of Boston, John O'Hara of Philadelphia and Franz Koenig of Vienna. Koenig's appointment manifests John's open-minded and pragmatic approach.[4] Vienna traditionally had a cardinal but certain persons, hoping to pressure the Austrian government to accept a new concordat with the Vatican, urged bypassing the then Archbishop Koenig. They felt that the Austrians should get a cardinal only after they signed the new agreements. John reversed this thinking, preferring the carrot to the club: give them a cardinal, he said, and perhaps they will sign. Besides, it was a good way to show esteem for the Austrians, a people who felt that Pius XII considered them second class Germans.

John's three speeches while creating the new cardinals offer insight into the changed spirit he brought to the Vatican. One speech is cold and lifeless, an official text obviously prepared by the Secretariat of State to express its diplomatic concerns. The other two are warm and personal, sprinkled with historical references and anecdotes about Roncalli's favorite saints. In this way John began to personalize the ceremonies so as to engage all involved, including the new cardinals, and to attract them to lives of deeper faith and service.

The speeches delivered on the occasion of this first consistory, as gatherings of the College of Cardinals are called, also illustrate how John both cooperated with the offices that served him and introduced a new tone and spirit. He personally collaborated with others and asked their help so they would collaborate with him. Thus on November 17 he visited the offices of the Secretariat of State and announced officially that Monsignor Domenico Tardini (soon to be Cardinal) would be the first full-fledged Secretary of State since 1944. (Pius XII had served as his own Secretary of State.) He invited the bureaucrats there to adopt his own manner and style — simplicity, humility, familiarity and goodness. "Human brilliance and grandeur can't do a thing," he said. "What attracts people is goodness."

John sought also early on to bring the papacy closer to the people, in two ways. He established good relationships with the media, and he took his role as Bishop of Rome seriously.

John had a long and deeply honed sense of the media and their impact on public opinion. The morning after his election he called in the editor of the Vatican's newspaper, *Osservatore Romano*. It was six in the morning! Pope John instructed the editor to refer to the pope in simple language rather than with the florid and triumphalistic circumlocutions that were traditional. As the son of a humble farmer, he found it clumsy to use the papal "we" rather than the more direct "I." The pope after all remained a person! John's style and tone showed up in other public usages. He did not permit the cardinals to kiss his feet but restored the Holy Thursday custom of washing the feet of others. He spoke humorously and in common terms of his peasant family, comfortably identifying with them. Millions of others around the world could identify with them as well, and so felt closer to John.

John also revealed his sensitivity to effective communication with the public during these early days by visiting Vatican Radio and by holding a news conference for the 400 journalists who covered his coronation. Pius XII would surely have met with them too and delivered a lecture. John's style was more direct and ultimately more impactful: he spoke with them off the cuff. In the following months John agreed to a newspaper interview and was the willing subject of a TV-documentary on a day in the life of the pope. In addition he cooperated with Leone Algisi in the preparation of an accurate biography. Before he died he edited his spiritual notes of a lifetime (*Journal of a Soul*) for publication. In the spring of 1963 he signed his last encyclical, *Pacem in Terris,* on international television. John understood the importance of the media from the very beginning and used it throughout his pontificate.

Pope John brought the papacy closer to the people also by immediately taking his role as Bishop of Rome seriously. Within a month he visited the Roman seminary and met with the Roman pastors. On these occasions he emphasized the pastoral and spiritual dimension of his responsibility, encouraged effective catechesis of the people, and set a model by his own clear yet colorful communication. Most importantly, he conveyed an enthusiasm for his role. He soberly noted that Rome had changed a great deal since he had lived there (1901-1904 and 1921-1925) and urged churchmen to take advantage of the practical possibilities offered by new times. He regularly emphasized getting doctrine into the fabric of one's own life and into the life of others. That was what being pastoral meant to him.

John set the pace for others by his example. He frequently left the Vatican to visit people — to go to a parish, to comfort the sick in the hospitals, to encourage the imprisoned, to walk the streets where people worked and lived. By the time his first Christmas was behind him, John had won the affection of the Romans, even of the world. The world was watching this new Bishop of Rome. His Christmas visit to a Roman jail ended a centuries-old British tradition of burning the pope in effigy. How, reasoned the people of Cornwall, could you burn a man who visited prisoners at Christmas time?[5]

In these first hundred days John also resumed the series of

diplomatic and other official contacts demanded of a pope. His experience as a diplomat enabled him to throw himself into this work as well. By Christmas he had carried out at least eight diplomatic functions, including a formal state reception for the Shah of Iran. Before he died, John would formally receive 34 other heads of State, a 4½ year total which far surpassed the 21 formal visits paid to Pius XII during the 19 years of his pontificate.

John also resumed the general audiences which Pius XII had made so popular, but changed their style. Rather than deliver formal lectures, this "Good Shepherd" spoke simply, often spontaneously, and catechetically to the people, much to their delight. He was a humorous man and his aim was to touch people's hearts, not to impress them. According to some estimates, John saw as many as 200,000 people a year in these weekly meetings.

John's private appointments became famous for running beyond their assigned limits because of his friendly and engaging conversations with his visitors. He did business to be sure, but first he met each person as a friend and brother with whom he had much to discuss!

In all these "official" duties Pope John remained very much Angelo Roncalli. He was not overwhelmed by either duties or honors. He remembered his origins, kept in touch with family and friends, indulged his curiosity and expressed his sentiments. The papacy was confining, but he maintained a sense of himself within it and beyond it. The result was a natural and attractive freshness in the papal office.

During his first hundred days and indeed throughout his first year, John set a tone, consistently signaling the character of the pontificate he intended to conduct. Near the end of his first year in office, he shared something with his secretary, Msgr. Loris Capovilla, that highlighted John's deep concern with setting a clear example at the beginning of his service:

> Christ has left us on earth to become beacons that give
> light, teachers who give knowledge; so that we may

discharge our duty like angels, like heralds among men, so that we might be grown men among the young, men of the spirit among men of the flesh, and win them over, so that we might be seed and bring forth fruits. It would scarcely be necessary to expound doctrine if our life were radiant enough. If we behaved like true Christians there would be no pagans.[6]

John told Capovilla that these words of St. John Chrysostom said all that was necessary about the nature of his pontificate.

On November 15, 1958, just days after becoming Pope, John spoke to the conference of Latin American Bishops in his first official audience. His speech was evidently prepared by one of the Vatican offices, but there is a section titled "Fatherly Suggestions" which has the ring of Roncalli. He encourages the bishops to distinguish the essential from the secondary, and to concentrate on the first. He urges them to keep their eyes on a distant horizon, and to elaborate a vision and adopt a program which will attract everyone's sincere contribution, not just their dutiful compliance. Finally the speech as a whole recommends a sober assessment of reality and a twofold program in response to that, one short-range and the other long-range. These three points were organizational common sense. Pope John himself followed them during his first hundred days. The results of his sober assessment of reality, the purposes he envisioned and the program he adopted flowed out of the tone he set during his first hundred days. As we shall see, he focused on essentials and set clear short-range and long-range goals.

Questions for You from John's Model

1. Are you mindful of the tone you set, especially at the beginning of a job?
2. Do you reach out to others in the way you lead?

3. Do you see value in being meek and humble in the way you lead?
4. Do you seek to bring your role closer to your colleagues in a personal way?
5. Do you seek to bring your role closer to the people served by your work — your clients or customers?
6. Do you deal with your work associates only as boss or also as friend, as mentor, even as brother/sister?
7. What is essential, what is secondary in your role?
8. Does your style *attract* everyone's contribution or merely require dutiful compliance?
9. Are you projecting both long-range and short-range goals?

CHAPTER 2

Setting a Course

Setting a tone is good. It can make people feel
good. But "without vision the people perish" (Prov-
erbs 29:18, KJV). Translated into management wisdom, a leader must have a program — one with a visionary quality, a sense of purpose that will attract and
engage others.

Clarity of purpose that one can and does share with
others, and definition of the program of action that
will enable people to accomplish that purpose, are
vital. Pope John modeled these critical aspects of
managerial leadership admirably, to most people's
surprise. This chapter presents John's purpose and
program in a way that might help you imitate his
model.

Defining a Program

On January 25, 1959, the one hundredth day from Angelo
Cardinal Roncalli's arrival in Rome for the conclave and three
months to the day after the start of the conclave that elected him,
Pope John XXIII went to the Roman basilica of St. Paul's Outside the Walls and announced his pastoral program. Who he
was and where he came from should have prepared people for
his announcement. Roncalli had learned early the importance
of a well-defined program from "his bishop," Radini Tedeschi.
He criticized Radini Tedeschi's successor for not having a firm

plan of action. Throughout his career, most recently as Patriarch of Venice, he had developed and systematically executed a
program of pastoral activity. Therefore, in setting for himself
and the Church a sweeping plan of action, Pope John was simply being true to himself and his established pattern of work.
Most people didn't know that pattern and, consequently, what
John did on January 25, 1959 came as quite a surprise. Some
individuals still do not believe that he really meant to do what
he did.

The occasion was the closing ceremony of the annual Week
of Prayer for Christian Unity. John's two speeches[1] on that occasion drew the blueprint that guided his entire pontificate. First,
his homily during the Mass reflected on Rome's united devotion to Saints Peter and Paul. He saw in that a sign of the unity
of bishops and pope in the teaching office of the Church. That
unity in turn symbolized the unity of faith of the Christian
people, which had implications for the whole world:

> Think how the perfect unity of the faith with the prac-
> tical living of the gospel would result in tranquillity
> and happiness in the whole world, at least to the ex-
> tent possible here on earth. This is not just a matter
> of promoting the great principles of a spiritual and
> supernatural order which concern the individual per-
> son.... It is also a matter of helping along the sound-
> est elements of civil, social and political prosperity in
> the nations.[2]

The first fruit of such unity would be a proper use of liberty. Every historical abuse of liberty, he pointed out, came from
violating gospel principles, a thought that led him to lament the
condition of the many Christians deprived of freedom. He closed
affirming that unity-liberty-peace constituted a motive for rallying to human and Christian brotherhood.

His second speech that day was a private address to seven-
teen cardinals who attended the ceremony. He began by telling

them that he wanted to share some of the main ideas for apostolic activity "which these first three months of presence and contact with the ecclesiastical circles of Rome have suggested to me." His concern was pastoral, the good of souls in keeping with the spiritual needs of the present time. People were looking for something distinctive by which his pontificate could be identified. He had two principal and inseparable responsibilities: one to be Bishop of Rome and the other to be Pastor of the universal Church in the world. As to Rome he felt there was a need for "an increase of energies, a coordination of individual strengths and collective acts" to produce a better result. With regard to the world, he saw many good things but he also felt that too many people abuse their liberty. They get so wrapped up in their lives on earth with its technical wonders that they lose sight of the fact that "the heavens are open."

To meet the situation, John told the cardinals he had "resolutely decided to reactivate some old forms for affirming doctrine and Church discipline that have proven extraordinarily effective in epochs of renewal in the history of the Church." Trembling a bit but "with humble resolve," he told them he intended to hold a Synod for the Diocese of Rome and an ecumenical Council for the universal Church. These two events would be crowned by an updating (*aggiornamento*) of the Code of Canon Law. He asked all cardinals, those present and those being informed of his intentions by mail, to let him know how they felt about it and to offer him any suggestions they had "concerning the implementation of this threefold plan." He closed by asking the assistance of the saints in this "demanding undertaking" which was for the "enlightenment, edification and joy" of the entire Christian people. It was also, he said, a "renewed invitation to the faithful of the separated communities to follow in a spirit of love this search for unity and grace."

For three busy months John had executed his immediate program of setting a tone. On that January 25 he announced his long range plan: Synod-Council-Updating of Canon Law. He would spend the rest of his pontificate making it happen.

John's critics considered his announcement ill-advised and his program brash.[3] It had not been carefully studied. How could he call a Council, the Church's most solemn and significant assembly, just three months after arriving in Rome? John himself described the Council as a sudden inspiration that had come to him during a conversation with Cardinal Tardini only five days before he made the announcement! John struck many as he did John Cardinal Heenan of London: "No one seemed less like a great thinker and planner than the Pope John who talked to me."[4] How could he call a Council?

Cardinal Lercaro of Bologna pointed out that Pope John's culture was deeper than met the eye. So too was his ability as thinker and planner. John's whole life was a preparation for calling the Council. His announcement on January 25 both expressed his personality and grew out of his varied experience.[5] He had been secretary of the 1910 Diocesan Synod in Bergamo. As a diplomat from 1925-1944 in Bulgaria, Turkey and Greece, he witnessed Orthodoxy's standard mode of doing Church business through Synods and Councils. His deep reading in the history of the Church, his experience of the important role of bishops during the postwar years in France, his own fresh memory of the recently held Synod in Venice — all of this made the calling of a Synod for the Diocese of Rome and a Council for the universal Church a logical and fitting thing for him to propose.

Pope John was not the only high-ranking prelate who felt that the time was ripe for an ecumenical Council. Two cardinals, Alfredo Ottaviani and Ernesto Ruffini had recommended a Council to Cardinal Roncalli during the conclave. They visited Roncalli's cell on Monday evening (October 26) knowing that he was about to be elected pope. They suggested that it would be a "fine thing" (*bella cosa*) to call an ecumenical Council, to combat the many errors circulating in both Church and world. Other evidences of John's intention to call a Council long before January abound. On October 29, John told Maurice Cardinal Feltin of Paris, "I shall summon a Council."[6] On October 30, his secretary heard him comment "on the necessity of celebrating an ecumenical Council."[7] On November 2, Pope John had several audiences, including one with Ruffini and the idea of a Council came up again.[8] John mentioned the Council to at least two other Italian bishops in November.[9] Finally, on November 21, Pope John spoke to his secretary, Msgr. Loris Capovilla and his confessor, Msgr. Alfredo Cavagna about the possibility of calling a Council.

By November 28, one week later, John's ideas were beginning to gell. Capovilla conjectures his thoughts as follows:

> A month has passed and everything has come about with naturalness. I announced the consistory for the creation of 23 Cardinals, thereby surpassing the number set by Sixtus V; I've taken care of Venice (by appointing Urbani patriarch) and have made several other nominations; I have gone about to meet everyone; I have taken possession of the Lateran and the same day I made a stop at the Church of Saint Clement so my respect and love for the Christian East would be known to everyone. I have taken care of affairs at Castel Gandolfo; the day after tomorrow I will visit the Urban College of Propaganda Fide. I feel in my heart the problems of the whole world. But my soul is in peace. If a commission of cardinals came to tell me that, all things considered, I should return to Venice… it would not cost me anything to set aside myself. I am not afraid of adversity and do not refuse suffering. I think of myself as the last of all, but I have in mind a program of work about which I am not fussing anymore. In fact I am pretty well decided.[10]

Capovilla himself had serious reservations about the Council. He felt John should mold his pontificate around his great appeal as a father-figure. Something as arduous as a Council might be too much, more than he should try. John knew

Capovilla's concerns, so one night after praying the rosary together with the rest of the papal household, John told Capovilla that he (Capovilla) was too concerned with cutting a "fancy figure" in the world. "One has to trample underfoot one's ego," he said, "if one expects to be free enough to lead well and carry out the designs of providence."[11]

John himself struggled with the idea of a Council. At first he thought it a temptation and tried to put it out of his mind. But it persisted. So he began to take it seriously, praying over it and sounding it out with persons he trusted.[12] He watched their reactions. On January 9, he told an old friend of his, Father Giovanni Rossi, what he intended to do.[13] On January 20, John asked some people whom he visited to pray for a special intention of his. That same day he took the project to his Secretary of State, Cardinal Tardini.[14] Two notes describing the meeting have been published, one by Pope John and one by Cardinal Tardini.

John wrote his note the very evening of the meeting:

> In my meeting with Tardini, Secretary of State, I wanted to test his attitude toward the idea which had come to me of proposing the project of an Ecumenical Council to the members of the Sacred College when they met at St. Paul's on the 25th of this month for the closing of the week of prayer. The Council would meet in due time when everything was prepared. It would involve all Catholic bishops of every rite and from every region of the world. I was a bit hesitant and uncertain. The immediate response was the most gratifying surprise I could have expected: "Oh, that's some idea, a brilliant and holy idea. That comes right from heaven, Holy Father! You ought to work on that, elaborate it and spread it around. That will be a great blessing for the whole world!" I didn't need anything more. I was happy. I thanked the Lord for my plan, which received its first seal of approval here below.[15]

Note that John mentions neither the Synod nor the updating of Canon Law. The Council was clearly his principal concern. Cardinal Tardini left a note in his agenda for January 20
as follows:

> Yesterday afternoon his Holiness reflected on the pro-
> gram of his pontificate and specified it. He had pro-
> jected three things: a diocesan Synod, an ecumenical
> Council and an updating of the Code of Canon Law.
> He wants to announce these three points next Sun-
> day to the Cardinals after the ceremony at St. Paul's.
> I said to the Holy Father (who asked me): "Good
> things which are new please me. These three points
> are quite fine, and the manner of making the an-
> nouncement to the cardinals is new (though it traces
> back to ancient papal traditions) and most oppor-
> tune."[16]

Two points deserve comment. One, where did the Synod
and updating of the Code originate as elements of John's program since John himself does not mention them in his note?
Two, was John testing his idea of a Council with Tardini or
announcing his intention to call one? Light regarding the first
question is provided by then Archbishop (subsequently Cardinal) Pericle Felici, Executive Secretary of the Second Vatican
Council and eventual overseer of the updating of Canon Law.
He reports a conversation he had with the pope on February
10, 1960:

> As far as the Council is concerned... he told me that
> the idea of convoking it was his. The other two un-
> dertakings were suggested to him by others after he
> had begun speaking about the Council "They said to
> me, 'before the Council it would be best to have a
> Synod for the Diocese of Rome. It would be a good
> preparation.' 'Fine!' I replied. 'Let's hold a Synod.'

Another said to me, 'It would be a good time to think about revising the Code, which is a little out of date.' 'That's good, let's think also about the Code. But in any case, let's make the Council our main concern.'"[17]

In fact, the idea of holding a diocesan Synod came from Monsignor Angelo Dell'Acqua, a high official in the Secretariat of State who had once been a trusted aide of Roncalli's. He subsequently became Pope Paul VI's Vicar for the Diocese of Rome. Nor was the idea of updating the Code originally John's. It may have come from Felici himself, at that time a trusted protege of Tardini's. So John's main concern was the Council but he elaborated his overall program in collaboration with others, adapting his own favored ideas according to suggestions of his closest advisors. He was willing to "bend but not break" as he put it.

John gave another account of his inspiration for the Council to a group of pilgrims from Venice. It throws further light on his January 20 meeting with Tardini and on his style as Pope. On May 8, 1962, John was talking "family style" with Venetians whom he formerly had served as Patriarch.[18] This was three years after the meeting with Tardini and just five months before the Council was to begin. Speaking "with great simplicity and from the fullness of his heart," John explained to the people "how much a simple and humble disposition of spirit before God enables us to hear the inspirations God always provides and to carry out his will." To clinch his point, he offered them the example of his idea of holding a Council:

How did it arise? How did it develop? To tell the truth, the thought of it and even more its application and implementation was so unforeseen that it seems unlikely.

A question arose in a meeting I had with the Secretary of State, Cardinal Tardini, which led to a discussion of the state of the world with its serious problems and disturbances. Among other things we noted how there was a general desire for peace and harmony, but, unfortunately, things usually ended up in aggravating dissensions and increasing threats. What could the Church do? Should the mystical barque of Christ just stand there battered by the waves and driven by the tides? Isn't she rather expected to provide not just warnings but, more importantly, the light of a great example? What could be that light?

My colleague listened with reverent respect and attention. Suddenly I had a great idea. It came to me precisely at this instant and I welcomed it with unspeakable confidence in the Divine Master. A word sprang to my lips which was solemn and weighty. My voice expressed it for the first time: a Council!

To tell the truth, I was immediately afraid I had disturbed, not to say dismayed, my listener. Without a doubt I would now have to listen to an initial list of severe difficulties. If for no other reason, this unforeseen announcement would make one think of the natural and long preparation which such a proposal would entail.

To the contrary! The response I got was unexpected. Emotion was evident on the face of the cardinal. His assent was immediate and exultant!

It was a first sure sign of the will of God. Everyone knows the intent caution with which the Roman Curia usually examines the questions which are presented to it, both great and small, and that is really necessary.

In any case, my "I'm ready to go" was immediately confirmed by my closest collaborators. In those very hours, one can say, the initiatives concerning the Roman Synod and the updating of the Code of Canon Law were concretized. I was able to make the triple announcement to the Sacred College on the morning of January 25 in the monastery of St. Paul's Outside the Walls.[19]

Later that same year, on September 15, 1962, in his private journal, John commented again on what had happened:

> Without any forethought, I put forward, in one of my first talks with my Secretary of State, on January 20, 1959, the idea of an Ecumenical Council, a Diocesan Synod and the revision of the Code of Canon Law, all this being quite contrary to any previous supposition or idea of my own on this subject.
>
> I was the first to be surprised at my proposal which was entirely my own idea. And indeed, after this everything seemed to turn out so naturally in its immediate and continued development.[20]

John's 1962 narratives seem incompatible with the facts as I have described them. In no way was the idea of a Council new to John when he took it up with Tardini, nor were the ideas of a Synod and a reform of the Code his own. Several interpretations have been offered.[21]

In my view, these discrepancies are best explained by the context of John's recollections. He was speaking to the Venetians in order to clarify a point of spirituality, not to establish an historical account. He simplified the matter to make it neat, striking and illustrative so his listeners could see the same dynamic working in their own lives. He was teaching people how to be open to good ideas and inspirations from God whatever their immediate origin. He was catechizing.

While John referred to the ideas he discussed with Tardini on January 20, 1959 as a "direct inspiration of the Most High," "the flower of an unforeseen spring,"[22] and something he put forward "without any forethought," his program was clearly not a sudden bright idea. It was a carefully matured decision. The seedling was planted in his past, took root in the earliest hours of his pontificate, and sprouted through extensive consultations with others during his first hundred days in office. He listened carefully to what others thought of the challenges facing the Church and what they felt should be done, starting with the cardinals whom he held in conclave a day longer than necessary. As pope he tested his idea of a Council with his closest personal advisors (Capovilla and Cavagna), then with the inner circle of his official family (Tardini and select other cardinals), and finally with all his colleagues in leadership, the curial cardinals. His idea grew and various elements were added to its central inspiration, but the whole gradually became his own.

The January 20 meeting with Cardinal Tardini is best understood historically as Pope John's first effort to win the support of the Vatican bureaucracy. To Roncalli, a Vatican outsider, Tardini was the master and symbol of the Curia. John made him Secretary of State for that very reason. The peasant pope's shrewd purpose in meeting with Tardini that January day was not simply to discuss the situation of the world. It was not even aimed at broaching an idea. Tardini's notes leave little doubt that John's mind was set. His purpose was to inform Tardini of his intentions but to do it in such a way as to confirm the idea, win the Secretary of State's support ("to test his attitude toward the idea," as John put it), and through Tardini to secure the backing of the Curia. In fact, when Pope John spoke with Tardini, he had already prepared notes for his January 25th announcement![23]

When John recounted these central events of his pontificate to the Venetian pilgrims in May of 1962, he commented on another dimension of his January 1959 experiences. Referring to the actual announcement to the cardinals on the 25th of the month, John said:

> Humanly speaking one might have expected the cardinals, having heard my allocution, to gather around me with expressions of approval and best wishes. In-

stead there was a devout silence. It was quite impressive. It was explained only during the subsequent days when the cardinals came into private audience and told me one by one, "Our emotion was so intense and our joy so deep over such a precious gift, altogether unimagined, given to the Church by the Lord as the work of the new pope, that we couldn't find words enough to express our jubilation and our unreserved obedience. We are ready to work."

And behold, immediately, from all parts of the world, came news of the consent of others. There was not one discordant sound nor even warnings of insurmountable obstacles. A veritable chorus of heartfelt applause arose, to which was soon added the good wishes of even the brothers not yet perfectly participating in the unity foreseen and established by the Lord.[24]

Some commentators are less positive in their interpretation of the initial silence of the cardinals. They read it as first evidence of curial resistance to the Council.[25] To be sure, Pope John's intentions were a surprise to practically everyone, both inside the Church and outside. The definition of papal infallibility at Vatican I (1870) and Pope Pius XII's exercise of infallibility in defining the Assumption (1950) caused most people, especially the Curia, to consider Councils obsolete. The pope could do all that a Council could do. Vatican insiders may have remembered that both Pius XI (1922-39) and Pius XII (1939-58) had considered holding a Council (the latter at the urging of Ruffini and Ottaviani) but nothing ever came of their ideas. Pius XII even had a secret commission spend three years studying the possibility, but in the end — nothing![26] To those who knew this history, Pope John's announcement sounded an old melody. It had not carried before; they doubted it would carry now.

The cardinals of the Roman Curia probably accepted

John's program. Most cardinals did not know quite what to make of John's plan and so had little to say. The idea of a diocesan Synod would have seemed especially odd since Rome had *never* had one before. Some may have wondered just what John had in mind. He spoke of an "ecumenical Council" and expressed hopes for Church unity. Did this mean that all the churches — Orthodox and Protestant included — would come? Such a direction would disturb the Curia and meet with resistance. Still the Roman Curia was basically content with John's announced program.

Cardinal Tardini, for example, was exultant in his agreement with Pope John. Perhaps he felt, according to a Roman dictum, "The Pope reigns but the Secretary of State governs." Let John call a Council. Tardini would run it and all would be well. Another major figure in the Curia, Cardinal Ottaviani had suggested a Council to Roncalli even before he became Pope. He surely supported John's program though his vision of the scope and purpose of the Council, Synod and reform of Canon Law differed from John's. Other Roman cardinals, who had helped elect John, felt that in part he was their creature and was by and large following the path they had suggested. True, some felt that he was a bit clumsy as pope. His deeds and actions lacked proper balance and dignity. Nevertheless, they believed that he was in the process of learning to be pope and his program as such was acceptable. If he succeeded in holding a Council, it could be used to put to rest the "errors" circulating in the Church.

This early curial acceptance was not to last. Opposition developed as John unfolded his ideas. The disagreement was not with the program, but with the finality of the program, its purpose. It was not a debate over *whether* a Council, but *whither* the Council. There was a seminal indication of opposition in a blunting of the January 25 announcement as it was printed in both the *Osservatore Romano* (the Vatican's daily paper) and the *Acta Apostolicae Sedis* (the Vatican's record of official documents).[27] Such opposition was destined to grow.

Stating a Purpose

Pope John issued his first encyclical letter to bishops and faithful on June 29, 1959, eight months exactly from his first full day as pope. He titled it *Ad Petri cathedram,* "to the chair of Peter." In it he stated what he wanted the program of his pontificate to mean in three words — truth, peace, and unity.

Ad Petri cathedram argues that knowledge of truth is the basis of a united and peaceful society. Ignorance of the truth is the source of errors, divisions and conflict. Using a pattern of reasoning developed in the 1800's, the encyclical asserts the necessity of embracing the Gospel, the "completeness and fullness of truth." It points to the role of the press and the media as means of spreading the truth, but does so negatively and with many admonitions.

The second section deals with peace and strikes a more positive note. It argues that attachment to truth by all, especially those responsible for leading society, will bring unity, human brotherhood and peace. Justice is affirmed as the most important avenue to peace. Its pursuit is discussed in terms of social classes, labor and families. Here John formulates one of his basic tactical principles:

> Salvation... is to be expected from a great outpouring of love, ... which is always prepared to yield to the convenience of others. Such love is an effective antidote against the brashness of the world and immoderate love of self.[28]

Finally the encyclical discusses the unity of the Church "which is closest to our heart and with which this pastoral office... is most particularly concerned." It recalls Christ's prayer "that all might be one" and expresses the hope that the Council will help those not of the flock to desire to return.

Bishops from every corner of the globe will come to

consider the serious problems confronting religion. The Council's special concerns will be the growth of the Catholic Church, the renewal of the spirit of the Gospel in the hearts of people everywhere and the adjustment of Christian discipline to the exigencies of modern day living. This will surely be a remarkable display of truth, unity and love, a display which those who are cut off from this Apostolic See will observe. We sincerely hope that they will receive it as a gentle invitation to seek and acquire that unity which Jesus Christ prayed for so ardently to His heavenly Father.[29]

The encyclical describes the unity of the Church at length in terms of doctrine, government and worship. It notes along the way the potentially unifying effects of controversy and affirms the axiom, "In essentials, unity; in doubt, freedom; in all things, charity." John urges others to come together and presents himself as "Joseph, your brother."

Ad Petri cathedram is an obvious hybrid, lacing two distinct tones and two different styles throughout. It reflects a struggle of viewpoints, one defensive and negative, the other affirmative and positive, a struggle between John's "fresh air" mentality and the integralist mentality of the Curia. Perhaps that is why the encyclical is explicit about the potentially positive role of conflict as affirmed by Cardinal Newman, a 19th century forerunner of the Church's 20th century renewal.

The encyclical situates concern for Church unity in the broader context of the unity of humankind and the peace of the world. The concern for both unity and peace rests on a concern for truth, but the encyclical as a whole, insists that knowledge of truth, even with good intentions, is not enough. Rather, practical living and loving action based on known truths are needed to bring about unity and peace in both Church and world.

Ad Petri cathedram strongly attests that the Council was the keystone to John's approach to Church unity, and that

Church unity in turn was the supporting arch in his blueprint for world unity and peace. His intentions for the Council finely balance concern for the Catholic Church itself — its growth, its renewal and the adjustment of its disciplines — with concern for the problems of religion in general. John wanted the Council to be a "remarkable display" of unity gently inviting those cut off from the Church, indeed all persons of good will, to gather together. The bold lines of John's broad pastoral strategy are in this document.

The tension apparent in *Ad Petri cathedram* reflects the budding opposition to Pope John and his idea for the Council. John had wide horizons and was trying to expand the horizons of the Church; the Curia preferred to keep things focused within and tightly controlled. John was concerned with the internal condition of the Church, but his ultimate goal was to make the Church a better agent of peace in the world.

The goal John set for his papacy in *Ad Petri cathedram* was intense pastoral activity based on the Church's doctrine with an eye to promoting unity in the Christian Church and peace in the world. Pursuit of his goals demanded the reform of certain attitudes and practices prevalent in the Church. John understood and fully accepted that consequence.

During his first eight months as Pope, John established a clear image of himself, a tone for his administration, and a clear course for the Church. His plans were visionary yet his approach to implementing them was pragmatic. He diligently acquainted himself with the situations for which he felt responsible — the Roman Church and the Universal Church — and he incisively applied his sharp intuitive powers to what he learned. He arrived quickly yet prudently at decisions and immediately acted upon them. His program was not the result of a study commission nor of labored calculation. It was simply his best judgment as to what was needed based on his past experience, many consultations, his current insight, and his prayerful, obedient sense of what God was calling him to do.

John's approach and program were so basic a departure from those of his predecessor that John's determination to change things would, in the end, create opposition and make him seem a revolutionary. His first eight months constitute a determined beginning, but eight months do not make a pontificate. The real question was whether this old man could effect his program and achieve his purpose before he died.

Questions for You from John's Model

1. In terms of your own background and experience, what is the logical and fitting thing for you to do in your job?
2. Do you challenge your own bright ideas before you presume their validity?
3. Are you free enough of ego-concerns to lead well?
4. Are you willing to test out your ideas with trusted advisors before you proceed with them?
5. Can you bend and adapt your plans without breaking them, integrating the thoughts of others without losing sight of your central goal?
6. Are you prepared to pursue your plan, even if it meets with incomprehension and resistance?
7. Are you willing to yield to the convenience of others as you pursue your program?

CHAPTER 3

Setting a Strategy

The question underlying the last chapter was this: Do you, like John, have a clearly focused purpose and a fittingly designed program to achieve it? But a program without a strategy, a vision without a pragmatic capacity to make it come into being, is little more than a dream. A manager without a program manages toward no end. He just happens to be "in charge." A manager with a program but no strategy is like a person with good ideas who is entrusted with power but then has no idea what to do with it, how to use it.

This chapter is about strategy. John XXIII had a program, but his amazing success in pulling it off is due to his strategy. Programs don't make themselves happen. Once John got the job, he not only had ideas about what to do but also about how to do it, and he did it. His strategy was complex yet very simple. This chapter provides an overview of his formula for success. Subsequent chapters will look more closely at the individual factors involved and follow the dynamic of their interplay as John executed his program. The question behind this chapter is: Do you have a strategy? How does yours compare with John's? What might you learn from John to make your strategy as a manager and leader, whether pastor or president, more effective?

John's Three Goals

John XXIII was by all accounts a lovable person. He was also a highly successful leader and a change agent of the first order. His record and achievement is clear. The present state of the Catholic Church has been deeply affected by the three goals that constituted the purpose of his pontificate — truth, unity, and peace. Historically it is still too early to make definitive judgments, but change in Roman Catholicism since 1958 has clearly run along the broad lines intended by John.

As regards truth, the dominant scholastic and legalistic way of thinking about and within the Church has been broken. Catholic scholars and Catholic people today explore the truth of Catholic tradition in all its richness from many perspectives and disciplines. Further, the Church has begun to address the truth of her past and her present condition in the context of modernity, dramatically evidenced by the numerous apologies made by Pope John Paul II before, during and after the Jubilee Year of 2000. Finally, Catholics today are more open to the truth of Judaism, other Christian traditions, and even of other religions.

With regard to unity, the Catholic Church has abandoned its former aloofness towards other Christian groups, is now in respectful dialogue with nearly all of them on an organized and sustained basis, and is actively collaborating with other Christians on many fronts.

With regard to peace, the Church has played a meaningful and significant role in the major changes between the historically Christian West and the formerly Communist East and plays an active role in pressing for peace and justice throughout the world.

Pope John's goals have not been fully attained, nor has movement toward them been an unmitigated success. Some of the change has weakened the Church and confused the meaning of Catholicism for members and nonmembers alike. There has been some loss. Many Catholics left the Church. There is not universal agreement that what has happened is good. But all agree that Pope John started a process of massive change. He alone did not provoke all that has occurred, but without doubt the Church has been moving in the direction of John's overall purposes.

How did he manage to do that in light of the low expectations people had for him? What was the secret of his success? This chapter argues that John XXIII had a strategy consisting of five interrelated factors: his person, his program, his ability to communicate, his reliance on an institutional ally, and his consistency. This strategy accounts for his success.

One of Pope John's best biographers, Meriol Trevor, wrote that "the Joannine impact was of a person, not a program."[1] Trevor is only half right. John's person was important, but so was the program outlined in our last chapter. As a person, Pope John surely impressed the whole world. But without his program, his personality would have been little more than a shooting star briefly lighting history's firmament, an attractive but inconsequential luminary. To the contrary, John's impact has grown with time. His pontificate marks the beginning of a new era, possibly even a new epoch, in the life of the Church,[2] signaled by the assuming of his name by two of his three immediate successors in the papal chair. This larger impact is due to Pope John's program more than to his person. The two go together. John without his program would have had little effect. John's program without John would never have been created, for his program reflected his person.

John's Person

It is no accident that John's person was a major factor in what he accomplished. Providing a good example was a conscious part of his strategy as seen in notes from his August, 1961 retreat, a turning point in his administration. These notes identify major dimensions of John's person — his personal qualities, his vision, and his style.

"Everyone calls me 'Holy Father,' and holy I must and will

be,"[3] he wrote. Pope John was a humble man, an individual without pretense who identified fully with the human condition. He walked with his fellows as one among them. He never felt himself above others nor did he want to be treated that way. John esteemed his own ideas, inspirations, and abilities but no more than he regarded the thoughts and suggestions of others. He respected others, revered their prerogatives, and held himself open to their ideas. He held a position of high authority, but he did not use that either to set himself above others or to control them. He was gentle and meek. He delighted in the many trappings of his high office (though he eliminated some), yet he never lost his spontaneity. In fact he restored a refreshingly human tone to papal protocol.

John was a sincere man, simple, direct, and honest. He believed what he professed and lived it. At 77 he tackled the challenges of his office with a vigorous courage which others found infectious. Once convinced that God wanted something of him, he pursued it. He undertook projects which frightened younger men and had been shunned by the previous pope, supposedly both stronger and more skilled than he. When difficulties arose he faced them with good humor and with faith. He remarked one day, "They say that the pope runs the Church with the help of the Holy Spirit. But that's not true. It's the Holy Spirit who runs the Church. The pope helps him!"

John's most important quality was "integrity." He was not humble *and* sincere, but sincerely humble; not a man *and* a believer, but a believing man; not fully human *and* deeply religious, but a thoroughly religious human being. In those regards, he embodied the essence of what the Church represents. This specific dimension, his integrity, lent him a compelling force when he was chosen to be the Church's leader and most public figure. John's integrity enabled him to restore the credibility of the Church and the attractiveness of Catholicism. He personified Christianity in an appealing way. He made "holiness" attractive.

A second note from John's retreat suggests his visionary, even "mystical" approach to his role:

> In the eyes of the whole world it is this mutual love
> between Jesus and... Simon or Peter, the son of John,
> that is the foundation of Holy Church, a foundation
> which is at the same time visible and invisible, Jesus
> being invisible to the eyes of our flesh, and the Pope,
> the Vicar of Christ, being visible to the whole world.[4]

John grasped his role and events in a context with deep perspective, wide horizon, and sharp detail. His vision arose from within his own heart, was rooted in a detailed acquaintance with his own cultural heritage, was nourished by his personal and refreshingly original contact with the prime sources of Christian tradition, and enriched by his open and enthusiastic contact with other peoples and traditions. His outlook embraced the whole world, and stretched out toward the transcendent horizons of that human stance which accepts as real God the Creator, Lord, and Father of all.

John's vision was non-clerical, even non-ecclesiastical. He saw the Church as part of society's structure and envisioned that whole social order as an instrument to serve humankind by promoting human living together in peace (*convivenza*). John's vision transformed the Church, shaking it out of a narrow concern with itself, opening it up to other institutions and problems, forcing revisions of its structure and policy. His vision induced a corporate re-visioning.

John communicated his vision in many ways. He spoke it and he enacted it. More importantly he brought the two phases together so that his actions embodied his vision and his words explained his action. He frequently related his vision to specific feasts or events, such as Pentecost and the feast of St. Charles Borromeo. His communication was highly symbolic. He himself became the symbol of a new way of being Catholic, and he generated other symbols: the Council, the "new Pentecost," the Secretariat for Christian Unity.

John assembled a team of capable publicists to help communicate his vision. They were sensitive to public opinion and knew how to work with the media so as to spread John's perspective to a larger public than those directly involved in the Vatican or the Catholic Church. In this way the majority of the bishops attending the Second Vatican Council, millions of Catholics, and countless persons throughout the world came to share John's personal vision.

John's vision produced optimism in him and in others. He was enthusiastic about what he saw. He believed that great things could be done and helped others believe that together they could accomplish things they dared not dream. John's goals formulated the deepest yearnings of the human heart, and when he energetically set in motion a program aimed at attaining them, others began to believe that it could be done. They mobilized with him, around him.

The third note from his 1961 retreat highlights John's style:

> Meekness and humility shown in the approaches made to clarify ideas and give warm hearted encouragement; tranquillity and constancy from which the faithful and my collaborators must receive light and encouragement from the Pope, the head priest.[5]

Angelo Roncalli came to the papacy with a developed administrative style, one fully consistent with his personality. It was both considerate of other persons and concerned with implementing a vision. The result was a distinctive style that can be characterized as "purposeful laissez-faire, innovatively responsive." Both phrases imply a collaborative manner of exercising authority.

"Purposeful laissez-faire" indicates that Pope John combined a sharp sense of purpose with an insistence that persons and procedures be allowed to operate freely. John set his administration in a definite direction, but he kept it flexible. He allowed others to play a role according to their own competence and insights, within certain very broad limits. This is most evident in his preparation and celebration of the Council. The freedom he allowed astounded the Protestant and Orthodox observers, most of whom came to Rome with visions of monolithic poparchy dancing in their heads. Yet John had called the Council for some very definite reasons, and he kept working until he persuaded the Council fathers to follow his lead. He tolerated a great deal of ambiguity and waited years in some instances for his vision to take concrete form.

"Innovatively responsive" suggests that John was a creative leader, but his creativity came largely from reacting to the initiatives of others. Even his greatest project, the Council, was suggested to him by others the evening before he became pope. Almost all his other important steps came in response to the ideas or initiatives of others: the Secretariat for Christian Unity, *Mater et magistra*, communication with Russia, and intervention in the Cuban missile crisis were all initiated by others. John's creativity consisted of the unique twist which he gave to the ideas of others, and this arose from the way he made events implement his vision. He had only a few basic themes — truth, unity, and peace — but like a master weaver he worked everything around them. The result was an integrated tapestry that made everything seem new. John changed the Church, not by destroying the old but by situating the old in a new context which opened new horizons and possibilities.

Besides being a visionary, Pope John was a pragmatist. He took one step at a time toward his goal, capitalizing on every opportunity while refusing to force situations. He did not seek to control events. He sought to be fair and balanced. He persuaded rather than dictated. He used his position to lead, not command.

The first element of John's strategy then was his person, specifically his integrity. He personally embodied the vision he had of the Church's essential meaning and value and expressed it by his style. Others could identify with him, and through him with his vision.

John's Purposive Program

John's program (Synod-Council-Updating of the Code of Canon Law) for achieving his purpose derived from his attitudes and was shaped by his vision. It was his tool for making the Church a better instrument to serve humankind in its quest for truth, unity, and peace. John's pontificate consisted of an unflagging but never grim or overbearing implementation of his program in pursuit of his purposes. He initiated all three elements of his program though he completed only one, the Synod. The Council continued after his death and was concluded in 1965. The reform of the Code of Canon Law was not completed until 1983, 20 years after his death.

John's program came from John himself. Its qualities were his qualities, its vision his vision, its style his style. This is most evident in the Council. It was a broad process that encompassed everything relevant to his vision. It was conducted in an atmosphere of freedom within which all persons could play their proper role. It had certain goals toward which it progressively moved, and the goals that it adopted were in large part the goals John had set for his own pontificate. With hindsight it is clear that the times were ripe for John's program, but at the time it was unimaginable. It was John's program, designed to achieve his purposes of truth, unity and peace. (See Part I, Chapter 2 above for details.)

John's Symbolic Communication

John consistently combined word *with* action in communicating his purposes and programs to the public. This aspect of his integrity invested persons, offices, events, and things with the meaning and values he wished to promote. The combination of word *with* action made John credible, persuasive, attractive to the media, and known to the world. Communication with all Catholics and with the public at large (i.e., not merely within official Church channels) is a crucial dimension of this factor. John's symbolic way of communicating his message is what this element of his strategy is all about. (See Part I, Chapter 7 below for details.)

John's Institutional Ally

While John acted largely alone in launching his program, he was aided enormously in implementing it by one person in particular, Augustin Cardinal Bea, and by the organism that he and Bea instituted, the Secretariat for Christian Unity. The Secretariat brought together within the conciliar process a large and talented group of persons fully committed to John's purpose and program. Because the Secretariat was there, John did not have to rely on an overt use of his own authority to promote his vision within the process. Cardinal Bea and the Secretariat for Christian Unity, his institutional allies, did the work for him. Both outlived John: Bea until a few years after the Council, the Secretariat as the Pontifical Council for Promoting Christian Unity. Next to John himself, Cardinal Bea and the Secretariat for Christian Unity best embodied and symbolized John's program. Both played a crucial role in its ultimate success. (See Part I, Chapter 4 and Part II, Chapter 1 below for details.)

John's Consistency

John gave internal coherence to the four factors of his strategy sketched above. John's program and his way of communicating were a reflection of himself. Similarly Cardinal Bea and Pope John were kindred spirits and the work of the Secretariat for Christian Unity was an institutionalization of John's purposes and program on a small scale. Thus each factor in his strategy reinforced the others. This gave the whole as well as each part a credibility and impact that would have been greatly diluted, even fully dissolved, had there not been such coherence.

All four elements of the strategy are essential and linked. The connection of "person and program" has been suggested above. John embodied in himself a new vision of the meaning of Church, but for that new self-consciousness to pervade the whole Church a process involving the entire Church was necessary. John's "person" needed a "program" to give effective direction to the organization, but just as much the "program" needed John's "person." A conciliar process without a clear model of what the Church needed to become could have gone in many directions, some highly undesirable. Indeed certain forces within the Curia conceived the conciliar process as an occasion merely to solidify past meanings and enforce pertinent discipline. Without John's person serving as a model, the Council might have solidified the integralist model of the Church adopted at the beginning of the 20th century rather than pointing the Church forward to the 21st century.

John's skill in using "symbolic communication" beneficially complemented both his person and his program. John had to project his vision beyond himself and beyond the narrow confines of the Church's structure. He was implicitly proposing a shift in the Church's meaning, not merely a revision of its structure or procedure. John's concern was the conception of the Church held by the mass of its own members and the larger public. Since his vision was not shared by many of his collaborators in the Vatican, he had to communicate over them. Messages sent through them would not have gotten out. Abstract verbal communication alone would not have been grasped by most believers, even by many bishops, much less the general public. John's person and his program needed symbolic communication to generate broad support.

Finally, John needed an "institutional ally." Presence is power in the Church as in other bureaucratically organized institutions. Those outside of Rome had neither the organization nor the skill to overcome the strength that the Roman curialists and their allies enjoyed by virtue of the positions they held. A well-disciplined and skilled group favorable to John's purposes and working within the process was essential for the forces out-side of Rome to find a rallying point from which they could influence the flow of events. The alternative was a forceful use of papal authority by John over and against the Curia. That would have contradicted both his own personality and the very values he was attempting to instill in the Church.

In summary, without John's example and vision, the process might have ended in a sterile reaffirmation of old positions. Without the open process, the Church at large might never have adopted John's personal example as it freely did at the Council's first session. Without John's ability to communicate his vision to the Church in a concrete form, the thousands of Catholics struggling in a scattered variety of movements would not likely have been drawn together in sufficient force to convince the bishops that a new model of the Church was available and worth-while. Without an internal ally, the conciliar process might never have brought to a head conflicts over central issues, thereby pro-viding the bishops with an opportunity to choose. Without con-sistency John's leadership, lacking organizational coherence and integrity, would not have been credible. John was opening the window to some very dramatic changes. People had to have confidence that he knew what he was about and somehow had to experience the effectiveness of a new way of doing the Church's work and living the Christian life. The consistency of John's leadership gradually merited that confidence.

This five-factor formulation of Pope John's strategy defines a pattern found in John's papal record. It helps account for his effectiveness. The formula offers one explanation of why John was so successful in accomplishing his program. His strategy was quite astute in its combination of factors, all of them together being more important than any one of them alone. The single most striking element of John's strategy is the "institutional ally," for this factor freed John from any need to quarrel openly with others or to use his authority hamfistedly to forward his own sentiments and vision. Such steps would have been distasteful to John, perhaps impossible for him to take. He would have avoided them at almost any cost. They would have broken the consistency of his strategy and would very likely have been disastrous. By developing and using an institutional ally John did not have to play a strongly directive role himself, nor did he let the Council labor without direction. His strategy both prevented others from imposing their direction and enabled him to gently lead his flock to new pastures.

Pope John was an effective pope, a successful manager and leader. His strategy explains in large part why he was. It was the secret of his organizational success. Subsequent chapters will observe his strategy at work as John did his job day-by-day.

Questions for You from John's Model

1. Do you have a strategy? Can you articulate and critique it, or are you flying by the seat of your pants?
2. Is your program consistent with your person? Do people find it credible coming from you or do they think it extraneous, strange, even alien?
3. Do you feel one with your program? Can you pursue it with full integrity? When others identify with you, do they identify with your program?
4. How are you getting your purposes and your program across to the various constituencies that are important for your success?
5. What means are you using to communicate your vision? Are you using symbolic communication? Have you engaged publicists? Are they concerned with integrity?
6. Do you have an "institutional ally" in the structure of your organization?
7. Are you comfortable letting the process of your program work out any conflicts that exist or do you feel you have to get in there and battle opposing factions yourself?
8. Is your leadership consistent across its various dimensions?

CHAPTER 4

Assembling a Team

"No man is an island." Neither is any manager. Without a supportive team, associates whom one manages, no one can get the job done regardless of how clear the purpose, how good the program, how potentially effective the strategy.

Like most managers, John inherited a staff to help him do the job he took on and had to develop it, with hands both old and new. This chapter offers a model that might help you choose and develop your administrative team, even if you, like John, don't have total choice in the matter!

John's Five Main Collaborators

Angelo Roncalli was a strong personality but he was not a loner. He had no illusions about his own talent or importance and enjoyed working with others. In that regard he was a good choice to reverse the isolated style of Pius XII.

John assembled a team of three main types of "collaborators," as he called them, to help him with his papal responsibilities. They were (1) persons holding official positions and working immediately with the pope; (2) persons with whom John felt a certain affinity and on whom he depended for execution of particular decisions; and (3) intimate advisors, persons with whom John enjoyed not only a close official relationship but a deep spiritual friendship as well.

John inherited most of his official collaborators. With time he was able to appoint increasing numbers of individuals to key posts, but even there he was constrained by Vatican traditions and established career lines. His attitude toward this first type of team member was respect and loyalty. He was open with them regarding Church business and expected them to be open with him. He recognized their experience and expertise, but he was not ashamed of his own background before them. The most important persons in this group were the officials of the Secretariat of State and the heads of the Curial Congregations.

A second group of collaborators consisted of individuals with whom John felt a certain affinity, men such as Monsignor Angelo Dell'Acqua, a high official in the Secretariat of State, and Monsignor Pietro Pavan, a respected professor and author on social questions. Others in the group were Gustavo Cardinal Testa from the Vatican, Léon-Joseph Cardinal Suenens from Belgium (once the Council started), and Franz Cardinal Koenig of Vienna.

Three persons comprised the third group, John's close friends: Monsignor Alfredo Cavagna, his confessor; Augustin Cardinal Bea, the eventual head of the Secretariat for Christian Unity; and Monsignor Loris Capovilla, John's personal secretary. John trusted these men deeply and totally. He responded readily to their suggestions yet never in a way that obscured his position as the pope. Profiling five of these individuals at some length will deepen our grasp of how John managed and led: Capovilla, Bea and Cavagna from the third category, and, from the first, John's two Secretaries of State, Domenico Tardini and Amleto Cicognani. We start with Capovilla, Cavagna and Tardini here, delaying profiles of Bea and Cicognani until later in our story.

Loris Capovilla

Loris Capovilla was a priest of Venice, born in 1915 of a working class family, ordained in 1940. Short, thin, wiry and youthful in appearance, he was 43 years old when John became pope. He first met Roncalli in 1953 as part of a Venetian delegation that went to Paris to meet their newly appointed patriarch. Capovilla was presented as a man who did a little of everything. Soon after Roncalli made him his personal secretary.

Capovilla's ability to do "a little of everything" derived from his varied background: military chaplain, popular radio personality, newspaper correspondent, and director of the Venetian diocesan paper, *La Voce di San Marco*. Eventually he became part of the diocesan staff, assuming responsibilities for liturgical functions among other things. Capovilla was a public figure, one well acquainted with the media, a man sensitive to effective public presentation. In addition he was reputed to be well read in contemporary French, Dutch and German theology.

When Roncalli became pope, Capovilla had already spent five years as his close associate. The two were not only collaborators but had become friends. Capovilla accompanied Roncalli even on his visits home and became acquainted with his family. Their closeness is revealed by an excerpt from a letter Roncalli wrote to Capovilla in July 1956 while Capovilla was sick in a hospital. After expressing his sadness at Capovilla's illness and encouraging him spiritually, Roncalli discussed some business:

> I had an initial conversation with and I have written to Bishop Gianfranceschi that he should suspend for now the provisions which had been made. Then we'll figure it out. In handling these cases there are certain laws which must be followed: laws of meekness, of patience, of charity. "First correct him privately ... then bring in witnesses ... then take it to the Church. As a last resort hold him as a foreigner and publican."

There is also the parable of the fig tree. A little time and waiting to see whether the correction hoped for arrives. Do you understand me? I know you do. May you be blessed and let's continue to pray together.[1]

Through the years Capovilla came to know John's style. An affectionate trust grew up between them. Capovilla assumed toward John the role that Roncalli himself held years before serving Radini Tedeschi. Capovilla lived with Pope John and had immediate and constant access to him. They ate together, listened to music together, read things together, talked things over together, prayed together. John confided in Capovilla as he did in no one else, making him his literary executor when he died.

John's appreciation of "Monsignor Loris" comes through most clearly from his deathbed. As he lay dying he called Capovilla "a faithful executor, intelligent collaborator, and most devoted son. He has interpreted my thoughts and carried out my will. I'll not cease thanking him and blessing him from heaven." More explicitly still, on the 31st of May, three days before he died, John wrote:

> My dear secretary don Loris. For ten years he has been near me like an angel, interpreting my thought, never distancing himself from me in anything. He has collaborated obediently and with most ardent zeal. He has sacrificed everything to be united to my ministry, with a spirit of sacrifice, love for the Church, and disinterestedness.[2] …We've worked together and served the Church without stopping to pick up and throw back the rocks on the road which sometimes blocked the way. You have supported my defects, I yours. We will always be friends…. We have many friends; more than that, you'll see, we'll have more. I'll protect you from heaven.[3]

John is referring to rocks thrown at them by others.

Capovilla was with Roncalli in the conclave when John was elected. He spoke of returning to Venice, but John insisted that he stay with him as the first member of his team. Capovilla was not Roman trained, he was not intimately acquainted with the Roman system, and he was not interested in a Vatican career.[4] He served John faithfully and exclusively, doing what John wanted done and what he thought needed doing. At times this caused friction with Vatican veterans.

Estimates of Capovilla's influence vary, but practically all accord him a significant role. He was certainly one of John's closest advisors and therefore a powerful man. He helped John work his inspirations into ideas and at times helped John stick to decisions that various Vatican circles resisted. Capovilla had a major hand in most of John's speeches.

Perhaps Capovilla's greatest contribution was the publicity that Pope John received. He was a professional in these matters and monitored what was being said of John. He knew how to make the real Pope John known to the public and succeeded in developing a believable and true public image for him. Capovilla himself gave lectures on Pope John. He arranged for a television documentary about a day in Pope John's life (shown in Italy on February 23, 1959) and set up an unprecedented papal interview with Italy's most esteemed daily paper, printed in March of 1959 in Milan's *Corriere della Sera*. These steps, taken just months into John's pontificate, helped crack the papacy's isolation from the people. Numerous decisions are attributed to Capovilla's influence including the selection of Cardinal Cicognani, former Vatican representative to the United States, as John's second Secretary of State.

Alfredo Cavagna

The position of the Pope's confessor is not part of the Vatican's administrative structure. However, the Pope's confessor sees the pope regularly and deals with an extremely delicate and confidential realm — the pope's conscience. Further, the individual who holds this position can serve as a channel for getting concerns and information to the pope. The pope gives his confessor full attention weekly with a kind of obediential reverence!

Pope John customarily confessed every Friday and seldom postponed the appointment. He named his confessor the day after he was elected. The man he chose was a friend from his early days in the priesthood. Alfredo Cavagna was ordained to the priesthood in 1902, two years before Angelo Roncalli, as a priest of Milan. He was secretary to Bishop Morganti of Ravenna in northern Italy during some of the very years that Roncalli served Radini Tedeschi of Bergamo in the same capacity. Like Roncalli he was involved in a diocesan synod conducted during that time. Like Roncalli he wrote for his diocesan newspaper. In 1922 he became the highest ecclesiastical officer in the emerging women's section of Italian Catholic Action and so, like Roncalli in those same years, was engaged in putting together an effective national organization. Their ways parted when Roncalli was sent on foreign diplomatic missions, but they kept in touch and Roncalli would stop to see Cavagna and confess to him whenever he passed through Italy.

Cavagna was a holy and cultured man. He traveled extensively in Italy and abroad, working primarily with clergy. He wrote many ascetical and pious books and helped develop national clergy weeks in Italy to promote collaboration between clergy and laity. He was highly esteemed, knew most of the bishops of Italy and served as spiritual director for several of them. He also knew many leaders of the international Catholic Action movement and of Italy's postwar Christian Democratic party. He knew well the personnel and methods of the Curia.

In many respects Cavagna was like John — quiet, humble and pious but at the same time knowing and capable. He had a good mind, an accurate memory and good judgment. He had an absolute sense of commitment to the papacy. Knowing four popes personally, he had organizational savvy — he was *furbo,* shrewd — though that was not his forte. He was perspicacious, reserved, tightly disciplined, and a man who exercised what authority he had lightly and with respect for others.

While Cavagna's official position was spiritual, he had the background to assist John in other respects and did so. Capovilla considered him one of John's intimate friends, a man with whom Roncalli shared his most private thoughts and inspirations — such as that of calling a Council — a man whose reactions and judgments John sought and respected.

Cavagna served as John's official liaison with the Central Preparatory Commission for the Second Vatican Council. John was unable to attend all the meetings but wanted someone he trusted present who could report and interpret them for him. One of Cavagna's special roles was to serve as a backdoor channel to the pope to help Italian priests who had resigned their ministry and married. At that time these individuals experienced severe discrimination, both ecclesiastical and civil. The condition of some was desperate. Given Cavagna's reputation and his role as the Pope's confessor, many of these married priests appealed to him for help and got it. Finally, Cavagna may have played a behind-the-scenes role in advancing some of John's new ideas on how the Vatican related to Italian politics.

Domenico Tardini

Monsignor Domenico Tardini has been called the "compleat curialist."[5] Born in Rome in 1887 and ordained in 1912, he early became a professor at Rome's Lateran seminary where he was trained. He began helping at the Vatican's Congregation for Extraordinary Affairs, a branch of the Secretariat of State, as early as 1921 and from 1929 on spent practically his entire career there. Under Pius XII he served as Pro-Secretary of State with Monsignor Montini, the future Pope Paul VI. Pius XII served officially as his own Secretary of State. In an episode reported to have involved a serious disagreement be-

tween Montini and Tardini, Pius XII sent Montini to be Archbishop of Milan while retaining Tardini as sole Pro-Secretary.[6]
When Roncalli became pope, Tardini was the ultimate Vatican
insider, an entrenched force.

Tardini's strength is illustrated by a Roman saying that "A
Pope reigns, but the Secretary of State governs." In John's days
that was transmuted to "Tardini reigns, Ottaviani [of the Holy
Office] governs, John blesses!"[7]

In fact, Tardini had a low opinion of Roncalli before he
became pope. When Roncalli was appointed Nuncio to France
in 1944, the highest post in the Vatican diplomatic corps, he
passed through Rome on his way to Paris. Roncalli remarked
to Tardini that he was quite surprised at his nomination. Tardini
replied that he was too, and let Roncalli know that he had little
enthusiasm for the decision. It was Pius XII's idea, he said, no
one else's.[8]

The two men had quite different viewpoints. Diplomatic
letters and dispatches from Roncalli breathed a different spirit
than Tardini's. They provoked amused smiles from Tardini and
his types in the Vatican. They considered John "good Roncalli,"
a nice and pious man but for all that a bit naive.

Many people were surprised when, a few days after his election, Pope John named Tardini his Secretary of State. That quick
decision is variously interpreted. Some see it as a part of a deal
made in the conclave, others as an expression of John's kindness toward career personnel, others as something Tardini
wanted badly. Whatever the motive, it made good sense for John
to appoint Tardini. The appointment was a fitting crown for
Tardini's long career, and John was sensitive to such matters.
But there was more to it than that.

John knew Tardini to be a master of the Vatican. Tardini
was respected in the Curia and John needed someone skilled to
help him run the bureaucracy. Neither he nor Capovilla knew
much about the place. Moreover, he saw in Tardini a good man,
a loyal priest who loved the Church, and an obedient collaborator.[9] Finally, Tardini was a man of conservative mentality

somewhat allied with the Vatican "Pentagon" mentioned above. His appointment also reassured those who may have favored Siri or Masella to succeed Pius XII.[10]

Moreover, Tardini, "wily, narrow, and witty in his earthly Roman way,"[11] was an engaging character. Authoritarian himself, he not only expected others to obey him but obeyed his own superiors. He was an intelligent and opinionated man, as Romans tend to be. Once he made up his mind he had no further doubt. He tended to surround himself with people who thought as he did. For Tardini, that meant other Romans, by training, if not by blood.

Tardini's good mind was yoked to a tough and passionate nature. He was an imposing character, controlled and methodic in the way he ran his office. But he could be explosive and fiery in dealing with others, even the pope. He would sometimes shout so loudly during his meeting with John that the doorkeepers felt impelled to close as many doors as they could to muffle the noise. At times Tardini sought to cow John. Face to face he would accuse John of ruining everything for him. On such occasions John would maintain his customary calm and invite Tardini to sit down beside him so they could talk things out. Tardini's excessive emotionalism at the end of his career may have been due to a heart condition that finally took his life.

Tardini's health had not been good in the waning days of Pius XII. He bounced back to life when he became Secretary of State, but John's willingness to grow, to change his views and to adjust Vatican policies seemed to wear Tardini out. Tardini would discuss matters with John and, thinking all was settled, proceed to act. John, however, would talk about these matters with others and not infrequently revise his position. Tardini then had to backtrack and set things going along another line. One of those with whom John discussed most things was Capovilla, who saw many things differently than Tardini. Friction developed. Within a year, in December 1959, Tardini asked that Capovilla's job be defined and limited.[12]

Tardini knew how to govern, but in his view papal leadership was best conducted by a twosome — the pope with the Secretary of State — not by a team.[13] By January 1960, the month following Tardini's complaints about Capovilla, rumors circulated that Tardini wanted to resign. He became ill, withdrew for a while, and on March 17, 1960 held a Vatican news conference (rare in those days) to announce his resignation.[14] Some saw this as a Tardini ploy to strengthen his hand.[15] After consulting with Tardini's doctor, John accepted the resignation, then immediately re-appointed him. On March 28 he told an assembly of cardinals, "Behold the old and the new Secretary of State."[16] Officially nothing changed, but Tardini's responsibilities were alleviated. Among other things, he no longer served as general coordinator of preparations for the ecumenical Council.

The differences between John and Tardini were partly style and partly emphasis, but they were largely a matter of substance. John was calm, Tardini tempestuous. John was a pastor who loved to roam around dealing with people first hand. He told Tardini right away he did not intend to be a prisoner of his office. Tardini, on the other hand, was a desk man. He knew "the world through official dispatches."[17] John was spontaneous, Tardini operated by the book. John's sympathies were democratic, Tardini's monarchist. John saw things with the eyes of the poor, Tardini with the eyes of the aristocracy. John saw the Church at the service of humankind and bound to reach out to people everywhere; Tardini saw the Church as a perfect society inviting all to join, but they — not the Church — had to move. John's aim was "tactfully and patiently to make improvements in everything."[18] Tardini's aim was to correct and improve John in any way he could!

The inevitable result was friction. It appeared first with regard to the direction of the Council and later, when Tardini was relieved of involvement in that phase of John's program, in the formulation of the Church's teaching on social problems (as we shall see in Part II, Chapter 3). Still, Tardini was invaluable to Pope John. Their conflict was a way of dealing openly with one another, even of getting along. It had certain benefits.

Tardini was a man of faith, a man of obedience, and a man of considerable discipline. He supported John in his decision to abolish the limit of 70 in the College of Cardinals, he made John's decision to raise Vatican salaries a reality, and he worked with John in such a way that the Curia and certain individuals within it did not get out of control. In fact, little by little John took many steps to break up the power groups that existed, with Tardini's support.

Tardini's greatest help to John was getting the Council under way. He apparently had serious reservations about the project as time went along.[19] Archbishop (later Cardinal) Pericle Felici, a Tardini protege who became General Secretary of the Council, comments:

> Cardinal Tardini was a man of great faith. His harsh, somewhat rude, exterior and his typically Roman sarcasm notwithstanding, he lived out of devotion to the Pope. Whatever exalted the Church and the Pope lifted up his own spirit. The positive response which he gave to Pope John when he so simply announced to him his proposal was dictated by those sentiments.[20]

He may have thought John was mad, but he did what he had to do as John's "closest and strongest collaborator... in governing the Church."[21] John genuinely appreciated, respected and trusted Tardini. Tardini served as John's mentor in the papacy. By the time Tardini died in 1961, the pupil had learned enough to take control of the Vatican bureaucracy himself and to move it in the new directions he favored. John's choice of Tardini's successor proved to be one of the crucial decisions of his pontificate. By then John knew how to be pope, how to make the Vatican respond — and how to run a Council. We shall profile

Tardini's successor, Amleto Cicognani, in Part I, Chapter 8 and the last member of his inner circle, Augustin Bea, in Part II, Chapter 1 below.

Questions for You from John's Model

1. Are you a team player? Or are you a loner?
2. Do you have any close work associates whom you would count also as close friends?
3. Who constitutes the inner core of your team?
4. Is your disposition to "get rid" of colleagues you have inherited so you can put in your own team? If so, what is the loss and what the gain?
5. What outsiders might you add to the keepers in your work group to enhance your capacity to implement your program?
6. Do you have a "father confessor," a spiritual mentor, one who thoroughly understands you and the organization in which you must function, one with whom you can share and discuss any and all work-related matters you wish?
7. Who is your mentor in the position you hold, the seasoned pro who can guide you to success?

CHAPTER 5

Establishing an Administrative Routine

To be effective, every management team must establish a routine, an administrative habit that will enable all to work together harmoniously. Management teams that lack such habit may be adventurous, exciting and always interesting places to work, but they are likely to be high stress zones with significant inefficiencies, lots of burnout, and failures. Leadership that intends to accomplish something significant on a far horizon — or even a near horizon — cannot afford to risk such lack of discipline.

The person who holds the lead job — the leader, the manager, whether pastor or president — sets the pace. His/her personal habit will evoke imitation on the one hand and the kind of response it merits on the other. Though John seemed to the world a happy-go-lucky pope and an undisciplined person, he actually functioned within a steady pattern and with a discipline that is remarkable once one sees it. Those qualities had much to do with his success. This chapter offers managers of all types an example they might follow.

John's Daily Schedule

Angelo Roncalli's life as Pope[1] was busier than it had ever been but also very well ordered. Nine months after assuming

81

his job he wrote to his family that

> my daily work here takes up all my time. I have a great
> deal of work, but it is all ordered and so it is less tir-
> ing and absorbing than it was in Venice.[2]

The well-ordered aspect of life in the Vatican at once
pleased and provoked John. Many in the Vatican wanted to do
things for him. That pleased him. But they also wanted to tell
him how to do and/or say things. That provoked him. The heavy
structure of roles and protocol bothered him. Several amusing
stories derive from his reaction to the expectations put upon him,
such as the oft-quoted, "I'm in a sack here!"

John's daily routine of a disciplined life was the fruit of a
lifelong effort. He generally retired about ten in the evening and
usually arose by four in the morning, sometimes as early as two
or three. He used the early morning hours to read, pray, and
work on speeches or documents. This pattern is reflected in a
note dated December 26, 1959, a full year into his pontificate:

> I had hardly gone to bed when my thought of last
> evening took the upper hand and interrupted my first
> slumber. It invited me to get up from eleven until two,
> pulling together ideas and images for the composi-
> tion of the first talk I intend to prepare for the open-
> ing of the Synod on the 25th of January at St. John
> Lateran. This nocturnal conversation with the cruci-
> fied Jesus from my prie-dieu [prayer kneeler]...
> marked the beginning of my spiritual elevation to-
> ward an approaching event. The whole Church is
> looking forward to it as a sort of introduction to the
> more distant celebration of the Second Vatican Coun-
> cil.[3]

One sees here that John's program was the stuff of his
prayer and spiritual life. He read a great deal in such fields as

the Fathers of the Church, lives of the saints, spiritual theology, and history. He read deeply in areas that touched on his immediate work, such as the biographies of a person he was about to name a saint. His favorite subject was history. To prepare himself for the Council he read copiously on past Councils, particularly the Council of Trent and the First Vatican Council.

Yet, John's reading was not limited to the past. One of the last books he read was *The Joannine Council,* an interpretation of the first session of Vatican II by moral theologian and Council expert Fr. Bernard Häring. John himself distributed copies of this volume to others. John also kept up with current developments and news through the daily summaries developed by the Vatican's Secretariat of State. He scanned a few papers daily, such as the one from Bergamo for which he once wrote.

During the early morning hours John prepared speeches for the coming day. His usually talked these over with Monsignor Capovilla the previous evening, throwing out reflections and ideas. When John went to bed, Capovilla would put John's ideas together and flesh them out. Capovilla was thoroughly familiar with John's style and could organize and present ideas as John would himself. When he finished, he would slip them under Pope John's door, or, if John was already up, deliver them personally. John in turn would review the draft. He often revised his talks right down to the time of delivery.

Following morning Mass and prayers, John and Capovilla would breakfast together and then review the morning news and reports. They monitored how John's words and actions were being received.

At nine in the morning John started his daily appointments (called audiences) beginning with the Secretary of State. His schedule ranged from private meetings with individuals to formal visits with heads of state, from daily meetings with small groups to Wednesday's general audiences with thousands of people in St. Peter's Basilica. Audiences were an important part of John's day so he made the most of them. He reached out to whomever he met first as one human being to another, next as a priest and pastor, and only then, if at all, as diplomat, head of state or supreme authority in the Church. He sought to break down the barriers that distanced him from others. He spoke freely, even abundantly in his meetings, usually from his heart. Many reports describe him as a chatterbox, talking constantly. Yet he could also listen well and took an interest in the problems of those who were visiting, particularly the concerns which bishops from around the world carried to him. John met others without preset agendas. He allowed each meeting to be what it would.

John the pastor used general audiences to catechize people. Many of his speeches were given in settings like this. He wanted what he said to be well understood and quickly grasped by everyone, without their least effort, and so instructed Capovilla and his other aides. He successfully strove for simplicity and clarity. Felici overheard a mother comment about Pope John to her child, "How well the Pope preaches! Everything is clear." He avoided obscure erudition, citing only the scriptures, the liturgy, and the Fathers and Doctors of the Church. For him the task was

> to break the bread of truth for the Christian people in a simple and intelligible form so that it can be remembered, thought about, and passed on within families as a precious heritage.[4]

His account of how he decided to call the Council, described above, provides a good example. This was one of John's most important and pleasing functions, to "catechize with love" and "to walk side by side with his brothers [and sisters] whom he wanted to listen to and question."

John's appointments usually ran from nine until one o'clock. He often ran late. After lunch, he took a short nap, relaxed by walking in the Vatican gardens, and gave some time to prayer. Later in the afternoon he addressed the paper work which came to his desk or met with Vatican officials and friends who did not have scheduled appointments. Often he would leave the Vatican to go visit someone in Rome.

John's guiding principle in addressing his workload was to "See everything; overlook a lot; correct a little." In the spring of 1960 he noted the importance of seeing everything "while holding the person of the pope in reserve" and of being to all a *pater amabilis,* a loving and lovable father. He prioritized his work and did not waste energy on secondary matters. As the years passed he concentrated more and more on the Council. That was the essential.

John's day was capped at 8 p.m. by evening prayers and a meal with his household family. After supper he reviewed upcoming events and dictated notes for Capovilla to elaborate into speeches. An accurate summary of Pope John's work ethic is provided by the booklet developed to argue the cause of his canonization:

> He applied himself to work with method, tenacity and above all with sacrifice. He dedicated himself to work with a strenuous rhythm. If the daytime did not suffice, there were always the hours of night, and he used them many times.[5]

John's preferred style of working with others was direct personal contact. This contrasted sharply with Pius XII's extensive use of the phone, reflective of his isolation. Those he called were reputed to take Pius' calls on their knees. John made it known that the telephone worked both ways and that Cardinals who wanted to reach him could use it. He gave his private number to many. He wanted memoranda, when used, to be short and to the point. He could type but wrote many things longhand. Often he just jotted notes on the margins of documents: "Good!" "Excellent!" "Most interesting!" He was a rapid reader and used his archivist's talent to go quickly through a great deal of material, rapidly sifting what was important from what was not. He kept Vatican operations moving by dispatching the paper on his desk quickly. For example, conciliar texts moved swiftly through his office and out to the bishops of the world. He read them all, making brief comments in the margins as he forwarded them for the next phase of work.[6]

While John did desk work efficiently, he preferred to be out and about, talking with people, learning what they were doing, listening to their concerns. Within the first few months of taking office he made a general tour of the entire Vatican complex. At the beginning of 1961 he visited all of the Vatican congregations. During these visits he regularly spoke with the people working there, emphasizing their ministry rather than their job. He physically covered the building from top to bottom, including the archives — one way to indulge his love of history.

John used every possible channel to keep himself well informed — Vatican reports, diplomatic dispatches, his own conversations with others — and he acted on what he learned. He once instituted a raise for all Vatican employees after conversing with a Vatican gardener. He used personal contacts when official channels proved ineffective. American author and editor Norman Cousins helped establish good communications with Russia, and Cardinal Koenig of Vienna made contact with Cardinal Mindszenty of Hungary on John's behalf.

John's major decisions were generally marked by vision, balance and firmness. He saw matters in terms of the mission of the Church and the good of humankind. At the same time he was capable of making fine distinctions which permitted him to act without compromising himself and to introduce significant changes of emphasis. His distinctions sometimes seemed naive and unrealistic, such as the one he made in 1960 between the apparatus of the Council and the normal administrative structure of the Curia. Since the conciliar structure was modeled on that of the Curia and the same people were put in charge of both, it seemed a useless distinction. But with time it became clear that the Council had a life of its own, one which eventually escaped and overrode the control of the Curia. In like manner John distinguished the pastoral goal of the Council from the Church's traditional doctrinal concern. In *Pacem in terris,* he distinguished ideologies in their pure state from their historical incarnations. All these distinctions had an important impact on the policies and practices of John's pontificate and on his success as a manager.

When John distinguished it was not to set parts against one another but to unite them in a fresh and balanced way. He believed that "the truth is expressed not in a disjunctive but in a conjunctive way: not with an 'or' but with an 'and.'"[7] He did not allow intellectual analysis to override his common sense. He examined everything, tested it, distinguished it and made appropriate applications within the scope of his general purpose. Once John perceived something to be valid, he held to it firmly and acted upon it. He respected the thoughts and viewpoints of others, but unless they convinced him of fault in his own position he would not compromise his own stance for muddled middle ground. He could enlarge his objectives (as he did in adding a Synod and Reform of the Code to his decision to convene a Council), but he did not abandon his own intuitions for the sake of consensus. His clarity, courtesy and firmness resulted in good organizational morale.

Overall, John saw clearly and when necessary acted quickly. For instance, he determined to establish the Secretariat for Christian Unity within two days of receiving the proposal calling for it. John easily delegated responsibility, but with equal ease he made decisions himself. He was low key, could tolerate considerable ambiguity, and did not panic before crisis. An example was his behavior during the Cuban missile crisis in October 1962. The Council was barely begun when the world went to the brink of nuclear war. Rather than send the bishops home, John remained calm, acting to help resolve the problem while the Council did its work.

John grew in his role as leader and as he grew the policies and practices of the Vatican changed. They moved from the often negative positions of Pius XII toward a more positive stance, such as the new attitude toward communist nations taken during his pontificate. (See Part II, Chapter 3.)

Ironically, the more John grew into his role as leader the less important he saw himself to be. He conceived himself as only one in a line of persons serving something bigger than all of them together. He esteemed the past, trusted the future, and sought only to do the best job he could in his own time. Thirteen days before he died, he said:

> I'm ready to go.... After me will things be done in another way? It's not my business. I experience the joy of truth contemplated, of duty done. I rejoice to have responded to every impulse of grace.... Everything has come without excessive effort: the audiences, the moving out of the pope [from the enclosure of the Vatican], the resumption of the liturgical and penitential celebrations [during Lent with the Roman people], the Synod, the Council. It's beautiful to repeat the phrase, "My merit is the mercy of the Lord." In that way together with the pope others receive praise and honor. That's what's happening in the Council.[8]

That was how John worked personally as pope — the way he ran his own office. He seemed casual but was deeply disciplined; he was detached spiritually but intensely involved. He ran the Vatican bureaucracy and the Church as a whole in much the same way, with what can be called a responsive laissez-faire administrative style.

John's Laissez-faire Mode

To be pope is to be chief administrator of an historic, global organization. Like every complex apparatus, the Catholic Church has a structure with which its head must work. In fact it is only through this structure that the pope can effectively administer and lead the Church. The Catholic Church's structure has three main components. Two of them constitute the Vatican bureaucracy, namely the Curia and the College of Cardinals. The third, the College of Bishops, is scattered around the world. John's manner of working with all three was rooted in his person, his style of being pope, and his concept of authority.

John's ideal was not to be "the authority," "top banana" or "big shot," but to be a *pater amabilis,* a lovable father. To him this meant to

> Ask for the more generous obedience to the rules [i.e., the ideals, goals, and regulations of the Church], but at the same time have understanding for your colleagues. Favor in each of them the development of natural attitudes. The duty of authority is to make obedience attractive, not by obtaining a merely exterior conformity, still less by imposing insupportable burdens.[9]

John's ideal helped him avoid the ecclesiastical vice known as clericalism. Its secular equivalent is officiousness, authoritarianism. It derives from "an insufficient acknowledgment of natural rights, personal and political."[10] John harbored no illusions about himself. He knew that papal infallibility did not extend to everything he said or did. He did not see himself as an authority but as *a pastor* and *a pater,* a person who cares, one concerned with the well-being of others. In that spirit he managed the bureaucracy and led the Church.

John's basic attitude resulted in several important administrative postures. First among them was freedom. Respect for the dignity of other persons demands that they be allowed their freedom. He considered liberty one of the four pillars for a peaceful society, and the Church was no exception. He took pains to assure the freedom of the bishops at the Council and did no less with his own Curia. They had a job to do, and he gave them the freedom they needed to do it.

It follows that John used persuasion rather than command to lead. He trusted others to work responsibly in their own field, but he energetically shared with them his own convictions and offered them his example. If they did not agree with him, he would say, "I have not convinced them, but little by little I will."

He was flexible, able to bend without breaking, willing to adjust to the suggestions of others without losing sight of his own original purpose. This quality made it possible for him to get his own projects through. Once John explained to certain prelates how he had broached the idea of a Council to Cardinal Tardini. He told them that he was afraid that Tardini *would not permit* him to go ahead with it! But, he said, "I am from Venice. I know how the gondolas pass within one inch of one another but never collide. If you cannot go this way, you go that way and so get by!"[11] Indeed he did.

John's sense of perspective and detachment also contributed to his administrative style. John did not imagine that he had to do everything. He was willing to "see everything; overlook a lot; correct a little." Correcting a little meant taking one thing at a time. A program of a thousand projects ends in nothing. His principle of action was gradualism: do what you can when you can and let the next step follow from that.[12] "Slowly, slowly" ideas will grow in men's minds and hearts. If things are not yet ripe to do something, don't do it! But help things ripen if you can. He was patient. He did not feel that he had to force things, "get them done." He lived in the present with a deep sense of the long past. He felt no compulsion to force the future.

It is enough to take thought for the present; it is not necessary to be curious and anxious about the shape of things to come. The Vicar of Christ knows what Christ wants from him and does not have to come before him to offer him advice or to insist on his own plans. The Pope's basic rule of conduct must be always to content himself with his present state and have no concern for the future; this he must accept from the Lord as it comes, but without counting on it or making any human provision for it, even taking care not to speak of it confidently and casually to anyone.[13]

The opposite of forcing events is to allow persons to develop and situations to unfold, *laissez-faire*. John kept an eye on developments and intervened when the "signs of the times" suggested he should. America's James Cardinal Gibbons at the turn of the 20th century called that "masterful inactivity while keeping a vigilant eye."[14] In the interim, John could tolerate considerable ambiguity. An example is his response to the first greetings to be received by a pope from a Russian Prime Minister since the Russian Revolution of 1917:

Today Mr. Khrushchev sent me greetings for my 80th birthday. It could be an illusion. I must watch out for that. But it could also be a thread woven by Providence, and I do not have the courage to cut it. Leave what is to be done [*Lasciar fare*] to the Lord. Let myself be led by the Lord. Let the Lord decide and say the last word.[15]

Lasciar fare, laissez-faire, "let things unfold as they will." The episode portrays a mainstay of John's administrative philosophy. John respected the competence of others and trusted them to do their work as they saw fit, including God! Still, John stood staunchly by his responsibility to provide direction. "It is my intention," he said, "to work hard and to make others work hard." And he did. But he did not do so by closely monitoring others, controlling their activities, and constantly intervening if things were not being done the way he wanted them done. Rather he gave general directives and let things be carried forward by others. He kept aware of what was happening and would intervene at certain points if that seemed necessary. An instance is his approach to naming saints:

> John XXIII seems to have toward the saint-making process the same direct and common sense approach that he shows in other matters. On several occasions he has shown impatience with the overly cautious, slow and legalist attitude of the officials of the Congregation of Rites who deal with such matters. He has told them that if they were convinced of the saintliness of a certain person, they should go ahead and bring to a favorable conclusion the causes of that beatification and canonization.[16]

General directives, sub-delegations, and non-directive symbolic activity suggesting what he felt should be happening — this was John's basic way of running the Vatican bureaucracy. He gave the thrust while leaving detailed work to others. But if they did not pick up his lead or if their results did not accord with the direction John was giving, he might intervene to make things more to his liking. It depended on what was at stake. The most dramatic instance was his intervention to give direction to the Council. (See Part II, Chapter 2 below.)

A particular instance of this administrative style is the seating of observers from other churches at the ecumenical Council. John left the organization of St. Peter's aula to the secretariat he had established for that purpose. But approximately a month before the Council opened, on September 3, 1961, John visited the aula to see how things were going. He specifically asked where the observers were going to sit. Told, he was not satisfied with the plans. So he directed that the observers be placed nearer the altar so they could see everything that was happening. So it was done, much to the delight of the observers who came.

Moderating the Curia

John's respect for others and his laissez-faire philosophy inclined him to work as part of a team — collegially, rather than alone. Many of his administrative moves manifest this: reestablishing regularly scheduled meetings with important Vatican officials; seeking advice from various elements of the Curia with regard to matters which touched upon their concerns; accepting help from individuals who had a particular contribution to make. John neither pretended to do everything himself nor did he impose himself on others. He was not threatened by the contribution others made, but rejoiced in it and worked with them. He wanted consensus, but he did not insist upon it. He took account of the views of others.

Little by little John had an effect. He worked slowly with persons and congregations, urging them to be more open in their ways and more respectful of others. The Curia was staffed mainly by persons with an integralist background, and "integralists, …when they turn from abstractions to persons, are not given to nice discrimination."[17] They inclined to treat both with the same absoluteness and, when error is involved, severity. John preferred mercy and respect. In fact, as time passed, the spirit of Vatican directives changed in tone, dropping their customary negativism and condemnation. An instance of this change is the way he handled the French worker-priest problem. Initially the Holy Office directed that the experiment end. Pope John made personal calls and sent supportive letters to leading French bishops, thus softening the Curia's severity, thereby helping the movement continue in a limited form. It was formally reestablished in 1965, after John's death.

By 1960 Pope John was so sure of himself in dealing with Vatican congregations that he flatly reversed a decision of the Holy Office, an unusual step for any pope. That decision regarded the language used in Oriental liturgy. In early 1962 he rejected early versions of a document eventually issued entitled

Veterum sapientia because he found it rigid and harsh. Even its revised form proved controversial. A famous *monitum* (warning) regarding the writings of Teilhard de Chardin issued by the Holy Office in the summer of 1962 reflected Pope John in at least three ways: it did not include the usual mention that the pope had seen the *monitum,* thus weakening its force; it was merely a *monitum* rather than the more severe "indexing" or "condemnation"; and it was respectful of Teilhard's person even as it was critical of his thought. These instances give evidence of a change of tone in the operation of the Vatican bureaucracy during John's term.

John did not radically restructure the Curia during his administration. His contribution was to erect other structures — the Council and the Secretariat for Christian Unity — which both co-opted and bypassed the entrenched bureaucracy. That opened the possibility of change. Then when the Council re-oriented the entire Church, curial reform became possible. It became a reality, at least partially, in Paul VI's 1967 restructuring of the Curia, in the Reform of the Code in 1983 and in subsequent reforms of the Curia.

John did change the atmosphere of the Curia. He worked personally with Vatican personnel, spending time being himself with them and treating them as persons. This was in marked contrast to the aloof style of Pius XII. Pope John was Angelo Roncalli from Sotto il Monte, and he never forgot it. Cardinal Ottaviani, a leader of the integralists, confided that John often spent three quarters of the time allotted for official business in familiar conversation talking about mutual memories, sharing anecdotes, recounting interesting episodes.

Another of John's methods was to send photographs with personal meaning to others, often after one of his systematic visits to a Vatican office. For lifelong bureaucrats, the visit of a pope to their workplace was a memorable event. John strove to personalize their service. He took an interest in who they were and what they were doing. By such steps John touched the minds and hearts even of those who disagreed with some of the things he was doing. Giving people an experience of his goodness and fatherly concern made it harder for them to obstruct his efforts should they have been so inclined.

John preferred being a lovable father but could be a stern disciplinarian. When Cardinal Ottaviani involved the Vatican in Italian politics, John rebuked him by canceling their regularly scheduled meeting. At other times he crisply deflated persons who were important in their own eyes. Still, John preferred persuasion to confrontation when dealing with his collaborators.

John made what changes he could in the staffing of the Curia. He added persons to the ranks of those who controlled Vatican finances; he induced individuals holding several important posts to resign from one or more of them; and when he could fill openings without violating established career patterns, he chose men he esteemed and trusted.

Pope John is rightly criticized for never taking the Vatican bureaucracy totally in hand. He refused to dismiss persons who opposed him and to favor unduly those who supported him. This surely slowed the process of change. He engaged in no housecleaning. His "new boss" strategy was gradualism. As a result he influenced the Curia but did not change it: he softened the tone, distributed some power at the top, and offered an alternative style of service, but the Curia remained what it was. (Some would argue it remains the same still!) The integralist mindset continued to prevail, and since men of that mind were supreme organizers and good administrators with dynamic personalities, the fundamental structure and operation of the Curia changed little if at all. The eventual consequence was conflict between John with his program and the Curia with its customs.

Changing the College of Cardinals

Pope John did four things with the College of Cardinals which taken together symbolize a significant change of perspective. First he increased their number. The traditional limit had been 70 but there were 82 when John died, 45 of whom he had appointed. In making these appointments John used two criteria: merit and universality in terms of both geography and spirituality. He continued Pius XII's policy of internationalizing the College but also strove to name representatives of the major spiritual traditions in the Church (e.g., Jesuit, Franciscan, Dominican, Benedictine and the like).

A second aspect of John's policy regarding the College of Cardinals was that he did not use appointments to the cardinalate to assure the continuation of his own approach and policies. John made cardinals of several members of the Curia who subsequently opposed his initiatives in the Council together with several cardinals who subsequently became progressive leaders in the Council (e.g., Suenens, Alfrink, Koenig). John's appointments were more pastoral than political, more a matter of due recognition than of ideological calculation. On balance his cardinals were decidedly conservative, reflecting the condition of the Church.

Third, John actively involved the College in his administration. He saw the cardinalate not simply as a reward for past services but as a call to new responsibilities. Individual cardinals were not as important as all of them together. John met regularly with the College as a group in a spirit of collaboration. The first meeting started when he kept the conclave in session after his election. Then in January of 1959 he announced his program to the cardinals and asked them to share their reactions with him. He named new cardinals yearly — in December of 1958, December of 1959, March of 1960, January of 1961, and March of 1962. He missed only in 1963 when he was dying.

Finally John altered the relationship of the College to the episcopacy. The tradition was that only some of the cardinals were bishops, namely those *in cura animarum* (i.e., in charge of dioceses) plus seven cardinals who were *in curia* but also the governing bishops of the seven dioceses surrounding Rome.

Originally the bishops of those seven regions had served the popes as cardinals (advisors) but with time the situation became reversed and advisors to the pope came to serve as ordinaries of Rome's suburban dioceses. Further, the cardinals in the Curia enjoyed a "right of option" according to which the oldest among them who was not the bishop of one of these suburban sees would assume the diocese which became vacant through the death of its cardinal-bishop. John, knowing from experience how much work it took to properly shepherd a diocese, wanted a greater division of responsibilities. Curial cardinals had enough to do in taking care of their regular jobs without heading a diocese on the side. John took two steps (and two years) to make a change. In 1961 he stripped the curial cardinals of their right to choose these dioceses for themselves. Then in 1962 he relieved them of the governing jurisdiction of the suburban dioceses. In their place he named an ordinary bishop to each of the seven sees involved. By these steps John both split up the accumulation of positions by a few persons and increased the likelihood of good pastoral service to the people living around Rome.

John's most important move came on April 15, 1962, when he decreed that all cardinals had to be bishops. Theologically, those responsible for governing the Church are bishops. Since the members of the College of Cardinals helped the pope govern the Church, he felt they should share in the dignity and grace of the episcopacy. In addition John made bishops of several other ranks of persons who helped the pope more or less directly. By these steps John symbolically affirmed that the episcopacy was more important than the cardinalate and that the College of Bishops was more central to the Church than the College of Cardinals. This was brought home in the Council dramatically as the voting of the bishops determined what was to be done. Since John's death, a Synod of Bishops has become an established and regularly functioning organism helping the pope govern the Church.

Making the Bishops a Governing College

John's esteem for the episcopal function in the Church was the foundation of his Council. A Council is a gathering of bishops for the sake of making basic policy decisions. In John's eyes the episcopacy was the important office in the Church. He knew and respected the importance of the papacy and its auxiliary offices, but he believed that the local bishops played the central pastoral role. His own greatest glory was serving as Bishop of Rome.

Pope John vigorously promoted the episcopacy. He established six native hierarchies in place of missionary (i.e., foreign) leadership in less than five years. He also encouraged the formation of national and regional bishops conferences, something which was just beginning when John became pope. Finally, by calling the Council John caused the bishops throughout the world to begin working together. That was especially true when they finally got to Rome. There they experienced the value and necessity of sub-grouping for effective work. Until that time each bishop tended to work alone, an independent prince in his own diocese but an easily controlled pawn in confrontations with the Roman Curia. John taught the bishops to relate with one another, to think and act like a college, and to govern the Church like the successors of the Apostles they are. In that respect, John transformed the bishops and left it to them in Council to transform the Church.

Questions for You from John's Model

1. Do you work with a disciplined and routine order that enables others to work well with you?
2. Do you read materials that will enrich your perspective on the matters you have to address?
3. Do you seek to see everything? Can you do so without feeling you have to be all over everything?

4. Can you overlook a lot, let things be?
5. Can you correct just a little at a time? Do you feel you must make a big difference, now?
6. Are there informal channels people know they can use to get your attention and feed you information?
7. Are you able to make careful distinctions that allow you to make decisions now that will not compromise your options in the future?
8. Can you act quickly and firmly about essential matters when circumstances require?
9. Are you comfortable persuading rather than commanding? Do you respect the freedom of others and allow them to use it?
10. Can you tolerate ambiguity? Are you able to allow things to unfold as they will rather than as you will them?
11. Do you have a sense of Providence? Do you trust it?

CHAPTER 6

Crafting a Message

The management of contemporary political campaigns has made nearly everyone aware of the importance of leaders having a message, keeping on it and using the media effectively to get their message across.

John understood all that instinctively and proved to be a master of this aspect of leadership. By projecting his person and personality to all persons of good will, he won attention for his program. By articulating his program in a few basic images, a few fundamental concepts and a few major projects, he effectively shaped his message so anyone who listened could get it. Then by using the available media, he succeeded in getting his message across.

This chapter focuses on the way John articulated his message. In doing so it offers a model for all leaders by which they can measure their own efforts to make clear to others what it is they hope to achieve.

John's Pastoral Intent

Every pope is charged to bring the message of Jesus to the people of his time. Each pope does this in his own way. Pope John was no exception. In some respects John's message was his purpose (truth, unity, peace) and his medium was his program (Synod, Council, Code). But a six-part message is too complex to be effective so we can look on those elements as the foundation of John's message.

John's coronation speech made clear that he aimed above all to be "pastoral." What did he mean? In general he wanted to communicate the gospel to the people of his time in a way they could understand so they could then apply the gospel to their daily lives. To be pastoral was to be doctrinal, but it went beyond doctrine by enabling the doctrine to penetrate the consciousness and consciences of people. To be pastoral was to be concerned with the well-being of those who belonged to "the Church," but it went beyond the boundaries of the Church to all people. To be pastoral for John meant using "new forms of approaching the whole world with the doctrine and grace of Christ."[1] To be pastoral was to adapt the teaching of the gospels for the good of individual persons[2] and of society. "The good of persons" was the heart of the matter. Being pastoral therefore demanded that the truth of the gospel be effectively communicated. If doing this involved stirring up all of Christian life,[3] including the structures of the Church,[4] then that would have to be done. That is why John called the Council — to be pastoral.

John expressed his pastoral intent in the two speeches he used to open the Council (September 11 and October 11, 1962). He asserted two major concerns. The first was that

> doctrine may influence the numerous fields of human activity with reference to individuals, to families and to social life.... [That there be] a step forward toward a doctrinal penetration and a formation of consciences in faithful and perfect conformity to the authentic doctrine.[5]

John's second concern was that the Church approach people with the medicine of mercy rather than the severity of condemnation, even in her teaching. To John "pastoral" meant a concern that doctrine be known and accepted, approaching people with warmth and respect for their human dignity, using laws to serve and authority to love them.[6]

John's notion of being pastoral also meant to be missionary, to reach out to all peoples. This meant always searching for what was common, what united him with others. Pastoral concern led the peasant pope to base his whole teaching on human dignity,[7] an emphasis that enabled many persons who did not share his religious faith to stand with him. Being pastoral meant uniting himself with others, not insisting that others unite themselves with him. He sought to teach the truth with love, as a brother drawing all together, not as a superior driving them into one camp. He took the initiative.

Convivenza: A New Order of Human Relations

John's rhetoric reflects his concern to be a good pastor. *Convivenza* is one of his key terms. The Italian word has no exact English equivalent. Literally, it means "living together," coexistence, yet more. It suggests "real coordination and integration, a fraternity of love,"[8] community rather than mere society, communion rather than mere community. *Convivenza* evokes intimacy, not just togetherness.

John's notion of *convivenza* embraced the whole world.[9] His vision was rooted in his childhood experience in Sotto il Monte, but it extended the Church to work with other institutions to find solutions for the problems of the whole human community. In the fall of 1962 John made it clear that he called the Council to enable the Church to contribute more effectively to the solution of modern problems. The following Easter, shortly before his death and a few days after the publication of his greatest encyclical, *Pacem in terris,* John spoke about "Generous Service to Human and Christian *Convivenza*":

I love to give homage to the world organizations which work in every field — political, cultural, welfare — to serve man in his dignity as a person, as our brother, as a son of God. In this noble enterprise, Catholics are present and active, and I am confident that the number of those who apostolically undertake this service will increase.… The gift of peace will give to each a sense of his responsibility and of his limits, so that he can communicate to his fellows what they expect and have a right to get. In that way it will be less difficult to enter with a resolute mind into the complexity of human problems and relationships in order to extend the *pax christiana* which puts everything together in due order and eliminates the sources of social and civic disturbance.[10]

The "life together" of the human community that John envisioned gave special attention to the lower and oppressed groups of persons. Indeed, his first great social encyclical, *Mater et magistra,* was a solemn cry for greater social justice on behalf of the poor and disadvantaged of the world. Humankind heard its own cry in John's words and knew that John meant what he said. John was one of the 20th century's few international leaders to voice the theme of global unity with conviction and make it believable. John's sweeping vision of a united humanity's *convivenza* is what gave rise to *Pacem in terris* and its unprecedented global reception.

John's vision arose from faith, not ideology. Ideologies are closed and tend to be absolute. They make everything fit their core idea. If it is a religious idea, it is a religious ideology. Ideologies tend to respect neither the nature of things nor human persons. Integralists tended to be ideologues. John was not.

John's faith confronted the various ideologies abroad among humankind and within the Church. He was convinced that only through the sacrifice that such conflict entailed could the Church render a genuine service to the modern world. John promoted his vision confidently because he experienced it as a work of God, an inspiration of the Spirit, not something he thought up. *Convivenza* for him was not a product of human endeavor. It was principally God's work, the Spirit's work, the fruit of a "new Pentecost."

"New Pentecost" was another key term in John's rhetoric. On July 7, 1959, he said, "I love to think that Divine Providence is elaborating one of the great mysteries of history, which will be the mystery of the mercy of the Lord for all peoples."[11] John wanted to see a "new Pentecost,"[12] but he harbored no illusions about its attainment:

> The Church does not pretend to expect each day a miraculous transformation such as occurred in the apostles and disciples on the first Pentecost. The Church does not pretend to that. But she works for this and asks God without ceasing for a renewal of the prodigy.[13]

A sub-theme of John's rhetoric similar to his notion of a "new Pentecost" is the concept of a union of heaven and earth. John first used the image in the January 25, 1959 speech in which he announced his intention to call a Council. As he reviewed the situation of the world, he felt

> sad... in the face of the abuse and the compromise of man's freedom which turns entirely to a search for the so-called goods of the earth, not knowing that the heavens are open.[14]

To meet the situation John turned to the extraordinary measures he announced for the benefits they could bring, "even in reference to the well-being of life here below, an abundant richness from the dew of heavens and the fertility of the earth"[15] (Genesis 27:28). More familiar is his use of the image in the opening speech of the Council:

> The Second Vatican Ecumenical Council... prepares,

> as it were, and consolidates the path toward that unity
> of mankind which is required as a necessary founda-
> tion in order that the earthly city may be brought to
> the resemblance of that heavenly city where truth
> reigns, charity is the law, and whose extent is eter-
> nity.[16]

The theme of "new heavens and a new earth in which justice dwells, according to the promise of Jesus" was on John's
lips until the day he died.[17]

No term in John's lexicon became more famous than
aggiornamento. It became the symbol of everything he was about,
an emblem of his program, a kind of slogan or motto. Literally
aggiornamento means to "update." It was John's word for pas-
torally motivated changes in ecclesiastical legislation and discipline. In 1953 he used the term to describe the results of a Synod
which had been held by the churches in the Triveneto region
of Italy.[18] In announcing his program on January 25, 1959 he
used *aggiornamento* to describe what he proposed to do specifically with the Code of Canon Law! The Synod and the Council would, he said,

> happily lead to the hoped for and awaited *aggiorna-
> mento* of the Code of Canon Law which ought to ac-
> company and crown these two examples of a practi-
> cal application of the provisions of ecclesiastical dis-
> cipline, which the Spirit of the Lord will be suggest-
> ing to us along the way.[19]

The same usage is found in his first encyclical *Ad Petri
cathedram* (June, 1959) and is repeated in the 1960 document
establishing the Council's preparatory commissions (*Superno Dei
nutu*). *Aggiornamento*'s primary meaning was the adjustment of
laws in order to bring them into greater conformity with contemporary life and practice.

In spite of the fact that the term had directly a restricted and legalistic denotation, *aggiornamento* quickly came to connote much more. It became the term most typically connected with John and the Second Vatican Council. People understood that not only the Church's legislation needed updating, but the Church's meaning as well. The sense of the term grew even for John. By June of 1961 this is what it meant to him:

> The Ecumenical Council wants to touch, and embrace under the outstretched wings of the Catholic Church the entire heritage of Our Lord Jesus Christ. Alongside our work on the conditions of the Church and for her *aggiornamento*, God wants that ... there be added as well another objective..., the recomposition of the whole mystical flock of Our Lord.
>
> We must reject facile illusions.... It will take a great deal before all the nations of the world take perfect account of the gospel message. Beyond that no little efforts will be needed to change mentalities, tendencies, prejudices, all of which have a past behind them. Indeed, in some way we will have to examine what time, traditions and usages have sought to establish, setting themselves over against reality and truth.... All of us ought to work tirelessly with the living forces of our person for what our Lord wants, for the diffusion of his gospel, which fills the whole world with serenity and joy, spreading everywhere grace and love.[20]

John's original meaning is still there but is no longer limited to Canon Law. This fuller notion of *aggiornamento* was both advantageous and disadvantageous. On the one hand it helped make Catholics aware of the need for continuous reflection on their own "mentalities, tendencies and prejudices." Indeed John's *aggiornamento* thoroughly shook the static, closed and self-assured mentality typified by integralism. That was good. But on the other hand, what John meant was often received and interpreted subjectively, distorting his meaning.[11] John's use of *aggiornamento* was actually conservative.[22] He and the Council intended only accommodating to the modern world without changing anything essential from the past. For many, the term continues to summarize what John and Vatican Council II were all about.[23] *Convivenza* should hold that place, for *convivenza* was *aggiornamento*'s goal.

John's talk about the "signs of the times" flowed right out of his concept of *aggiornamento*. If the Church was to "update," it had to do so in terms of what was happening in the world. Hence John was always taking stock of the contemporary situation through the "signs" it presented. John tended to read the signs with hope. In the document formally convoking the Council, issued on December 25, 1961, he distanced himself from "distrustful souls [who] see only darkness burdening the face of the earth." He preferred confidence based on faith: "We seem to see now, in the midst of so much darkness, a few indications which augur well for the fate of the Church and of humanity." He listed several such indications, as he did also in his two major encyclicals, *Mater et magistra* and *Pacem in terris*.

John's optimistic sense of *convivenza* was based on his conviction that something new, all-encompassing, and good was developing in history. This spirit pervades all of his speeches. He opened the Council in October 1962 saying

> In the present order of things, Divine Providence is leading us to a new order of human relations which, by man's own efforts and even beyond their very expectations, are directed toward the fulfillment of God's superior and inscrutable designs.... It is easy to discern the reality if we consider attentively the world of today, which is so busy with politics and controversies in the economic order.[24]

The most explicit expressions of this new order are found in John's last will and testament, *Pacem in terris*.

All human beings ought to reckon that what has been accomplished is but little in comparison with what remains to be done: because organs of production, trade unions, associations, professional organizations, insurance systems, legal systems, political regimes, institutions for cultural, health, recreational or athletic purposes — these must all be adjusted to the era of the atom and of the conquest of space, an era which the human family has already entered, wherein it has commenced its new advance toward limitless horizons....

There is an immense task incumbent on all men of good will, namely the task of restoring the relations of the human family in truth, in justice, in love and in freedom: the relations between individual human beings: between citizens and their respective political communities; between political communities themselves: between individuals, families, intermediate associations and political communities on the one hand and the world community on the other. This is a most exalted task, for it is the task of bringing about true peace in the order established by God.[25]

John's sense of a "new order of human relations" here was equivalent to his notion of *convivenza*. The chief values of both were truth, justice, freedom and love. Together these values could found a peaceful human condition. By being pastoral, the Council and the Church would "contribute more efficaciously to the solution of the problems of the modern age... [to] the whole collection of human activities."[26] The Council had been called to enable the Church to do this. *Aggiornamento* was the name given to the process; *convivenza* was John's term for the goal. The Church thus engaged would experience a new Pentecost thereby giving birth to a new and more youthful Church.

In summary, John envisioned an emerging new order of human relationships within which the Church's pastoral role is to promote *convivenza* by bringing the truth of its life to bear on every human situation. To carry that out the Church had to be renewed. Renewal first had to be spiritual and profound, a new coming together of heaven and earth, a new birth, a new Pentecost which would affect the Church's deepest sense of herself. But that would only be the beginning. A renewed awareness that the heavens were open would sharpen the Church's sensitivity to what was happening on the earth, to the "signs of the times." The Church would have to update its own discipline and laws — and more. It would have to undergo *aggiornamento* in a broad sense. Still John's Church would remain in essence the institution it had always been, a body characteristically "one, holy, catholic and apostolic," but with a personal emphasis and spiritual tone rather than an institutional one.

John's message called for change of the deepest kind — change of meaning. His call arose from a penetrating grasp of the condition of the Church in the broader social context. He firmly insisted that the Church had a role to play in the new world which was emerging, but to play it well it would have to change. His message threatened the integralist mindset and the comfort of those in its thrall.

Pope John spent four years articulating his message in such unique and refreshing yet pleasantly muted themes as those sketched above. Only on October 11, 1962, in the speech with which he opened the Second Vatican Ecumenical Council, did John transform his voice into a mighty trumpet blast. Soon other trumpeters playing the same melody — a new tune indeed — joined him. By the end of the first session of the Council the question was not whether the old walls would come down but whether the integralist forces would succeed in holding anything up. To breach those rigid walls and to enable the free movement of the Spirit in and through the Second Vatican Council, John had to sound his message through every available medium — and he did, as seen in our next chapter.

Questions for You from John's Model

1. Have you translated your purpose and program into a coherent and communicable message?
2. Are you able to summarize your vision in a few key terms with several supportive subthemes?
3. Are you caught up in any particular ideology which will make your message rigid and subject to rejection?
4. Are you personally convinced by your vision and fully committed to it?
5. Do your key rhetorical terms relate to the current situation as your listeners experience it?
6. Is your rhetoric hopeful, pointing toward a future to be achieved, avoiding the extremes of both tired pessimism and mindless optimism?
7. Do you plan to express your message in a few major documents available to all and to repeat it regularly in fresh and reinvigorating ways?
8. Are you willing to persist in stating your message, giving voice to your vision repeatedly until others can grasp it and respond constructively?
9. Do you get discouraged when others don't get it?

CHAPTER 7

Using the Media

An ability to use the media to get one's message across and through is crucial to successful leadership, whether of a corporate unit, a parish or a nation. One of the key qualities distinguishing managers from leaders is the ability to communicate a meaningful message on a large scale — at least to all the members of one's work unit and all those beyond on whose cooperation success of the work depends.

John not only grasped the importance of communicating his message but instinctively knew how to do it. This chapter examines some of the techniques he and his team used. It offers helpful options to leaders at every level of management as they face the challenge of getting their message across, thereby influencing others with their purposes and programs.

Symbols, Spectacles, Spectaculars, Language

John faced two major communication challenges. The first was to get his message across to the Curia and the bishops effectively enough that it would take hold of day-to-day operations. Second, he had to get it out to Catholics, other Christians, and well-disposed non-Christians (whom John called "men of good will") worldwide. He needed the public, so to speak, to rally behind his drive for *convivenza* through *aggiornamento*. To meet these challenges, John used a variety of media.

Every individual communicates something by his bearing, his presence and his manner. John was a naturally communicative person. What he communicated was attractive and infectious. He went from being an unknown and at first disappointing figure to a popular and beloved pope within 48 hours of his election. He exuded a sense of peace and security, maturity and wisdom, genuineness and love. His chubby figure, peasant bearing, easy smile and twinkling eyes made Roncalli an immediate and stark contrast to the lean, aristocratic and ascetic Pius XII. This man struck one as being part of the human community, not above it. He could laugh, even at himself. He intrigued people. They liked him and were interested in knowing more about him and what he had to say.

John understood the importance of his own example. He risked being open to the public in order to invite and enable others to follow him. He did so confidently because of his own sincerity in attempting to live the gospel. On December 22, 1958, soon after being elected, he told the pastors of Rome that he would often leave his Vatican palace to exercise the fourteen works of mercy as an example to them. He told the prisoners he visited on December 26, 1958, two months into his pontificate, that he was pleased to be exercising an act of mercy toward them "because one calls forth all the others, one gives the tone to all the others."[1] This one act of Christmas charity established the legend of John's love worldwide.[2] At the other end of his pontificate, two months before he died, when *Pacem in terris* was released in April 1963, John said, "My own contribution to this encyclical is above all the example which I have wanted to give in the course of my existence."[3] John's example changed the image of the papacy from one of high and distant authority to one of ministry, service, and love. John's person was his first and most important medium for communicating his message.

Symbols — events or items that convey a message — were

his second. John was not ashamed to be a symbol himself, to "make a spectacle of himself" in a mild but literal sense of the term, if through it he could communicate with others. Thus he fumbled and stumbled with languages he did not know or pronounce well. That was embarrassing to those who were used to the impeccable linguistics of Pius XII. John felt it pleased people if he tried, even if he did poorly. So try he did. Such humble reaching out made John a symbol of grace to all, not just a select few.

John loved also to create spectacles, to give people events to attend, activities to watch, occasions that would move them to reflection. He created several in the course of his pontificate. Most were small but symbolic actions magnified by the media, such as visiting prisoners at Christmas time. But some were high profile. For example, he received in private but publicized his audience with Geoffrey Fisher, the Archbishop of Canterbury and official head of the Anglican Church. He took one of the first papal trips out of Rome since 1870, choosing to visit shrines at Assisi and Loreto, bastions of anti-papal feeling, with a full complement of the press in tow. He pushed himself off his deathbed to go to the Quirinal Palace, former home of the popes but current residence of the President of Italy, to receive the International Balzan Peace Prize. He made it a point to sit on a little chair on floor level when he met with the observers from other churches at the Vatican Council. He walked down the long aisle of St. Peter's when he entered to open the Council, choosing to be seen as a bishop among the others rather than as one carried aloft on the *sedia gestatoria*. He talked to newsmen in the Sistine Chapel where Michelangelo's *Last Judgment* is located to impress upon them the importance of their job to make the truth known. He received Alexei Adzhubei, son-in-law of the Russian Premier Nikita Khrushchev. He released *Pacem in terris*, his last will and testament, on Holy Thursday.

John at times combined several discrete symbols into a single significant event. His trip to Assisi and Loreto on October 4, 1962, one week before the Council started, both manifested his personal devotion and showed the watching world, especially the gathering bishops, that prayer was essential for the Council to succeed. That same trip highlighted qualities that John wanted to mark the Church: poverty, evangelical simplicity and a deep incarnation of religious ideals. The trip also symbolized John's promotion of a more cordial relationship between the Vatican and the state of Italy into whose territory he ventured, the first pope since 1870 to do so. Thus the pilgrimage to Assisi and Loreto was a journey of deep and multiple symbolism. Subsequent popes have followed John's pattern, most notably Pope John Paul II.

John also loved to create large spectacles, "spectaculars" in the proper sense of the term. His inauguration, the opening of the Council and the handling of his own illness and death exemplify this. In many respects the tradition and pageantry associated with such major Church events make them spectacles to behold in any case, but John loved such moments, adding special touches that transformed them into something truly glorious and significant. He scheduled his coronation on the feast of St. Charles Borromeo in order to proclaim the ideal of his pontificate — to be a pastor, indeed a pastor connected with a major Church Council. He opened the Council with one of the most significant speeches of papal history. He released his last will and testament in the form of an encyclical with truly global meaning, *Pacem in terris.* He did all these things with as much openness and publicity as he could, meeting with journalists covering the events and having as much television coverage as was then possible. In short, John enhanced the impressiveness of such moments and took as much advantage of them as he could to leverage his message. He sought to share such events with as many people as possible through the media. In fact, John's spectaculars reached large numbers of people, energizing persons and movements that would influence events long into the future.

John not only generated "spectacles." He thought in those terms. He used the word *spettacolo* frequently in his speech. One careful summary of John's intentions for the Council, based completely on John's published words, reads:

> Before one's eyes and in one's heart, a marvelous spectacle! A spectacle of truth! A spectacle of unity! A spectacle of charity! A work of the Lord with fruits both "ad intra" and "ad extra" for the Church.[4]

John's use of symbols, spectacles and spectaculars to get his message across was a key element of his strategy. He knew the importance of publicity and worked to get it. He once said that St. Paul would have been a journalist if he were alive today. He was aware that through the printed medium he could reach two to three hundred million people at a time, through the radio four hundred million, through television one hundred twenty million. In comparison to those figures the two hundred thousand or so he could see yearly in audiences paled to insignificance. So he had to have audiences on a larger scale, through spectacles which newsmen could see and hear and report to others.

John knew that the media created public opinion and that opinion was important to his effectiveness. Thus on December 27, 1958 he recalled a document published by the bishops of Lombardy when he was a young priest, remarking that it had received a "big hearing in the press and resounded in public opinion."[5] Near the end, as he received the Balzan Peace Prize in May, 1961, he again manifested his sense of the importance of public opinion:

> Carried by the wave of public opinion which has spread everywhere, a testimony of great significance is given today by your hands to the person who represents here below the Prince of Peace.[6]

Given this deep awareness of the power of the press, very likely planted in the days when he was himself a journalist, John courted the media. As we have mentioned, within two days of his election he visited the Vatican Radio station and called in the director of the Vatican newspaper, *Osservatore Romano,* to request a change of style. He collaborated in the writing of an accurate biography, allowed a television program to be done on a day in his life as pope, and granted an unprecedented newspaper interview. When the editor of the *Osservatore Romano* resigned in the spring of 1960 John replaced him with Raimondo Manzini, a professional journalist from Bologna and an active Italian politician. In John's mind, newspapers had to speak to the world and not simply provide a semiofficial record of passing events in timeless language, as the *Osservatore* of those days tended to do. Finally John took several steps to assure adequate coverage of the Council by the media. Others felt newsmen should get nothing save the most sterile bits of information. At the beginning, they prevailed, but in the end John did.[7]

Through the media John reached the public. He was open, human, humorous, warm, humble, spontaneous, energetic, clear, concrete and personal. All of this made him a favorite of newsfolk and their audiences. As the *New York Times* put it, "Not since the Reformation, perhaps not even since the separation of Eastern and Western Churches, has a Roman bishop had such a vast and well disposed public."[8] John with his Council carried the Vatican and Catholicism in general to an unparalleled pinnacle of public attention and esteem. Fittingly, John gave permanent status to a Vatican office concerned with communications and the media.

Part of John's appeal was the freshness of his language. Vatican communications traditionally consisted of theological jargon and/or vague, abstract expressions. These were strung together in long Latin sentences (called "periods") with multiple and therefore confusing subordinate clauses, one balancing off another. In the end nothing was clearly stated. The reader or listener of such statements was impressed but mystified. John's speech, on the other hand, was simple, direct and concrete. He spoke the common language of humanity, not the language of schools and books. When people heard him say, "I am Joseph your brother," they understood and listened.

John knew the impact of language. He chose words carefully. He spoke of "separated brethren" rather than "heretics" (or something worse). He struck the word "perfidious" from a solemn Good Friday prayer for the "perfidious Jews." He was careful about his language in what he wrote. He cushioned harsh phrases, such as "schism" when speaking of the situation in China.[9] Already in November of 1959, in an encyclical on the missions, he commented that the phrase "native clergy" held no "meaning of discrimination or belittlement such as must always be excluded from the language of the Roman pontiffs and from ecclesiastical documents."[10] John believed that

> We must bestir ourselves and not rest until we have overcome our old habits of thought, our prejudices, and the use of expressions that are anything but courteous, so as to create a climate favorable to the reconciliation we look forward to.[11]

John's effort to identify with others often led him to try to use his listeners' native language. He was not a gifted linguist, so he made mistakes. That simply showed that he was as human as they. Language was one small but significant way John reached out to the people of the world and touched them.

John was convinced that plain language would help doctrine enter more deeply into people's consciousness. That was his profound pastoral preoccupation. He was suspicious of theologians who complicated the teachings of Christ with complex reasonings and abstruse language. He is reported once to have said, "When I see a theologian, it is a little like an enemy.... I have to ward off a slight feeling of mistrust."[12] Before theologians he felt himself "like a babe saying ah, ah, ah" — for he could not speak their language. His concern was to speak the language of the people. That he could do very well.

John's sensitivity to language impelled him to support the

use of vernacular languages in the liturgy. His sentiment on the matter was quite clear even though Vatican publications consistently failed to make it known. He spoke publicly about his hope that the vernacular would occupy a more important place in the liturgy. Secular newsmen reported that to the world. On September 9, 1960, he took the unusual step of annulling a decision of the Holy Office forbidding the use of the vernacular in the celebration of Oriental liturgies. The Council eventually adopted vernacular in the liturgy as universal Church policy.

If John's gift for language did not show up in his mastery of many languages, it did show in his conversation. His gift of the gab drew both officials and visitors into his world, winning their confidence and trust. In meetings with others, John communicated both himself and his message. The famous saying that John wanted to open the windows of the Vatican to let some fresh air circulate originated in conversation during one of his private audiences.

John also saw the many speeches he had to give as an important opportunity to communicate. He often spoke to large general audiences or in rather formal settings, yet John used them to break curial resistance to his program. He worked hard on his speeches but did not become preoccupied with them. "I do not intend to be lost in discourses," he said soon after becoming pope, a reference to Pius XII's intense preparation for his many speeches. John relied on Capovilla to draft his speeches while he concentrated on acquainting himself with the people with whom he would meet. Often he would digress from the text as a way of putting himself in touch with others. A November 2, 1962 note reveals his attitude.

> A day spent in thought of my dear dead and in the preparation — often enough disturbed until the night — of my discourse for next Sunday. To speak to the crowds even off the cuff doesn't cost me much. More than that, it comes easily to me. But to write word for word what I will say in circumstances of some

> solemnity costs me quite a bit, and I don't know how
> to get away from my original proposal to write ev-
> erything personally. There's a bit of self-love involved
> — the Lord forgive me — and self-love makes one
> suffer a bit.[13]

We have seen his solution to the dilemma in his arrangement with Capovilla by which John suggested ideas and an outline and Capovilla completed the text. When John did talk, his purpose was to speak simply, wisely and lovingly so as to illuminate the consciences of his listeners, to help them grasp the Creed, to heal them, and, when the occasion called for it, to stir their enthusiasm.

John preferred the direct language of the scriptures, the liturgy, and the Church Fathers to the safer but more rigid and less intelligible language of theological schemes or legal systems. As he observed, "it is commonly believed and considered fitting that even the everyday language of the Pope should be full of mystery and awe. But the example of Jesus is more closely followed in the most appealing simplicity."[14] John was hurt by the way his words were sometimes ridiculed or abused, but he maintained his style. Eventually his language became the language of the Council and of the Church.

Statements and Documents

Formal statements and documents were another important medium Pope John used to communicate his message to both Church and world. He issued many of them in the four and a half years of his service. Three types deserve discussion: messages, *motu proprios,* and encyclicals.

Messages include such things as homilies given on important occasions, allocutions delivered to various groups, and formal papal speeches on such occasions as Christmas, Easter and Pentecost. John's Christmas messages invariably dealt with peace. His Easter messages dealt with the role of the Christian in the struggle of life and death, good and evil, light and darkness, peace and war, concluding with the call of the Christian to engage himself in the struggle. His Pentecost messages dealt with the Council in its various phases, as we shall see below.

The Easter speeches offer a good instance of John's balance, his recognition of different and sometimes opposed aspects of human life. He sees struggle in history, in the lives of nations, in families, in individuals, within the Church. In that context, the Church proclaims Christ as the source of the victory of life over death. She keeps the light of Christ shining before those engaged in the battle, with victory attained through sacrifice. John's messages are at once sober and joyous, realistic yet hopeful. They call Christians to provide generous service to the cause of human *convivenza* and express confidence in ultimate success.

A *motu proprio* is literally something which comes from the pope "on his own motion." It generally expresses a decision in which the pope is especially interested. The title suggests that there is something spontaneous about them, that they are actions of the pope himself whether in response to a request or simply out of his own creativity. John issued fifteen *motu proprios*. Of John's *motu proprios*, two revised the regulations governing the period of interregnum and conclave, four conferred higher rank on pontifical centers of learning, three revised certain aspects of the College of Cardinals as noted above, three dealt with the Council (discussed below), and one introduced certain liturgical reforms originally promoted by Pius XII.

Encyclicals constitute the final and most important category of John's formal papal documents. These are authoritative teachings of the pope on doctrine or discipline that are addressed to the Church's bishops and faithful. John expressly addressed *Mater et magistra* to all clergy (not just the bishops), and later surprised everyone by addressing *Pacem in terris* to all "men of good will," whether Catholic or not![19] John issued six encyclical letters altogether:[20]

Ad Petri cathedram ("Truth, Unity, Peace") on June 29, 1959, a statement of John's purpose and program, as discussed above.

Sacerdotii nostri primordia ("The Curé of Ars" or "On the Priesthood") on August 1, 1959, commemorating the hundredth anniversary of the death of St. John Vianney, the patron saint of priests and pastors.

Princeps pastorum ("Prince of Shepherds" or "On the Missions") on November 28, 1959, commemorating the fiftieth anniversary of an apostolic letter of Benedict XV (*Maximum illud*) that gave great impetus to missionary work after the First World War. Roncalli was called to Rome in 1921 to help implement Benedict's document. John's encyclical stresses the importance of native clergy, the work of the laity as catechists, and the role of Catholic social action.

Mater et magistra ("Mother and Teacher" or "On Christianity and Social Progress") on May 15, 1961, to commemorate the great social encyclical of Leo XIII, *Rerum novarum*. It recalls the teaching of Leo as developed by Pius XI and Pius XII, then further develops their teaching on such topics as the role of the state in the economy, "socialization," wages, justice in economic structures, and private property. Part three discusses new aspects of the social question, including the relationships between different segments of modern economies, especially agriculture; the relationships between developed and underdeveloped countries; and the challenges to justice such relationships entail. The encyclical then considers the renewal of human relationships as a "convivium" (a happy living together, *convivenza*) of truth, justice and love; deals with the problems posed by incomplete and erroneous ideologies; discusses the Church's social teaching in that context; and strongly urges the laity to involve themselves in the work of establishing a just social order. The encyclical closes insisting that teaching and principles have to be pondered and put into action. As Mother and Teacher, the Church helps humankind find effective ways of dealing with the evils and imbalances that afflict the world. Pope John helped with the original drafting of this encyclical and intervened at a critical point to change its direction and tone. Though dated May 15, the encyclical was not actually published until July 15. A few weeks later Cardinal Tardini died. The two events were connected. Together they mark an important turning point in John's pontificate, as will be seen in Part I, Chapter 8 below.

Aeterna Dei sapientia ("God's Eternal Wisdom" or "On Pope Leo the Great") on November 11, 1961, the 1500th anniversary of Leo's death. John made it an expression of his own sense of the papacy being at the center of Church unity.

Pacem in terris ("Peace on Earth") on April 11, 1963, John's last will and testament. Addressed to all men of good will, it proposes a peace between all nations and peoples based on truth, justice, freedom, and love. It insists that peace can only be established if it respects the order God has established in the nature of things. It unfolds in four parts. The first deals with the order between human individuals, discussing both the rights and the duties of persons. The second concerns the relations between human individuals and public authorities within political communities, discussing authority, the common good, the competence of public authorities and the rights of persons, the structure of public authority and the importance of citizen participation in public life. Part three discusses the relationships between political communities or nations, recognizing that political communities have rights and duties too, and that their relationships must be regulated by truth, justice, a spirit of solidarity, collaboration, and freedom. The fourth and final section discusses the relationships of individual political communities with the world community, asserting their interdependence and the insufficiency of current organizations to deal with problems of the worldwide common good. The document goes on to consider a number of specific issues, including the fact that the human person must be kept at the center of any concept of the universal common good and the importance of the United Nations. A fifth and final part is devoted to pastoral recommendations. Here Pope John introduces two crucial distinctions, one between the person who errs and the error he makes. He insists that persons always retain their dignity and must be respected as such, even when they err seriously. Secondly, he distinguishes ideologies in their pure and original form and the historical movements to which they give birth as they develop over time. On the basis of these two distinctions Pope John suggests that Catholics can and should be engaged with persons of many different persuasions in addressing the challenge of peace, and that they can do so without compromising their own faith and convictions. He closes by noting the "Law of Gradualism" which proposes that social problems, like life, develop more by gradual evolution than by revolution. Persons must work patiently within institutions if they hope to see change take place. Pope John was the architect of this encyclical, though the man who actually wrote it was Monsignor (later Cardinal) Pietro Pavan. It received enormous attention from the world press and from statesmen around the globe.

The character and quality of these six encyclicals is uneven. Some clearly reflect Pope John; others do so to a lesser extent. His thought is best reflected in *Ad Petri cathedram, Princeps pastorum, Mater et magistra,* and *Pacem in terris.* The themes of his encyclicals were not chosen from a list of possibilities but rather were responses to prevailing conditions. John would generally indicate the overall theme and the pastoral line he wanted an encyclical to follow and then would allow others to prepare a draft. John's effectiveness as a communicator can be seen in these documents. Because two of the encyclicals, *Mater et magistra* and *Pacem in terris,* are particularly tied to Pope John in the popular mind, they deserve further discussion. Their story reveals a great deal about the rhythm of John's pontificate and how his leadership and management of events opened the windows of the Church.

Mater et magistra

The year 1961 marked the seventieth anniversary of the publication of one of the great encyclicals of the modern papacy, Pope Leo XIII's 1891 *Rerum novarum.* It dealt with social questions and had been solemnly commemorated by several succeeding pontiffs — notably by Pius XI in 1931 with a like encyclical, *Quadragesimo anno.* It was decided early in 1960 that a major document commemorating *Rerum novarum*'s seventieth anniversary should be issued. That spring Cardinal Tardini, John's Secretary of State, spent considerable amounts of time at his villa sketching the encyclical for release the following year.

In a sense, Tardini was a natural to work on the project. He had collaborated on a detailed study of the editorial development of *Rerum novarum* which revealed that Jesuits had played a key role in producing it. He knew also that Jesuits had been involved in the development of *Quadragesimo anno.* Thus Tardini asked the Jesuit General to assemble a team to write the commemorative document in 1961. The team labored over the summer of 1960 composing the draft. Tardini reworked it in September, 1960.

Tardini was aristocratic in his tendencies. His Villa for orphans aimed to raise the children of the poor to become aristocrats. He favored a laissez-faire economic philosophy with a strong emphasis on the prerogatives of private property. He tended to distrust the state and strongly emphasized subsidiarity, a social principle which urged that individuals and groups under the state be left free to do as much for and by themselves as possible. Pius XI formulated the principle in *Quadragesimo anno* (article 79). Pius XII reasserted it often. One of the authors of *Quadragesimo anno* (subsequently a ghost writer for Pius XII on social philosophy) was a Jesuit named Gustav Gundlach. He was included on the team of Jesuits assembled to update the Church's social teaching during the summer of 1960.

When Tardini received the preliminary text he followed the usual procedure of running it through relevant Vatican offices. Among those reviewing it were Msgr. Pio Parente, the second in charge of the Holy Office, and several individuals active in various sectors of Italian Catholic Action including Msgrs. Pavan, Ferrari-Toniolo, Quadri, and D'Ascensi. Msgr. Cardijn of Belgium, a well-known international leader of Catholic social action, is also reported to have received the text. Several of these individuals were acquainted with John's confessor, Msgr. Cavagna, some directly with John.

By Christmas, John had received the text himself, presumably with the reactions of such individuals. On December 29, 1960, he publicly announced that he intended to publish a document commemorating *Rerum novarum* in the spring. Things seemed on schedule. Apparently however John was not satisfied with the document. He found it arid, abstract, scholastic — a lecture more than a letter. John wanted to speak to his people, not add a file to academic archives. So around the turn of the year (1960-61) John consulted through Capovilla with at least one individual who had criticized the text. Capovilla indicated that John too was not comfortable with the document, even though it was already being translated into official Latin, and asked who might be able to rework it. Msgr. Pietro Pavan was recommended.

There was in Rome at this time a group of ecclesiastics concerned with agricultural questions. This group suspected that Pope John, being of peasant background himself, might be sympathetic to issuing a major document addressing the problems of agriculture in modern economies and of agricultural nations in international commerce. They submitted various suggestions to the pope, forwarding their project through every channel they could. One such channel was Msgr. Cavagna. This circle knew Msgr. Pavan well. When it became clear that John wanted the document commemorating *Rerum novarum* revised, this group intensified its activities to convince the pope and, perhaps more importantly, Cardinal Tardini, that agriculture deserved a major mention in the new encyclical. In the end, they won. For whatever reason, John turned to Pavan. Other hands may have been involved in the revision, but Pavan was the chief second author.[21]

By the spring of 1960 a new text had been prepared. The precise date of the anniversary was May 15. On April 19 John told a group of farmers that the encyclical was in preparation. On May 14 he told a group of workers:

> ...my plan was truly to be able to offer you, and to offer the whole Catholic Church precisely on the day of festive commemoration of the seventieth anniversary of *Rerum novarum* — May 15 — this... document.... I rejoice to assure you that my promise has been kept. The encyclical is ready. But the concern to make it available to all believers in Christ and to all upright persons scattered throughout the world at the same time, in the official Latin text and in various spoken languages, has suggested that we delay publication of the text a bit.[22]

The delay, in fact, lasted two more months and translation was not the only problem. A grim debate about its content raged within the Vatican. Though thoroughly grounded in the teaching of previous popes, the new draft contained several significant shifts on such crucial items as private property, the role of the state, the meaning of justice and natural law, the significance of the international order, decolonization, hunger, development, underdevelopment, and the collaboration of Catholics with persons professing anti-Christian or at least non-Christian ideologies. In short, John's encyclical abandoned the integralist vision of the world. It sounded a revolutionary note.

In fact, Pavan represented a new school of thought. Though once a student and colleague of Gundlach and other leading Jesuit social thinkers, he had broken with them. He developed a line of thought more reflective of a French approach than of the Germanic pattern of Gundlach. Thus the choice of Pavan represented a departure from the Pius XI-Pius XII-Gundlach tradition for which Tardini was now the spokesman.

Pavan was a clear thinker. He wrote limpid Italian prose. He knew sociological theory and philosophico-theological jargon well, but his own language echoed the gospels more than theories. His language was down-to-earth, not technical. He was more human and less intellectual. In short, he was understandable! That in itself was a refreshing break from the convoluted Latin circumlocutions which enshrouded most Vatican statements, including the proposed first draft.

John was delighted with what Pavan developed; the Jesuits and Tardini were not. As a result Pavan had to meet frequently through the spring with both John and Tardini. Tardini worked furiously to blunt the direction *Mater et magistra* was taking. To some extent he succeeded. But not enough. John with Pavan prevailed. The text was finally released on July 15 and received widespread attention, mostly favorable. Two weeks later, on July 30, Cardinal Tardini, whose health had been failing for some time, suffered a fatal heart attack. Meanwhile John was surprised and pleased by the tremendous popularity of his first social encyclical.

In the development of this encyclical, Tardini presented John with a first-draft *fait accompli*. By the time the draft got to John it had already gone through various Vatican offices and was presumed ready for translation. *Mater et magistra* proved to be what it was only because John acted on his discomfort with the first text, was open to the criticisms and suggestions it elicited, and decided to intervene. In the ensuing debate, he stood by his own sympathies, Cardinal Tardini, the Jesuits and others in the Curia notwithstanding.

That was not John's only contribution. The entire document breathed John's spirit. He personally contributed the title, something he picked up while reading about Pope Innocent III and the Fourth Lateran Council. The whole document was an instance of John's ability to communicate an inspiration so well that others could produce something which seemed to come directly from John himself.

Pacem in terris

The story behind *Pacem in terris* is nearly the reverse of the story behind *Mater et magistra*. In mid-November, 1962, after the opening of the Second Vatican Council and the resolution of the Cuban missile crisis (about which more in Part II, Chapter 3 below), Pope John decided to publish a document which would summarize and update the Church's teaching on peace. He saw such an encyclical as a fitting sequel to *Mater et magistra*, so he went directly to Msgr. Pavan. He told him that "only if there is peace can the enormous energies of the world be used in the struggle against social injustice and for the human and spiritual advance of man. *Mater et magistra* demands this renewed thought of the Church on peace."[23]

John received Pavan's first draft in January. When he and Pavan had the text in a condition with which they were satisfied, John circulated it through various Vatican offices. In effect he presented the Curia with a *fait accompli*! By March John put the finishing touches on the document and published it on April 11, 1963.

Mater et magistra and *Pacem in terris* played a significant role in John's papacy. *Mater et magistra* received a mixed reception. It was not permitted free circulation in Spain, but was unexpectedly given official attention in Poland. In the United States the conservative journal *National Review,* edited by William F. Buckley, a Catholic, called the encyclical an "exercise in triviality" and flippantly commented "Mater, si; Magistra, no." Even a long-time American commentator on papal social thought, Fr. John Cronin, wrote in the *Osservatore Romano* (July 17-18, 1961) that the document was too progressive for the prevailing mentality in the United States. The same was true for many in the Vatican.

The novel quality was not just the ideas John developed, innovative though they were, but the fact that he expected practical application. He wrote to be understood, personally acted on what he said, and urged all Catholics — indeed all persons of good will — to do the same. Being pastoral meant doing something, not just talking about good ideas. That was John's emphasis on June 29, 1961, the feast of Saints Peter and Paul, when he spoke of the forthcoming *Mater et magistra*:

> He who cares for life and wants to see prosperous days must keep his tongue from evil and his lips from uttering deceit. He must turn from evil and do good, seek peace and follow after it... (1 Peter 3:10-11).[24]

John himself set the pace, and he expected the entire Church to put the ideas expressed in *Mater et magistra* into action.

That was an exalted expectation, but more was needed than publishing encyclicals and giving good personal example of living by them. John needed something more powerful than that to shift the policies and practices of the Church as well as the rhetoric. That larger strategy was the Council, but his two great encyclicals played an important role in giving the Council direction. Initially they failed to do that. For instance, the first documents on morality prepared by the Theological Commission had almost nothing about the social teaching of the Church. As a result John explicitly reemphasized *Mater et magistra* in his major pre-conciliar speech on September 11, 1962, one month before the Council opened. That helped, but still was not enough. *Pacem in terris* served as his last effort to share his vision with the Council and to point the Church in a direction that looked beyond its own borders to the well-being of all humankind. Happily, *Pacem in terris,* together with other tactics John used, got the Council on the track he wanted and kept it there through its adoption of one of its major documents, *Gaudium et spes, The Church in the Modern World.*

Questions for You from John's Model

1. What is your personal style of communication?
2. What importance do you attach to your personal example?
3. Do you appreciate the impact of public events and strive to make them effective expressions of your message?
4. How much do you appreciate the role of the media? Do you see the media as friend or foe?
5. What skills do you possess to enable the media to amplify your message?
6. Do you seek to personalize the official and formal communications that issue from your position?
7. Have you articulated your vision in a coherent statement written by yourself or with the help of others?
8. Is the way you have shaped and stated your message intelligible to only a small "in group"?
9. Are your intentions expressed in common and understandable terms that appeal to the profound aspirations of all affected by them?

10. Do you value the impact published statements and documents can have?
11. How well do you listen to those who criticize things you say, draft or publish? Are you willing to change in response to such critiques?
12. Can you stand intense debate between opposing views within your own place of work?
13. How do you honor and respect those veterans who work with you but whom you must move beyond?
14. Do you have a seasoned advisor at your side who can guide and discipline you until you are ready to step out on your own in leading the organization in directions you feel it needs to go?
15. What steps do you take to make sure you are not the captive of your own bureaucracy?

CHAPTER 8

Using Time

Leaders manage in a context marked by time. Effective leaders and managers proceed with a sense of time, attentive to the calendar of events that transpire, recognizing opportune moments to take action, and making critical turns when the time is right.

John's success flowed in significant part from his ability to "read the signs of the times" and to act appropriately in response to them. A key turning point in his administration was the change of personnel in the office of Secretary of State. This chapter profiles the fourth member of John's core team, Cardinal Cicognani. Without forcing things, John used the forces at play, including the calendar and vacant offices, to enable those things to happen that he felt were important. His record manifests a remarkable pattern over the time span of his pontificate, and he recognized the moments he had to seize within that span. This chapter will sharpen your sense of time, the importance of pattern in your activities, and the necessity of making critical moves when the time is right.

A Pattern and the Turning Point

A distinctive rhythm marked the many events that filled Pope John XXIII's four and a half years as supreme pontiff. Clear divisions emerge in his overall record giving a logical order, a pattern, to what managers often experience as "one damn thing after another" and outsiders see as random facts.

One way to break down the flow of John's pontificate is to trace the implementation of his program. On that basis he spent from January, 1959 until January, 1960 concentrating on the Synod of the Diocese of Rome. It took place in January, 1960 and John promulgated its results that summer. Work on the Council began in May, 1959, but became the focus of John's attention only in June, 1960 after completion of the Synod. It remained his focus until his death in June, 1963. On March 29, 1963, two months before his death, John named a commission for the revision of the Code of Canon Law but no serious work was done during his lifetime.

Archbishop Capovilla has characterized the phases of John's pontificate by calendar year in terms of dominant themes: 1958 (two months only) — presenting himself as "Joseph, Your Brother"; 1959 — establishing himself as "Pastor and Bishop"; 1960 — reaching out to "Teach All Nations"; 1961 — emphasizing the Church's "Social Concern"; 1962 — "The Council"; 1963 — "Dying for Peace."

The best division is one based on the internal rhythm of the pontificate and John's vision of a "new Pentecost." In fact he initiated a significant new phase of his program each year either on Pentecost itself or about that time: in 1959, he inaugurated the Antepreparatory Commission for the Council on the feast of Pentecost; in 1960 he initiated the preparatory period of conciliar work. A few weeks after Pentecost in 1961 he met for the first time with the Central Preparatory Commission. By Pentecost 1962 preparations for the Council were rushing to a conclusion, so John used the feast to give the effort a final push in his preferred direction. John died the day after Pentecost in 1963, on June 3. This approach seems most authentic because it relates so closely to successive phases in the implementation of John's major project, the Second Vatican Council.

Another division profoundly reflective of the internal rhythm of John's administration can be based on the change in the office of Secretary of State. Domenico Cardinal Tardini served from October, 1958 to his death on July 30, 1961; Amleto Cardinal Cicognani served from August 14, 1961 until John's death in 1963 (and actually continued for several more years under Pope Paul VI).

Tardini represented the power structure that had long dominated the Vatican. He had worked as a close aide to Pope Pius XII in the Secretariat of State, indeed at the end as the sole Pro-Secretary. He was not a cardinal or member of various congregations and thus not a member of the so-called Vatican "Pentagon," but he was a master of the Roman bureaucracy. Within a week of Tardini's death on July 30, 1961 another pillar of the "Pentagon," Nicola Cardinal Canali, also died. The death of these two men shortly after the publication of *Mater et magistra* provided John an opportunity to change the emphasis and style of his pontificate. The encyclical's popularity provided him encouragement to do so.

John signaled a new direction by choosing Cardinal Cicognani as his second Secretary of State. Cicognani was vastly different from Tardini. Both were experienced, cautious and prudent, but Tardini knew the world from a Roman desk while Cicognani knew it from spending many years abroad, specifically as Apostolic Delegate to the United States. Tardini resisted change; Cicognani was flexible and open-minded. Most importantly, Cicognani was not by training, background, choice or pressure the captive of any Vatican faction.

Amleto Cardinal Cicognani

Who was Cicognani and why did John select him?[1] Amleto Cicognani was born in 1883, two years after John, and like him in a small northern Italian village. He studied at his local diocesan seminary and was ordained there in 1905 before going to

Rome's Lateran University to take degrees in philosophy, theology and canon law. He then became a professor of canon law, published two canonical books, and worked in the Vatican. From 1928-33 he served as second in command of the Oriental Congregation, years during which Roncalli was papal diplomat to Bulgaria and dealing largely with the Oriental Churches united with Rome. During those years Roncalli and Cicognani became thoroughly acquainted. Because Roncalli's relationships with the head of the congregation were not always pleasant, Cicognani did what he could to ease the situation. He earned Roncalli's lasting trust.

In 1933 Cicognani was made Apostolic Delegate to the United States, a job more ecclesiastical than diplomatic, and held the post until 1958. His unusually long 25 year stay in that post was taken by many as an indication that he did not get along with Pope Pius XII. Just why is not known, but the situation was aggravated by fact that Amleto's brother Gaetano had been made a cardinal by Pius. According to canon law that effectively excluded Amleto from attaining that honor as long as his brother was alive. Pius would not violate such regulations, but Pope John would. In 1958 Pope John held his first consistory, named Amleto Cicognani a cardinal, and called him back to Rome.

Though not close friends, Roncalli esteemed Cicognani and appointed him head of the Oriental Congregation as soon as Eugene Cardinal Tisserant resigned that position. John's many years in Bulgaria, Turkey and Greece left him with a special interest in the work of the Oriental Congregation, long a French enclave. John felt a need for change since the old regime did not allow the natural growth and free expression of the Orientals in their own culture. Cicognani's background made him the man for the job. When Cicognani became Secretary of State, John named a native Oriental churchman as his successor.

Cicognani mirrored John in being religious and spiritual as much as he was diplomat and jurist.[2] He was hard working, meticulous, serious, prudent and cautious. In this he reflected the conservative Roman orientation in which he had been trained. At the same time he had learned much from his years in the open and democratic setting of the United States. There the Catholic Church is but one religious institution among many. Cicognani knew how to deal with other leading churchmen and had a positive attitude toward the press.

Cicognani had a calm temperament — a marked contrast to the fiery, eruptive Tardini. He worked slowly, seeing only three or four persons a day, but was well organized and a careful planner. Perhaps most importantly, Cicognani knew how to handle delicate situations with calm and how to get things done. He had been an important link between Pius XII and Franklin Roosevelt during World War II. When the Council got started John made Cicognani the chair of two key groups, the Secretariat for Extraordinary Affairs and the Central Coordinating Commission.

In many respects Cicognani was a less prominent figure than Tardini. Never having been Roncalli's superior, as had Tardini, he was more docile and willing to stay in the background. He worked collegially, as part of a team, whereas Tardini tended to think in terms of himself and the pope. Cicognani's influence was not as evident as Tardini's. He fit in well with John's style.

John's way of selecting Cicognani reveals something of that style.[3] On August 2, the day Tardini was buried, John gave a late night call to Cicognani and asked him to come by. Cicognani did so, somewhat disgruntled. John told him that he had looked over the cardinals at Tardini's funeral mass and decided that he, Cicognani, should replace Tardini. Cicognani objected that he was old and asked for some time to think about it. John pointed out that he was two years younger than the pope and then chatted on for some minutes. Finally he said to Cicognani that he had had time to think about it and John presumed he would accept. He did!

The episode illustrates the speed and apparent ease with which John made important decisions. He relied on intuition more than calculation. It also suggests the persuasive tact with which John gained the help of others even when they were re-luctant.

The effect of the change of Secretaries of State on Pope John was striking. An Italian analyst of Vatican affairs charac-terized the first part of John's pontificate as "tempered with pru-dence" and the second as the "immediate translation of intui-tions into programs."[4] John's careful English biographer, Meriol Trevor, interprets the change in terms of John's gradual distanc-ing of himself from the style and tone of Pius XII. English church historian E.E.Y. Hales summarizes the second half of John's reign as "thirty revolutionary months."

John's retreat notes from August 10-15, 1961, published in his *Journal of a Soul*, reflect the change. The retreat took place between Tardini's death and Cicognani's official appointment. It was surely the most significant one he ever made. John's notes indicate why this change of Secretary of State was central to John's achievement and constituted a turning point in his pontificate. His notes also reveal his basic motivations as pope. His *Journal* entries from those days are the most extensive of any made during a given year since before his ordination as a sub-deacon (1903) and are the most copious for a single retreat in the entire *Journal*! They reveal his deep concerns at that time.[5]

The retreat was occasioned by the coincidence of several factors. John's eightieth birthday was approaching (November 25), it was the 57th anniversary of his ordination as a priest, and it was a time in which John wanted to reflect on his ministry as pope. All of this John mentions in his opening entries.

The most important reason for the retreat was the third — John's desire to reflect on his papal service. He was instinc-tively aware that Tardini's death (along with that of Canali) con-stituted a break point in his pontificate. John does not say this explicitly, but in the three previous years he had not set time aside for a summer retreat. Rather each previous year John had made his annual retreat at the beginning of Advent (December) with the rest of the Vatican. He would do so again starting in 1961, on November 26, the day after his birthday. That occasion surely would have been the time to reflect on his advanced age. Nothing about John's 57th anniversary of ordination to the priesthood was so special as to compel him to enter retreat. It was not pre-planned. Capovilla does not even mention it in his chronology of John's life, whereas he does note John's participation in the Vatican's annual Advent retreats.

John begins abruptly: "I have called for silence and a halt in the customary occupations of my ministry." His focus is clearly on taking stock of his pontificate. He notes that "this form of spiritual retreat has a purpose beyond the usual scope" and rapidly reviews the time between his ordination and the situation now when his "priestly service" is "to be at the head of the whole Church of Christ" and to have "my own hands extended in a blessing for the Catholics, and not only the Catholics, but of the whole world in a gesture of universal fatherhood." Marveling that he, Angelo Roncalli, has been "raised to the sublime height of a ministry which towers far above the loftiest human dignity," Pope John closes his introductory notes as follows:

> When on October 28, 1958, the Cardinals of the Holy Roman Church chose me to assume the supreme responsibility of ruling the universal flock of Jesus Christ, at seventy-seven years of age, everyone was convinced that I would be a provisional and transitional Pope. Yet here I am, already on the eve of the fourth year of my pontificate, with an immense program of work in front of me to be carried out before the eyes of the whole world, which is watching and waiting.... everyone calls me "Holy Father," and holy I must and will be.[6]

Two days later (August 12) he writes:

> So this retreat of mine is an attempt to make some progress in personal sanctification, not only as a Christian, priest, and Bishop, but as Pope, the "good Fa-

ther of all Christians," the good shepherd which the Lord has called me to be.[7]

The day after the retreat ended (August 16), he wrote a letter to Msgr. Alfredo Cavagna, his confessor and sole companion on this retreat:

> Alas, even on this occasion circumstances have not permitted us to realize our mutual desire and purpose of absolute and tranquil solitude. The departure for the highest spheres of two Cardinals, both most distinguished servants of the Holy See [Tardini and Canali], has caused me many grave preoccupations, inherent in my ministry, that of the servant of the servants of God.[8]

Two days earlier, on August 14, he had formally appointed Cardinal Cicognani the new Secretary of State.

Like any retreat, this one was concerned with John's personal life and sanctification. His "particular way of sanctification" however was to be the pope; he was striving to be holy as the "Holy Father." His reflections were not separated from what was happening in his life as pope. They throw considerable light on his experiences and intentions as he stood before the "immense program of work in front of me to be carried out before the eyes of the whole world." His notes reveal what had been happening in his administration up to that point and what would happen from then on.

His notes repeatedly refer to suffering, tribulations and sacrifice. Sanctity "consists in being willing to be opposed and humiliated, rightly or wrongly; in being willing to obey; in being willing to wait, with perfect serenity, … in sincere love; in tranquillity, resignation, gentleness and the desire to do good to all, and in unceasing work." He reflects on a Pietà:

Nothing could be more suitable: paintings and decorations. All round are scenes of the sufferings of Jesus: a permanent training school for any pontificate.... Of all the mysteries of the life of Jesus this is the most suitable and most familiar thought for the Pope's constant meditation: "To suffer and be despised for Christ and with Christ."[9]

Throughout the retreat he reflected on Christ's suffering. On the 12th:

The life still left for me to live here below must draw its strength at the foot of the Cross of Jesus crucified, bathed in his most Precious Blood and in the bitter tears of Our Lady of Sorrows, Mother of Jesus and my Mother, too. This inspiration, which has lately taken me by surprise, is like a new impulse, a new spirit in my heart, a voice that imparts courage and great fervor.[10]

On the 14th he notes that "Justice led him [Jesus] straight to love, immolated him. This must be my lot."[11] It was not that Pope John felt he *had* suffered a great deal. Indeed in a section he titled the "purpose of tribulations" he says:

I must admit that hitherto the Lord has spared me those tribulations which make the service of truth, justice and charity hard and distasteful for so many souls.[12]

Rather he seems to have had a premonition that suffering lay ahead:

If and when the "great tribulation befalls me," I must accept it willingly; and *if* it delays its coming a little longer...[13]

Those thoughts led him to seek being content with day-to-day events without "wasting time in predicting the future.... It is enough to take thought for the present: it is not necessary to be curious and anxious about the shape of things to come."[14] He repeats this notion a couple times over, then says:

> My experience during these three years as Pope... bears witness to this maxim and is a moving and lasting reason for me to be true to it. Absolute trust in God, in all that concerns the present, and perfect tranquillity as regards the future.[15]

With that perspective John next reviews his various pastoral initiatives, the tranquil and loving way in which he had acted on his inspirations, and the success they had enjoyed, almost as though to solidify his convictions and instincts. He wrote that note on August 14, the very day he formally appointed Cardinal Cicognani.

On August 15, he writes:

> "Vicar of Christ?" Ah, I am not worthy of this name.
> ... Yet that is what I must be; the Vicar of Christ.
> "Priest and victim": the priesthood fills me with joy,
> but the sacrifice implied in the priesthood makes me
> tremble.[16]

It was almost as though John knew that hard times were coming.

While Pope John was a realistic Christian who regularly took account of the harsher realities of life, his notes suggest why he reflected on them so extensively at this particular time. On the second day of retreat John examined his conscience about humility:

> I make a special point of cultivating this and practicing it. This does not mean I no longer feel hurt by

what I consider to be a lack of respect shown to me. But for this also I rejoice before God, as if it were an exercise in forbearance, or the wearing of an invisible hair shirt.[17]

And about charity:

This is the virtue which comes most easily to me; yet even this sometimes costs me some sacrifice and I feel tempted and roused to show an impatience from which, unknown to me, someone may suffer.[18]

Then on the 13th about the value of simplicity in his conduct as pope:

Wiseacres may show disrespect, if not scorn, for the simple man. But those wiseacres are of no account; even if their opinions and conduct inflict some humiliations, no notice should be taken of them at all: in the end everything ends in their defeat and confusion. The "simple, upright, God-fearing man" is always the worthiest and the strongest.[19]

A little further on he writes:

I must beware of the audacity of those who, with unseeing minds led astray by secret pride, presume to do good without having been called to do so by God speaking through his Church.[20]

From these brief, discrete and private complaints, one sees that John clearly felt the sting of disrespectful and even scornful criticism of the way he was conducting his papal office. The notes further suggest that the criticism regarded his "prudence" in two basic realms: his policy on the Church's relations to the political sphere and his style of evangelical simplicity.

The sublime work, holy and divine, which the Pope must do for the whole Church, ... is to preach the Gospel and guide men to their eternal salvation, and all must take care not to let any other earthly business prevent or impede or disturb this primary task. The impediment may most easily arise from human judgments in the political sphere, which are diverse and contradictory according to the various ways of thinking and feeling. The Gospel is far above these opinions and parties, which agitate and disturb social life and all mankind. The Pope reads it and with his Bishops comments on it; and all, without trying to further any worldly interests, must inhabit that city of peace, undisturbed and blessed, whence descends the divine law which can rule in wisdom over the earthly city and the whole world. In fact, this is what wise men expect from the Church, this and nothing else.

My conscience is tranquil about my conduct as newly elected Pope during these first three years, and so my mind is at peace, and I beg the Lord always to help me to keep faith with this good beginning.

It is very important to insist that all the Bishops should act in the same way: may the Pope's example be a lesson and an encouragement to them all. The Bishops are more exposed to the temptation of meddling immoderately in matters that are not their concern, and it is for this reason that the Pope must admonish them not to take part in any political or controversial question and not to declare for one section or faction rather than another. They are to preach to all alike, and in general terms, justice, charity, humility, meekness, gentleness and the other evangelical virtues, courteously defending the rights of the Church when these are violated or compromised.

But at all times and especially just now the Bishop

must apply the balm of sweetness to the wounds of mankind. He must beware of making any rash judgment or uttering any abusive words about anyone, or letting himself be betrayed into flattery by threats, or in any way conniving with evil in the hope that by so doing he may be useful to someone; his manner must be grave, reserved and firm, while in his relations with others he must always be gentle and loving, yet at the same time always ready to point out what is good and what is evil, with the help of sacred doctrine but without any vehemence. Any effort or intrigue of a purely human nature is worth very little in these questions of worldly interest. Instead he must with more assiduous and fervent prayer earnestly seek to promote divine worship among the faithful and above all he must encourage religious instruction because this also will help to solve problems of the merely temporal order, and do so much better than ordinary human measures can. This will draw down divine blessings on the people, preserving them from many evils and recalling minds that have strayed from the right path....

This is my pastoral thought and care, which must be for today and for ever.[21]

The second area of criticism was John's style of evangelical simplicity.

It is commonly believed and considered fitting that even the everyday language of the Pope should be full of mystery and awe. But the example of Jesus is more closely followed in the most appealing simplicity, not dissociated from the God-given prudence of wise and holy men.

He then refers to the wiseacres who scorn the simple man (cited above), convinced that the "'simple, upright, God-fearing man' is always the worthiest and the strongest." He continues:

Naturally he must always be sustained by a wise and gracious prudence. He is a simple man who is not ashamed to profess the Gospel, even in the face of men who consider it to be nothing but weakness and childish nonsense, and to profess it entirely on all occasions, and in the presence of all; he does not let himself be deceived or prejudiced by his fellows, nor does he lose his peace of mind, however they may treat him.[22]

Having thus contrasted the prudence of truly "wise and holy men" from the prudence of the "wiseacres," John goes on to draw a portrait of the prudent man. In large part, he describes himself.

The prudent man is he who knows how to keep silent about that part of the truth that it would be inopportune to declare, provided that this silence does not affect the truth he utters by gainsaying it; the man who knows how to achieve his own good purpose, choosing the most effective means of willing and doing; who, in all circumstances, can foresee and measure the difficulties set before him, and knows how to choose the middle way which presents fewer difficulties and dangers: the man who having chosen a good, or even a great and noble objective, never loses sight of it but manages to overcome all obstacles and see it through to the end. Such a man in every question distinguishes the substance from the accidentals; he does not allow himself to be hampered by the latter, but concentrates and directs all his energies to a successful conclusion; he looks to God alone, in whom he trusts, and this trust is the foundation of all he does. Even if he does not succeed, in all or in part, he knows he has done well, by referring to the will and greater glory of God.

Simplicity contains nothing contrary to prudence, and the converse also is true. Simplicity is love: prudence is thought. Love prays: the intelligence keeps watch. "Watch and Pray": a perfect harmony. Love is like the cooing dove; the active intelligence is like the snake that never falls to the ground or bruises itself, because before it glides along it first probes with its head to test the unevenness of the ground.[23]

These reflections on the pope's political stances and the pope's simplicity were recorded on the same day, August 13, the midpoint of the retreat. The next day, as mentioned, John formally announced the appointment of Cardinal Cicognani as Secretary of State, a move he had been contemplating since Tardini's death. Indeed John may have made the choice the day of Tardini's funeral (August 2),[24] but he wrote the letter naming Cicognani only on August 12.[25]

There is defensiveness in John's remarks. He was reflecting on the substance of his papacy and, it would seem, strengthening his resolve. Throughout he manifests a heightened sense of being an example to the Church. Early in the retreat he writes: "I always keep a careful watch over myself where they (ecclesiastical and human laws) are concerned, above all so that I may be an example for the edification of the clergy and all the faithful." On the 13th: "Faith, hope and charity are the three stars of the episcopal glory. The Pope as the head and as an example, and the Bishops, all the Bishops of the Church, with him." On the 15th:

Peter's successor knows that in his person and in all that he does there is the grace and the law of love.... And in the eyes of the whole world it is this mutual love between Jesus and himself... that is the foundation of Holy Church, a foundation which is at the same time visible and invisible, Jesus being invisible..., and the Pope, the Vicar of Christ, being visible to the whole world.[26]

The resolutions John makes in this retreat perfectly accord with his personality and his style of piety. Why did he suddenly choose to renew them in the summer of 1961?

Tardini's death surely led John to review the style he had used and the policies he had followed in his conduct of the papal office up to that time. He coupled this with an examination of the results his approach had produced, and used this evaluation as a basis for setting his course into the future. He did this because Tardini was one of his severest critics. Tardini resisted, or at least checked, certain of John's initiatives. On many things they did not see eye to eye. Tardini is known to have told Pope John, sometimes in a rage, "You are ruining everything for me."[27] To others he said outright, "This dumb ninny [referring to Pope John] doesn't know anything," yet somehow things worked out for him.[28] Tardini even tried to resign from his position in the spring of 1960. John refused to accept.

To summarize, during his first three years as pope, John chose to have a critic named Tardini at his side, where he could effectively temper John's instincts. Tardini's death raised this question: was John going to give his own intuitions freer play or was he to choose again a man who would temper them? The retreat obliquely but clearly throws light on John's choice. Even though he seemingly selected Cicognani early in August, he prayerfully reflected on the implications of what he was doing before he confirmed his decision and publicly announced it. His *Journal* of August 12 repeats his meditation upon the Crucified Jesus: "This inspiration, which has lately taken me by surprise, is like a new impulse, a new spirit in my heart, a voice that imparts courage and great fervor." He expresses what he felt in three resolutions: first, "total detachment from everything, with absolute indifference to both praise and blame"; second, "absolute obedience and conformity" with God's will "even if he wishes me to be wholly transformed by his pains and sufferings"; third, "perfect readiness to live or die, like St. Peter and St. Paul, and to endure all, even chains, sufferings, anathema and martyrdom, for Holy Church and for all souls redeemed by Christ."

By the 15th John wrote: "as my retreat draws to an end, I see very clearly the substance of the task which Jesus in his Providence has allowed to be entrusted to me." He summarized that task in terms of piety, meekness, and charity, with special emphasis on the latter:

> It is love, then, that matters; Jesus asks Peter for it, and Peter assures him of it.... My life must be filled with the love of Jesus and also with a great outpouring of goodness and sacrifice for individual souls and for the whole world. From the Gospel episode which proclaims the Pope's love for Jesus, and through him for souls, it is but a short step to the law of sacrifice.[29]

Before he died John would submit still more fully to that law. In the next year and ten months he escaped chains, but little else. He experienced sufferings, anathema and even martyrdom of a sort. From October, 1962 until the end he experienced the considerable physical discomfort and pain of deadly cancer. In November, 1962 he was attacked in Italy's largest daily paper as a "modernist," the worst form of contemporary heretic. The attack was almost certainly inspired by sources within the Vatican. In the spring of 1963 he was accused of contributing to the growing influence of the Communist Party (which made dramatic election gains in Italy) by receiving in audience Alexei Adzhubei, the editor of *Izvestia* and son-in-law of Soviet Premier Nikita Khrushchev. After the publication of *Pacem in terris,* he was treated to a personal visit from the head of America's CIA, John McCone. The purpose of that visit may have been to scare John away from the open attitude he was espousing toward persons who were communists. His final days were a virtual martyrdom from the attacks launched against him by rightist political groups and conservative Church groups but also in terms of the blood he lost through hemorrhaging cancer. In the end his illness chained him to the bed on which he died.

In his August, 1961 retreat, Pope John was calculating the

probable effects and costs of pursuing the line of thought and action which his own intuitions and instincts recommended. He had spent almost three years acquainting himself with the office and its demands. During that time he had maintained as his chief official collaborator a tough master of the system who was thoroughly grounded in the approach to papal governance prevailing over the previous hundred years. Tardini had been trained by Pius XII, the quintessential pope according to the old model. He tried to train Roncalli. But now he was gone. The question John had to answer was whether to replace him with someone similar or someone more like himself.

In John's "calculation," such as it was, the effects of choosing a man like himself could be only good, because his thrust was "evangelical simplicity." The principal costs would be ones he would have to absorb himself. The retreat brought him to "see very clearly the substance of the task which Jesus in his Providence has allowed to be entrusted to me." He chose Cicognani as his new Secretary of State and then proceeded to what Hales has called his "revolution."

The significance of this change of personnel should not be forgotten. The momentum of John's pontificate built considerably after Tardini's death and its direction became both more distinctive and more concretely expressed. The Tardini/Cicognani dichotomy is the major division of John's pontificate, defines its most fundamental underlying rhythm, and provides the best platform for getting a clarifying prospect of John's four and a half years in office.

Questions for You from John's Model

1. Would you consider making a personal retreat, calling a halt to your normal routine, when faced with critical decisions in the management of your job?
2. When you choose key collaborators, do you confirm your own best instincts or opt to check them?

3. How do you handle criticism from your closest collaborators?
4. Do you have a spiritual perspective you are able to bring to bear on the painful realities of your job?
5. What is the source of your courage?
6. Do you let the Gospel or your own spiritual tradition influence your style of management, or is it all set by some other book?
7. Are you alert to the signs of the times in your life, world, and work?
8. Are you able to perceive significant divisions and turning points in the calendar of your own administration?
9. How do you handle moments you perceive as turning points?

Part II
GETTING THE JOB DONE

CHAPTER 1

Execution One: Toward Ecumenical Unity

It is one thing to state goals, another to pursue them, still another to engage the organization you lead behind them, and still another to achieve them. One thing is certain: if you do not execute, pursuing them systematically, you will not get beyond the mere stating of them. In the end, execution alone is the test of an executive.

Early in his administration John established three goals — unity, truth, and peace, making them known to all through the publication of *Ad Petri cathedram* nine months into his term of office. He spent the rest of his pontificate executing, engaging his organization in pursuing them, getting them done.

This chapter begins an examination of how John pursued his goals and executed his program, thereby engaging the Vatican, the Vatican Council and the Catholic Church as a whole in pursuing them. It profiles Cardinal Bea, the final key member of John's team, and presents the specifics of the "institutional ally" factor of his strategy. John executed well, effecting significant movement toward the accomplishment of his goals. This chapter offers a model of how you might execute, engaging your organization in effective pursuit of your goals.

John's Pentecostal Leadership

When John announced his program on January 29, 1959, he spoke of an "ecumenical Council for the universal Church,"[1] extending "a renewed invitation to our brothers of the separated Christian Churches to share with us in this banquet of grace and brotherhood, for which many persons from all parts of the earth yearn."[2] Though the official Vatican news release put it somewhat differently, the radio announcement of what John said to the cardinals at St. Paul's Outside the Walls created quite a stir.

The thought of a Council in the Roman Catholic Church was surprising. The fact that it was to be "ecumenical" was puzzling. To Protestants and Orthodox believers the word "ecumenical" suggested a gathering of all Christian Churches. The radio announcement seemed to recognize other Christian Churches as ecclesial communities, implying a willingness to deal with them directly. This was not Rome's way! The official published wording of John's speech spoke rather of an invitation "to the *faithful* of the separated communities" (emphasis added). That was Rome's way. The radio announcement also connected the Council with an invitation to search for "unity," while the official text kept the Council and the question of unity distinct. One thing was sure: both texts spoke of "unity" and not of "union" or "unification," both of which would have implied a "return" to Rome and thus been unacceptable to Protestant and Orthodox Christians.

In the days immediately following, the Vatican officially put out nothing about a Council beyond the news release. It was broadcast over the Vatican Radio, distributed to newsmen, and printed in *Osservatore Romano*, the Vatican's official newspaper — which, however, tucked the announcement deep in its back pages.

The confusion grew four days later (January 29) when John met with the priests of Rome and spoke about his program. Apparently he again touched on its "ecumenical" aspect, but once more just what he said is not clear. John did not always stick to prepared texts! Within an hour one Roman news agency reported that:

> The Pope said that he is not hiding the difficulties that stand in the way of implementing his program because, he observed, it will be extremely difficult to restore harmony and conciliation between the different churches. Having been separated for too long a time, they are often torn by internal dissensions. The Pope intends to say to them to be done with discord and to come together, without holding minute historical proceedings to see who was right and who was wrong. It could be that there is responsibility on both sides. Thus the Pope intends to say only "Let's unite."[3]

Within another half-hour the news agency issued bulletins nullifying the previous release, seemingly under Vatican pressure. The subsequent issue of *Osservatore Romano* makes no mention of any reference to unity and ecumenism in what the Pope said to the pastors of Rome.[4]

The confusion surrounding these early announcements had an important impact on the course of events. The world — particularly the non-Roman Catholic world — became quite excited about what they heard. Imaginative reporters and commentators read all sorts of possibilities into the Vatican announcements, many going far beyond the information provided by the Vatican. Then when the Pope and other Vatican spokesmen began to speak more specifically about the Council's purposes, some felt John was backing away from his original intentions. To such observers the publication of the official text, in early March, was a "cold shower."

Unfortunately some people understood John to be calling for a coming together of all bishops or leaders of all the churches, simplistically proclaiming "Let's get together and all be brothers." John's long experience with Orthodoxy lent this interpretation particular credence with regard to a union of the Catholic Church with the Eastern Orthodox Churches. John's concern for such a coming together was well-known and the obstacles to such a union seemed fewer than those to a union of the Catholic Church with the Protestant Churches in the West. Cardinal Bea, the most authoritative commentator on these events, explains:

> ...the declaration of the ecumenical purpose of the Council concealed in itself the danger of misunderstandings and illusions, with the subsequent painful disillusionment. In fact, the news was taken by not a few non-Catholics in the sense that the Pope intended to convene a Council to discuss the problem of unity, with all the non-Catholic Churches and communions taking part. But the Pope soon made it clear that the Council would be ecumenical in the sense carried in the Catholic Code of Canon Law — one in which all the bishops of the Catholic world in communion with the apostolic see would take part. As far as the unity of Christians was concerned, the Pope explained that the Council would have to give a contribution that was indirect.[5]

Bea then shows how much John's statement to the Federation of Catholic Universities on April 1, 1959, and others like them, caused "a certain disappointment." John spoke of a "return to the flock of Christ, ... to the flock entrusted to the care and guidance of Peter." The same traditionally conservative, and to the ears of other Christians, offensive talk of "return" was repeated in John's first encyclical, *Ad Petri cathedram*. The first announcements of John's intentions notwithstanding, it eventually seemed to other Christians that even for Pope John "unity" meant submission to Rome. That was hardly what the other churches meant by being "ecumenical."

Yet there was another element in *Ad Petri cathedram*. John spoke personally to the other Christians with moving words:

Our sincere wish is that we be allowed to call you brothers and sons. Allow us to nourish the hope of your return, for which we strive with a Father's concern.... We all participate in the same divine vocation, each as he is able. Let us all imitate Jesus Christ, who is the guide and author of our salvation. Let us embrace that unity which uplifts the heart, that love which binds us to God, that faith in his mysteries. May we flee all division and avoid all dissension... taking strength from all conquering love.[6]

With such words John injected a fresh attitude into the traditional posture of the Roman Church with regard to ecumenism. If the hopes raised by the announcement of an "ecumenical Council" had been dashed, at least John affirmed "how intense was the longing for unity in the Christian world."[7] And with a man like John on the chair of Peter, Protestants and Orthodox at least felt that it was worth keeping in touch. That feeling would grow as John reached out to them.

Within the Vatican, the issue became whether the Council was an "internal event" or an "external event." Tardini made his position quite clear: the Council was "an internal matter for the good of the Church." Unofficially, he sometimes contradicted John's assertions about what needed to be done. This derived in part from the fact that the press and the world overread John's initial statements, putting Tardini and the Vatican in a defensive position. Correcting press exaggerations positioned them as fighting a rearguard action against John himself.

In fact, John's vision was broader than Tardini's and most others in the Vatican. To both sides an ecumenical Council was a gathering of the bishops of the Roman Church for the sake of making decisions about the Church, but John's idea of the kind of decisions to be made differed from theirs. The curial mentality tended to want a tightening of Church discipline, a reaffirmation of established doctrines, and a correcting of contemporary errors. That was the "*bella cosa*" that Ottaviani and Ruffini had in mind when they suggested a Council to Roncalli just before his election.

John saw a different need. Inward rejuvenation around doctrine was only a first step toward a more effective reaching out to all persons of good will. For curialists, the inner rejuvenation would ground a crisp call to other churches to return to Rome and a more authoritative reproval of a corrupt world, heading as it was for disaster. Others had to move to Rome, not Rome to them.

John took no particularly brilliant ecumenical steps early in his administration. He didn't even communicate a clear and consistent message. But he did reach out, including other churches in his vision of what his own Church had to do. He did so somewhat vaguely in the beginning, but with time his vision became better defined and his voice clearer. Eventually his intent would work a revolution. In fact it took a year and a half for John's ecumenical hopes to take concrete form.[8] A central figure in what transpired then and thereafter was Augustin Cardinal Bea, the third person Capovilla counted among Pope John's intimate friends (with himself and Cavagna). Bea was the final key member of John's team.

Augustin Cardinal Bea

Born in Germany in 1881, ordained a Jesuit priest in 1912, Augustin Bea[9] studied oriental (i.e., near eastern and Semitic) languages at the University of Berlin to prepare for a career teaching scripture. He studied under famous biblical scholars from many different Christian traditions, not solely Catholic. He began teaching in Holland in 1917, became superior of the Southern German province of the Jesuits in 1921, and was called to Rome to teach at the Pontifical Biblical Institute (Biblicum) in 1924. He served as rector there from 1930 until 1949 and continued to be associated with the Biblical Institute until 1960 when Pope John made him a cardinal and put him in charge of the newly created Secretariat for Christian Unity.

Bea was a successful academic. By 1962 he had published some 150 titles and won for himself an international reputation extending far beyond the boundaries of the Catholic Church. Already in 1935 he led the first delegation of the Biblical Institute ever to attend an international congress of biblical scholars and fostered such contact through the years.

Bea met Eugenio Pacelli (Pius XII) when both were working in southern Germany (1921-24). After 1930 both found themselves in Rome. Among other things they worked together on Pius's forward-looking encyclical on the scriptures, *Divino afflante Spiritu,* published in 1943. From 1945 to 1958, Bea served as Pius XII's confessor. In 1949 Bea was named a consultor to the Holy Office, one year after that congregation issued a highly restrictive warning about ecumenical relationships. Soon after he arrived, a new and more permissive "Instruction on the Ecumenical Movement" was published. It opened the door to Catholic ecumenical activities throughout the 1950's. That work laid the ground for the ecumenical advances of the Second Vatican Council.

Bea had other assignments within the Vatican. In 1931 he was associated with the Biblical Commission, in 1939 with the Congregation of Studies, and in 1950 with the Congregation of Rites. He was not a top official, but he was present and brought his insights and thinking to bear on the issues which came before these bodies. His scattered presence is what first brought him to Pope John's attention, for John met him more than once in the visits he made to different offices during his first year as pope. They got acquainted, however, only after John made Bea a cardinal.

John used appointments to the cardinalate for several different purposes. In Bea's case two motives came together. The first was John's desire to have the major religious orders represented in the College of Cardinals. When he became pope, there was no Jesuit cardinal. A second objective was to honor men who had worked closely with Pius XII for many years without public recognition. Bea fit both criteria, but he was not an ideal candidate on other scales. For one, he was 79 years old. For another, a recent illness nearly took his life and he remained quite weak. One Jesuit told Capovilla, "He's a little old man who isn't worth anything anymore." Making him a cardinal seemed little more than a gesture.

Nonetheless John made Bea a cardinal during his second consistory in December, 1959. A month later, in January, the two of them met privately to get acquainted. It was a profound experience for both. They found themselves to be "soul brothers" with a shared vision. Bea emerged and told his secretary, Fr. Stefan Schmidt, "We understood one another perfectly." John commented to Capovilla that he saw in Bea a humble, religious man, and a catechist, "the stuff of a pastor. He will be very useful." Two months later Bea gave John the proposal for a special organism to deal with ecumenical concerns. From that proposal grew the Secretariat for Christian Unity which became John's "institutional ally."

According to his secretary, Fr. Stefan Schmidt, S.J., Bea was an open-minded man and a team player with a great capacity for work. Brilliant but modest, he had a deep respect for others and a willingness to learn from them. He had his own thoughts and convictions and had the courage to stand up for them, but he didn't need to force his views on others. He was balanced, a realist, a man with refined sensibilities, a priest with a deep pastoral love for the Church, and himself a deeply spiritual individual. Genuine, good, meek and diplomatic, Bea did what he did out of deep conviction and commitment to the gospel and the demands he understood it to be making on him.

Bea was like Pope John in his basic dispositions, yet his background was totally different. Bea was an academician; John was an organizer, diplomat, and pastor. Bea was a renowned scholar; John was a simple catechist. Bea had spent most of his ecclesiastical career in Rome and was a Jesuit closely identified with the Biblicum and its mother university, the Gregorian. John was a diocesan priest whose training and loyalty were rooted in the rival Lateran Seminary. Bea was from Germany, a country John knew little about.

As usual, however, John worked on what united him with Bea rather than what distinguished them; and having established that unity, he allowed their differences to enrich them both. Together they became the rallying point for the forces for change abroad in the Catholic Church and the Christian world.

Bea was one of the persons permitted free private access to John's apartment in the afternoons. As a Roman veteran he had a well-developed sense of discretion. He did not go to see John often lest his visits arouse jealousy. In fact, John had to encourage him to come more frequently. They did see one another enough to coordinate their work effectively. As was his custom, John delegated the work of the Secretariat for Christian Unity to Bea, let him follow his own instincts, kept informed, and gave Bea all the support he needed. Meanwhile Bea brought his considerable intellectual talents to bear on substantiating and interpreting John's intuitions and intentions.

The primary charge to Bea's Secretariat was to keep Christians of other denominations informed about developments in the work of the Council and to keep conciliar bodies informed about the sensitivities and viewpoints of other Christian groups. This made him a publicist and, in spite of his age, he became an enormously energetic one. In the nine years between his elevation to the cardinalate (at age 79 just recovered from serious illness) and his death in 1968 he generated some 250 publications, including ten books. In the nine months immediately preceding the opening of the Council alone, he held 25 news conferences. He traveled everywhere — Germany, Switzerland, France, England, the U.S. — lecturing about the Council and spreading significant ideas that would eventually be contained in conciliar documents. Together John and Bea dissipated an anti-ecumenical tone issuing from other Roman sources, notably the Lateran and the Holy Office.

John entrusted more and more to Bea's Secretariat. It began as an office concerned with Christian Unity, primarily in terms of the Protestant Churches since concern for the Orthodox branch of Christianity fell under the jurisdiction of the Preparatory Commission for Oriental Churches. By Christmas of 1961, however, relations with the Orthodox too were entrusted to Bea. Next John asked Bea to prepare a statement on the relationship of the Catholic Church to the Jewish religion. Little by little the Secretariat for Christian Unity became the gathering point for questions concerning other religions and religious freedom in general. In short, the scope of its concerns and activities came to be as broad as the vision of Pope John himself.

Bea was a whirlwind driven by John's vision. He was uniquely equipped to translate that vision into acceptable and appealing terms for persons long antagonized if not offended by the style of the Roman Catholic Church. He became the chosen and willing champion of the way of approaching and thinking about issues in the Council that resulted in many of the changes introduced by Vatican II.

In sum, Bea enhanced John's core management team in three principal ways. First, John felt the need for change, and Bea possessed the academic expertise to formulate and confirm John's intuition. Second, Bea was a potent publicist, strengthening John's own efforts and those of Capovilla. Finally, Bea possessed organizational wisdom, complementing the talents of John and Cavagna.

The Secretariat for Christian Unity

Early in 1960 Cardinal Bea received a proposal for a "Commission for the Union of Christians" from Archbishop Lorenz Jaeger of Paderborn, Germany. Bea studied the proposal carefully before passing it on to Pope John on March 11, just three months after Bea had been made cardinal and two months from the time that Bea and John had their first private conversation. Within two days, on March 13, 1960, a Sunday, John had

Capovilla phone Bea to ask for a meeting that very day. John was pleased with the proposal. He considered it a perfect way to give practical expression to the unity component of his program. It was an instrument for achieving his aspirations. John told Bea that there should be a commission, and that Bea himself would be its head. Several weeks later John told Bea to call the new body a secretariat within the structure of the Council rather than a commission within the Curia. This would give the new organism greater freedom. Moreover, the Council was attracting the other churches while the Curia had historically repelled them. By making the body a secretariat and placing it within the conciliar organism, John made the move more acceptable to the other churches.

The Jaeger-Bea plan called for a permanent body within the Vatican structure but John decided to make it part of the temporary conciliar preparatory organization. He told Bea that they would determine the future of the body step by step. On May 30, 1960, he announced to the cardinals in Rome his plans for the preparatory organization of the Council, including three secretariats of which Bea's was one. On June 5, 1960, by a document titled *Superno Dei nutu,* John formally established the preparatory commissions and secretariats, publicly announcing the names of those responsible. From that day the man previously known as a scripture scholar and confessor of Pius XII became the President of the Secretariat for Christian Unity.

This sequence of events manifests several dimensions of John's management skill. He had waited more than a year for the right proposal from the right person. When it came he acted with startling swiftness and assurance. The idea for the Secretariat was not his own, but he adopted it, adapted it and made it a central part of his plan.

The Secretariat for Christian Unity was immediately well received outside the Vatican. For the first time other churches had an official office in Rome with which they could relate, an office not shackled by the prejudices and fears generated during a complicated past.

Its role grew. When convoking the Council in December, 1961, John commissioned the Secretariat to contact other churches, Orthodox included, to see if they wished to send observers. Later still the Secretariat assumed responsibility for all relations with the Orthodox (at their request). By January of 1963 the scope of the Secretariat was formally extended to include the Oriental Christian Churches and later the Jewish religion.

By making the new body a secretariat, John afforded it freedom of movement within the Vatican. Congregations and Commissions had established procedures and fixed limitations. The chief function of Commissions was to study, report and recommend while Congregations enjoyed executive authority. On the other hand, the Secretariat of State, the only existing secretariat in the Vatican, was eminently flexible. "Secretariats" connoted action. Their responsibility was specific and limited, but within that realm they could do what needed to be done. The preparatory commissions themselves, even though they paralleled the established Congregations, had no executive power. They could only prepare documents which, if accepted by the Central Commission, were sent on to the bishops as the basis for conciliar discussions. By making Bea's organism a "secretariat," John gave it both freedom and authority to decide and do certain things. The way John established the Secretariat for Christian Unity was not dramatic, but the effect was.

It soon enough became clear that nearly everything other commissions handled had ecumenical repercussions. So John logically asked that all the preparatory commissions cooperate with the Secretariat for Christian Unity. This gave the Secretariat a position in the preparatory structure of the Council matched only by the Theological Commission, led by Cardinal Ottaviani. This latter was charged to weigh "questions touching holy scripture, sacred traditions, the faith and its practices." Since that charge touched practically everything, the Theological Commission was able to influence, even control, everything every other commission was doing — as did Ottaviani's Holy

Office within the Curia. Bea's Secretariat was positioned to provide a counter-balance.

Superno Dei nutu established the Council's preparatory organization, proposing that the Secretariat for Christian Unity be "presided over by a cardinal" and be "organized in the same manner as the commissions" of the Council. Bea himself emphasized this likeness of his secretariat to the commissions. He pointed out that the difference of title did not imply *less* importance, but a different function. It was organized just like the commissions, with a president, secretary, several voting members, and a number of nonvoting consultants. Bea also pointed out that the members and consultants were chosen "in such manner that almost all nations with a notable number of non-Catholic Christian communities are represented in the Secretariat." It included seven from France, six from Germany, five each from England and the United States, two each from Belgium, Holland, Italy, and Switzerland, and one from several other countries. Notable was the fact that only two came from Italy. Such composition was practically the exact opposite of most other commissions. They were set up on the basis of Catholic strength rather than non-Catholic presence, and they consisted heavily of Italians. Bea's Secretariat had more international balance than most other groups assembled to prepare for the Council.

From the beginning this group was unique in other ways. Bea himself was one of only two non-Italians presiding over preparatory conciliar bodies. Further, Bea invited a man from outside Rome to be the secretary of his body, Monsignor Jan Willebrands from Holland. Though an outsider to Rome, Willebrands was well acquainted with churchmen of other faiths. Also, Bea held several plenary sessions of his group outside of Rome. All this was significant psychologically, both for the membership of the Secretariat and for the various churches with which the Secretariat was charged to communicate.

In September, 1962, when Pope John set up the organization and regulations for the Council itself (as opposed to its preparatory phase), he retained the Secretariat for Christian

Unity (and two other secretariats) as distinct organisms "because they have not finished their task, and they keep their characteristic nature and structure of the preparatory period."[10] Of the Secretariat for Christian Unity he commented that "it has given a good account of itself, so we'll leave it as it is."[11]

As the Council began, then, the Secretariat was responsible for dealing with the various Christian Churches that were interested in the work of the Council. In particular, the Secretariat took care of the observers representing various churches at the Council. When the first session started in October of 1962, it became apparent that the Secretariat needed authorization to present to the Council those documents it had prepared within its sphere of competence. This included statements on ecumenism, relations with the Jews, religious liberty, and mixed marriages. Only conciliar commissions had the right to present documents. So on October 22, John decreed that the Secretariat was to have the rank of a commission. This decision was made subsequent to the elections through which the Council itself established the membership of conciliar commissions. It left Cardinal Bea's special team intact and gave it parity with the commissions. The Secretariat for Christian Unity was uniquely positioned to influence the course of events.

Taken together all the aspects of the Secretariat for Christian Unity discussed above reveal extremely clever managerial leadership within a highly organized and traditional structure. By positioning the Secretariat as John did and entrusting it to Bea, he destined it to play a critical role in getting his purposes and ideals adopted by the Council. It was no accident.

How Bea and the Secretariat advanced John's Program

Cardinal Bea and the Secretariat for Christian Unity served as strategic partners to John in at least four ways: (1) publicizing ecumenism and the aims of the Council; (2) arranging meetings between leading Protestants and Pope John; (3) establishing relations with the World Council of Churches; and (4) providing for observer delegates at the Council.

As president of the Secretariat for Christian Unity, Cardinal Bea was a boon to Pope John in getting his message out and across to the world. Bea's new position enhanced his international reputation as a scholar, giving him added prestige. It put him at the cutting edge of Pope John's program and threw him into the midst of what General Secretary Willem Visser't Hooft of the World Council of Churches called a "general mobilization" for the union of Christians taking place at that time. As noted, the 79 year old Bea responded to his new situation with amazing vigor. In the first nine months of 1962 he gave 25 interviews. His impact through the media spurred growing interest in the Council and developed high expectations for it.

Bea was an excellent and faithful interpreter of John. When asked early in 1961 whether the Council intended to achieve immediate union, he responded:

> No. The Holy Father has expressly excluded this. He is not thinking in terms of a Council of reunion.... The Holy Father hopes that the forthcoming Council may be a kind of invitation to our separated brethren, by letting them see in its day-by-day proceedings the sincerity, concord, and love which prevail in the Catholic Church. So we may say rather, that the Council should make an indirect contribution to union, breaking the ground in a long-term policy of preparation for union.[12]

Like a good publicist Bea varied his emphasis according to his audience. In interviews aimed at audiences beyond Rome, he toned down the expectations for unity. But in Rome itself he emphasized the importance of unity as a goal of the Council. Thus also in early 1961 he wrote:

The movement in favor of our separated brethren has steadily grown and has reached vast proportions. One can almost speak of a general mobilization of all ranks in the Catholic Church in favor of these brethren. The plain fact is that the Holy Father has definitely designated union as the ultimate aim of the Council, even if it is not the immediate aim, and has asked the whole Church to make a united effort for prayer and purification in preparation for it. But the Council cannot reach the finishing point even if it is a point of departure.... It is clear then that at the moment there is no question of spectacular results, nor of successes in the near future, but of long, patient preparation.[13]

Bea also related the Council to John's concern for peace:

A realist will admit that the Catholic Church can be a worthwhile ally in the struggle for a securely peaceful coexistence of all races, people, nations.... The importance of the Council for humanity becomes still clearer if we consider that the Council intends to do more than cope with the Church's internal affairs.... Try to estimate what the effect would be on mankind if all Christians were in perfect agreement on the question of nuclear weapons, disarmament and peace.[14]

Bea was a clear and official voice for John's vision of the Church's role and his hopes for the Council — though not as official as the Secretary of State. He counterbalanced the "internal event" emphasis of Tardini. More importantly, he spoke often and everywhere, something which was not true of Tardini. And Bea's voice grew louder as the Council approached while Tardini's became silent.

Besides serving as publicist, Bea gave John's inspiration a

theological foundation that increased its respectability. He and his staff began to unfold the implications of the new attitude John was displaying and the new atmosphere he was creating. They presented baptism as the essential experience all Christians had in common, the basis of their unity. All else was secondary. Bea proposed that the Catholic Church had a responsibility to attend to all the baptized, whatever their denomination. Indeed, he went so far as to say that this responsibility was greater than the Church's responsibility to reach out to the unbaptized. He discussed the thorny questions of membership in the Church, mixed marriages, religious freedom, and authority within the Church. In all this Bea spread ideas that prepared the ground for positions the Council would eventually take.

The Secretariat was specifically concerned "to foster more frequent and wider contacts with separated brethren,"[15] frankly and lovingly. One possible place to foster such contacts was at the top. Previous efforts to bring together the pope and other Christian leaders resulted in many failures and only a few successes. John himself did little during the first two years of his papacy in that regard. He spoke about his concern, but he did not do much more than receive a few well-known persons of other faiths, not unlike previous pontiffs.

Actually Pope John was not a good ecumenist in a technical sense of the term. He knew little of the Protestant Churches and their traditions, an ignorance all too apparent in some of his audiences with Protestant leaders. Indeed for John the idea of Church union meant primarily a union of Roman Catholics with the Orthodox, about whom he knew a great deal. To his dismay, he had little chance to meet with them while he was pope.

On the positive side, John was adept at making friends with persons of good will, whatever their faith or tradition. His respect for others and their beliefs was such that he did not attempt more. But he envisioned more. He wanted others to be attracted to the truth in which he believed, which he lived and which he represented. Indeed he wanted others to join him in personal conviction, in common worship, and in institutional solidarity. But he knew it would take a long time to accomplish that and he accepted the fact that he had neither the skills nor the time to work out the details such ecumenism entailed. He could, however, bring people of different professions together. For him that was the essential beginning and he was satisfied to do that. When Dr. Fred Corson, a Methodist observer at the Vatican Council asked him, "How long do you think it will be before Christian unity is realized, perhaps 200 years?" John replied, "My dear Bishop Corson, you and I have achieved it already."[16]

How then did John become famous for meeting many different church leaders? The process was started by Dr. Geoffrey Fisher, the then Archbishop of Canterbury. The meeting took place on December 2, 1960. The initiative was entirely Dr. Fisher's, as Cardinal Bea frankly affirmed:

> The initiative was wholly from the Anglican side, and particularly from Dr. Fisher himself.... It was Dr. Fisher who sensed the change of atmosphere, pointed it out, realized the obligations entailed and took the necessary steps to bring the public to a greater awareness of the new atmosphere and to foster their interest.[17]

Fisher in turn attributed the change of atmosphere to John. He was responding to John's persistent expression of a desire to improve the relations of the Roman Church with other churches. However, the visit only took place because John accepted Fisher's proposal, a decision that caused much consternation in the Vatican. There was first a question as to who was responsible for handling the visit. Eventually John decided that the just organized Secretariat for Christian Unity, still finding its way, should make the necessary arrangements. The visit was delicate, with many implications and surrounded by a plethora of speculations as to what the visit was really all about. One author describes the scene the day Fisher finally arrived:

> On that afternoon of December 2, the Vatican was almost deserted and strangely quiet, but behind the scenes the eyes of all the Court and especially of the Curia, were fixed on this sprightly old gentleman in his strange half-lay, half-clerical dress who moved with a small following towards the Pope's apartment, and whom John XXIII left his throne to greet with open arms and with all the warmth of an old friend who had constantly awaited the day and hour of this meeting.[18]

John transformed the cold discourtesy of a suspicious Vatican and melted the ice left by four centuries of chilling distrust, even mutual contempt. The visit was a success in spite of the misgivings within the Vatican and the wild interpretations without. Bea's Secretariat had handled its first challenge well.

Fisher's visit led to others. On June 12, 1961, John received Canon B. Pawley, a representative of the Anglican Archbishops of Canterbury and New York, and eventually their permanent delegate in Rome. Next came the President of the Episcopalians in the United States, Dr. Arthur Lichtenberger (October 15, 1961); then Dr. I.H. Jackson, President of the National Baptist Convention in the United States (December 20, 1961); then Dr. Archibald Craig, Moderator of the Scottish Presbyterian Church (March 28, 1962); then Dr. Fred Pierce Corson, President of the World Methodist Federation (October 15, 1962). Many others of lesser rank also visited John. All such visits were reported widely in the press, and every visitor had good things to say about John when the visit was over.

John's manner in these visits was personal and familiar. Little if anything official was discussed. It was more a matter of getting acquainted than one of doing business. As a result the visits did not seem to add up to much. But after four centuries of not talking to one another, of accusing one another of bad faith, it was the first necessary step, a big one, on the long road to Christian unity.

The movement for ecumenical unity flourishing among the Protestant and Orthodox Churches had taken concrete form after World War II in the World Council of Churches. The question naturally arose almost as soon as the Secretariat for Christian Unity was formed as to what relationship should be established between the two. Bea brought the topic to John, asking whether "there was reason to contact" the World Council. John replied that "the time does not seem ripe." Bea decided to ripen it. He arranged to meet privately with the General Secretary of the World Council, Dr. Willem Visser't Hooft, twice. The first took place on September 22, 1960 — just a little more than two months after the Secretariat was founded — in Gazzada, a small city north of Milan, on the occasion of a meeting held by the Catholic Conference on Ecumenical Problems.

A second private meeting took place in Rome three months later, on December 3, 1960, the day after Archbishop Fisher's visit. One of the major points taken up at these meetings was Catholic representation at the approaching month-long third General Assembly of the World Council, scheduled to start in November, 1961 in New Delhi. Neither of the two previous General Assemblies (Amsterdam in 1948 and Evanston in 1954) had attracted official Catholic observers, only designated Catholic "journalists" who reported the proceedings to Rome. Here again there were "serious difficulties."

By January of 1961 Bea was working to make sure the times ripened fast enough for Catholic observers to go to New Delhi. In an interview with a German agency published on January 22, he talked about an association of the Secretariat with the World Council:

> There is no objection to this in principle. Since, in fact, the World Council of Churches does not hold

doctrines irreconcilable with Catholic dogma, association or cooperation would, in principle, be possible. First of all, there spring to mind non-doctrinal fields: social work, charitable activity, work for peace and the like. The whole of humanity, for instance, would be influenced by the fact that all Christians acted in agreement about such problems of decisive importance as atomic war, disarmament, the means to preserve and promote world peace! Obviously I do not mean to make any official pronouncement on these difficult problems — that is outside my competence; I merely wish to draw attention to the contemporary situation.[19]

While Bea took advantage of the independence the Secretariat gave him, he was sensitive to the limits of his "competence" in light of the "territorial rights" traditionally held by other Vatican offices. The Holy Office had the right to review the names of the persons nominated as observers to ecclesiastical functions. Accordingly Bea submitted a list of nominees for New Delhi to the Holy Office in the summer of 1961. Cardinal Ottaviani, the head of the Holy Office, neither approved nor disapproved the names. He questioned the right of the Secretariat to send observers at all. The Holy Office had previously (in 1948 and 1954) responded negatively to this same question.

Cardinal Bea was a member of the Holy Office. He argued the matter within that body and won the sympathy of several but lost the vote. So he took the question to the pope and convinced him that if they hoped to attract observers from other churches to the Vatican Council, they had to send official observers to this gathering of the World Council. In July the pope agreed. Bea had to submit a second list of persons and in the end, five observers attended. They were well-received and made important contacts. Good relations evolved so that by February 18, 1963 Bea himself publicly visited the World Headquarters of the Council in Geneva.

Sending observers to New Delhi was a second major step of the Secretariat for Christian Unity (the first having been Archbishop Fisher's visit). It consolidated the Secretariat's identity, role and its specific sphere of influence. Sometimes that meant redeciding things previously addressed by other powerful Vatican offices. It was new, it was small, but it was not insignificant.

Cardinal Bea clearly played the role of a spearhead within the structure. He promoted crucial items on the agenda, brought things to a head when they needed to be faced, and won John's support for the direction things had to take. Bea provoked a division of views within the bureaucracy, forcing decision upward to the pope. He helped many questions to "ripen." He saw things which John did not, grasped what had to be done and helped John do them. Without Bea, John may well have floundered; but without John, Bea would have had little if anything to do.

In assuring official representation of the Roman Catholic Church at the World Council's General Assembly, the Secretariat moved the Vatican beyond authorizing personal activity into developing institutional relationships. That was significant. But the relationship was going only one way: Rome was sending observers to the World Council. To the conservative Roman mentality, having Protestants and Orthodox come to observe the Roman Catholic Church in Council was another question. On October 30, 1959, Cardinal Tardini answered a question regarding those involved in the Council this way:

> The Council is an internal event of the Catholic Church. As such those who do not belong to her will not be able to take an active part in it. This however does not preclude that these persons can come as observers. In any case the problem is under attentive study.[20]

John personally brought this issue to a head on November 7, 1961, a few weeks prior to the opening of the General

Assembly of the World Council at New Delhi, when he placed it at the top of the agenda of the Central Preparatory Commission. The question was presented by the Preparatory Commission for the Eastern Churches. The Central Commission divided over whether non-Catholics should be invited.[21] So John decided the issue himself on Christmas Day of 1961 in the document that officially convoked the Second Vatican Ecumenical Council. He noted that he had established the Secretariat to facilitate such contacts.[22]

The Secretariat proceeded to contact all the other Christian Churches, Eastern Orthodox and Protestant alike, taking care to avoid the disaster of the First Vatican Council in 1870. The manner of issuing invitations for that Council insulted the invitees, worsening the situation rather than improving it. Monsignor Willebrands of the Secretariat became a travelling ambassador asking various churches whether they desired to be invited and how. The decision was eventually made to invite official "observer-delegates" from "world confessional families" only. Individuals interested in attending could come as guests of the Secretariat but not as formal delegates of their particular churches. No one would be embarrassed since only those accepting invitations were publicized. Those who declined the invitation were not mentioned.

Overall the Secretariat succeeded. Complications within the Orthodox community resulted in sparse representation on their part, but when the Council opened, 46 observers representing 17 different confessional families and communities were present, along with eight guests. The number of observers increased yearly. Pope John met with these individuals on October 13, 1961 in a session Bea called a "miracle." The situation had come far since March of 1960 when he forwarded Jaeger's suggestion for a "Commission for the Union of Christians." Far, but not far enough. The work of the Secretariat was just beginning and the first session of the Council was just getting under way. There the Secretariat would make its most significant impact.

If the chief agent of Rome's ecumenical activity was Cardinal Bea, John's contribution was not small. Cardinal Bea specified three things "due directly to personal decisions of Pope John XXIII." First, by explicitly stating "that the Council's aim was to be in part ecumenical … he contributed significantly to uncovering and strengthening the longing for unity which already existed in the world, though often latently." Second, by setting up the Secretariat for Christian Unity he actualized and symbolized the decision to officially enter the ecumenical movement. And third, he decided "in the midst of misunderstanding and, one may say, against opposition" to invite non-Catholic observer-delegates to the Council.[23] In short, Bea credits John with raising up the issue of Church unity, making it the center of attention in the Christian world, and making it an integral component of his program. John's seriousness about implementing his program moved others to take his concept of a united Christianity seriously. The ideal was not new in itself. It was new as a practical object of people's striving, especially Catholics. Bea, of course, did much to spread the word and do the work.

Both John and Bea were realistic about how much they could accomplish. They hoped to set a tone and establish an atmosphere. They knew they were initiating a long-term policy. They did not expect spectacular results. Indeed, they lived consciously under the law of gradualism, formulated in *Pacem in terris*:

> to proceed gradually is the law of life in all its expressions; therefore in human institutions, too, it is not possible to renovate for the better except by working from within them, gradually.[24]

Bea's second observation is that John institutionalized the issue and the Church's response to it. By establishing the Secretariat John went beyond his own person and even beyond institutional rhetoric. He made the concern institutional reality and by putting Bea in charge made it an effective force which led to major shifts in institutional policy. Without Bea, the Secretariat might have been empty rhetoric, window dressing, a line on an organizational chart, a step worse than nothing.

John's managerial shrewdness shows in his decision to establish an organism for unity with considerable independence, a secretariat. This decision broke the centuries-old Vatican pattern of congregations and commissions. It instituted a new way for handling new questions. It broke the conservative hold on Vatican policy and practice without offensive reforms or blatant confrontations. Through the Secretariat for Christian Unity John was able to do what he could not have done through the Holy Office or even through the Secretariat of State. John's notion of secretariats designated to cover specific areas of concern but free enough to operate in new ways opened up the Vatican bureaucracy.

Institutionalizing the Secretariat for Christian Unity enabled Cardinal Bea to play the crucial role he did in the Council. Bea emerged as the protagonist of an alternative vision of the Church in the modern world, articulating the Council's majority viewpoint. He might have done that as an individual cardinal in the Curia and a confidante of the Pope without the Secretariat, but that is unlikely. The Secretariat gave him a base of operation, a sizeable and highly competent group of assistants, a role that kept him constantly in the eye of the public in the years preceding the Council, and a distinct constituency whose interests he was commissioned to defend and promote.

Pope John's third personal contribution to the ecumenical effort, according to Bea, regards the observers. John decided that they should come, took pains to make sure they had prime seats in the conciliar aula, and directed that they attend all sessions of the Council and receive all the documents distributed to the Council fathers. This greatly impressed the observers. Their presence in St. Peter's exerted a moderating influence on the bishops of the Roman Church. It is one thing to discuss family problems with close members of the family and quite another to do the same thing when a banished brother or sister is present listening to everything said.

John's execution of his program for unity evidences the pragmatism of his ways. He would take a step, sometimes on his own initiative, sometimes on the initiative of others, see what happened, and then take the next step. This pragmatism is evident in his announcement of the ecumenical purpose of the Council itself, his handling of the proposal for a Commission for the Union of Christians, his openness to Fisher's desire to visit him, his approach to establishing relations with the World Council, and his determination that there be observers at the Council. He was not arbitrary. He did not cut others off. He allowed everyone to have his say, gave time for the "thoughts of many hearts to be revealed," waited for things to ripen, and then, with full awareness of what the situation was and where different individuals stood, he decided what to do. As Capovilla put it, John's Council was made day by day, step by step.

Questions for You from John's Model

1. Do you accept the limitations of what you can accomplish? Are you willing to lay the groundwork for achievements that will blossom only after you are gone?
2. Are you afflicted with ageism? Would you entrust a key dimension of your administration to someone 79 years old?
3. Are you conscious of the power of structural innovation in an organization? Can you skillfully play that card?
4. Are you able to conceive one element of your organization that will be significantly different from the norm, staff it with people who think differently from most, and allow it to play a countervailing role as events unfold?
5. Can you live with the law of gradualism, moving things

along day by day, step by step? Are you patient? Do you need to have it all now?

6. Do you need to specify not only where you want to go but precisely how to get there, determining each step along the way? Can you allow others to define and take those steps?

7. Are you willing to resolve disputed issues, even at the price of seeming to take sides?

8. Do you take advantage of the opportunities that are presented that can move your agenda forward? Or do you insist on making things happen your way, letting advantageous moments pass you by?

CHAPTER 2

Execution Two: Toward Pastoral Truth

The devil is in the details. Every effective leader knows that. Genius, too, reveals itself in the details. Genius does not so much consist in having a strategy or articulating it. Rather it consists of working strategically, thereby making something work.

This chapter, the longest in our look at Pope John as a model and mentor for managerial leaders, digs further into the genius and details of his leadership. The centerpiece of his program was his Council. It was an unexpected project and one deemed unlikely to happen much less succeed. But it did. By examining in some detail how he made it happen and how he gave it the direction he wanted, we will see his genius. The picture and pattern that emerge might enable you to look with new insight at the details of your own situation and at the pattern of your own leadership. You may see ways to apply John's model that will help you achieve your goals, exercising your own genius in the details of your job.

The Way to Truth: Vatican Council II

The centerpiece of Pope John's program, the heart of his entire pontificate and the key to his strategy was the ecumenical council which came to be called Vatican II. Everything else he did was either preparatory or complementary. His Council was one of the great events of modern Church history.

John structured his pontificate around the Council and paced it by Pentecost. Pentecost is the Church's annual celebration of the original outpouring of the Spirit that brought the Church into being. John used each year's celebration of Pentecost to initiate a new phase of activities toward his Council. In 1959 he established the Antepreparatory Commission (Phase One). In 1960 he set up preparatory commissions and secretariats (Phase Two). In 1961 he initiated the Central Preparatory Commission (Phase Three). In 1962 as events rushed toward the fall opening of the Council (Phase Four), John used Pentecost to focus the attention of both Church and world on the spiritual preparation which he considered essential to its success. As a prelude and test run for his larger project, John conducted the Synod of Rome. As a sequel and concluding institutionalization, he projected an updating of the Church's Canon Law.

Prelude: The Synod of Rome

When John introduced his program on January 25, 1959, he noted the city of Rome's tremendous growth, the relative inadequacy of diocesan resources, and the need for

> an increase in energies, of coordination of individual and collective efforts in order to produce... a more fertile fervor of parochial and diocesan life.[1]

To achieve this John called for a Synod, a consultative assembly of the clerics of a diocese with the bishop to discuss the pastoral care of the people and, if need be, to revise its laws. To John, synods were a normal if occasional instrument of ecclesiastical governance. But synods were not normal for the Diocese of Rome. There had never been one!

John intended for the Roman Synod

> to study the problems of the spiritual life of the faith-
> ful, to give or restore vigor to ecclesiastical laws, to
> root out abuses, to promote Christian living, to en-
> courage divine worship and religious practice; [and
> most especially] "to offer a humble example and en-
> couragement to the dioceses of the whole world."[2]

He hoped it would help the whole Church understand what the
Council could be.

The Synod was also part of John's early effort to establish
pastoral concern as the priority of his pontificate. Activities concerning the Diocese of Rome occupied much of his first six
months in office. After swift installation as Bishop of Rome at
St. John Lateran (November 23), he visited important institutions within the diocese, such as the Lateran and Propaganda
seminaries (November 27 and 30). He met with the priests of
Rome on December 22 and January 29 and made weekly visits
to Rome's parishes during Lent (February 22 through March
29). His Synod would cap these activities, so he moved quickly
to get it under way.

Within a month of his January announcement, a Synod
Commission was nominated (February 18, 1959) and initiated
its work (February 23) and within another month the pope met
with it and all its subcommissions for a progress report (March
17, 1959). Between January 25, 1959 and June 29, 1960 when
the decrees of the Synod were formally promulgated, John made
51 distinct interventions.

The Synod started precisely one year from the day John
announced it, on January 24, 1960 and ran through January
31. Formally it consisted of reading 800 regulations and listening to several discourses Pope John gave. Eight subcommissions
had generated 2000 regulations from which the 800 were chosen. They were organized into three books on persons (209 articles), on pastoral action (504 articles), and on ecclesiastical
properties (46 articles).

Reviews of this legislation are mixed. Some observers were aghast at the pettiness of some items, particularly those breathing opposition to the secular world and sheltering clerics from it. Others felt that the legislation was not legalistic enough, that it was too pastoral. To them it was not good law. Others, still, found in the Synod the beginning of pastoral planning. To them that was good.

John's intention was not to make good law, but to make a better Church. He hoped the Synod would establish an ideal of sanctity that would help the Romans — both priests and people — live better Christian lives. He developed that emphasis in his synodal discourses, speaking to the priests (three times) and to seminarians, religious and laity at the opening and closing ceremonies. John labored over the discourses himself, preparing them as early as a month ahead of time. Thus on Christmas day, 1959 he noted "in the evening my spirit opened up and put me in a state of thought about the Roman Synod for which I want to prepare myself well."[3] The next day he wrote:

> No sooner did I go to bed than the thought of last evening took the upper hand, interrupted my initial sleep, and invited me to get up from eleven until two in the morning. It furnished me with ideas and images for the composition of the first discourse which I intend to prepare for the opening of the Synod at St. John Lateran on January 25. This nighttime conversation with Jesus crucified… fixed the beginning of my spiritual elevation toward the event which the whole Church is waiting for as an introduction to the more distant celebration of the Second Vatican Council.[4]

John's focus was priestly and pastoral, but he included everyone in his vision. Pastoral ministry was not a work for priests alone.

In many ways John's Synod was a failure. Its methods were

disastrous, so the work done was poor. John communicated well, transmitting his pastoral concern, but the Synod generated poorly prepared legislation. It was little discussed, routinely approved, and then methodically neglected. If that was John's idea of a Council, it wasn't going to amount to much.

John's Synod disappointed in part because of inflated expectations, in part because of the state of development in the Diocese of Rome, and in part because John entrusted the Synod to authorities within the Roman diocesan structure who had a narrow cultural horizon. They molded the Synod more than did John.

Nonetheless, John learned many things from the Synod. He found that a great deal of work could be done by Church officials working with theologians, canonists and other experts in the space of a year. He learned that if the horizons of those preparing documents were closed, the documents would reflect that horizon. If he wanted a viewpoint different from that which prevailed in Rome, he would have to "leaven the dough" with persons from other lands and traditions. He also experienced various maneuvers to prevent his proposals from having final effect. For example, one provision he wanted in the Synod's legislation called for fraternal consideration of priests who had left the ministry — in those days a disgraceful step harshly punished. The revolutionary article was written by John himself, but somehow it kept disappearing from drafts of the synodal legislation. In the end John personally went to the printer and stood there while the man set it in type. In this and other ways, the "thoughts of many hearts were revealed" and with their thoughts their tactics. The Synod taught John how things got sidetracked in Rome — and how to retrack them.

The Synod of Rome reveals a pattern that John used later in approaching the Council. He set up an organization to do the work and let it proceed without interference. Meanwhile he kept up a steady commentary on what he expected. He monitored developments but did not intervene until it was proper that he should. His interventions sought "tactfully and patiently to make improvements in everything."[5] He saw everything, overlooked a lot, and corrected only a little!

John's approach to the Synod was like his approach to the Council in other ways: insistence on spiritual preparation; stimulation of public opinion; reaching out to all segments of the Catholic population; and making the Synod itself a public spectacle by solemnizing the opening and closing and inviting everyone to take part. Finally, John did not become directly preoccupied with the legislation as though that were the Synod's most important aspect. He entrusted its implementation to the appropriate officials but refused to set up a watchdog commission to assure conformity to the Synod's decrees, nor did he himself use those decrees as an instrument of control. The point of the effort was to inspire life, not to codify it.

In such light, the Roman Synod was a tempered success. John at least always spoke of it as such in public. Privately he responded to someone who called it a failure, "Well, at least we tried. Doing something was better than not doing anything at all."[6] He knew it had fallen short of the ideal, but it set a precedent. As he told Capovilla, the next one would be the *second* Synod of Rome. In any case, by the summer of 1960 it was over, freeing John to devote full attention to the Council.

Preparing Vatican II

May 1959-June 1960: Antepreparatory Period

In June of 1960 John projected four distinct phases for the Council:

1. Introduction and antepreparation — a general gathering of concerns.
2. Preparation for the assembly — decisions about agenda.

3. Celebration of the solemn and general assembly — the most splendid moment of the Council.
4. Promulgation of the decisions and teachings of the Council.[7]

John announced the Council on January 25, 1959, then waited four months before taking another step. During those months he started the Roman Synod and made pastoral Lenten visits to Rome's parishes. He spoke often about the Council, but until May he did not actually do anything. Finally the May 17, 1959 edition of *Osservatore Romano* for the feast of Pentecost announced the institution of an Antepreparatory Conciliar Commission with Tardini as president, Msgr. Pericle Felici as secretary, and the secretaries (those second in command) of the ten curial congregations as members. Its mandate was:

1. To establish appropriate contacts with the various national Catholic episcopates to obtain their counsel and suggestions
2. To collect the proposals formulated by the offices of the Roman Curia
3. To sketch the general lines of those matters to be treated in the Council, soliciting the viewpoints of the theological and canonical faculties of Catholic universities
4. To suggest the composition of different organisms (commissions, secretariats, and the like) responsible for making the proximate preparations for what the Council had to do.[8]

During Vespers in St. Peter's on Pentecost eve, John gave a special talk:

> At the end of January, on the feast of the conversion of St. Paul, I announced the project of a celebration of an ecumenical Council. It would call together especially all the bishops of the Church in communion with the Holy See as sort of a new Pentecost....

Well, look! Here we are today on the 17th of May, 1959, the feast of Pentecost, at the first act of this extraordinary undertaking, namely the announcing of the Antepreparatory Commission for the great event. … which is destined to move both heaven and earth.[9]

John met formally with the new commission for the first time on June 30 though it started its work as early as May 26. In a Tardini letter dated June 18, the commission wrote to all those persons entitled by Canon Law to attend and to several others such as auxiliary bishops and general superiors of religious communities. The letter invited these prelates to send the commission "with absolute liberty and sincerity, viewpoints, counsels and wishes which pastoral concern and the zeal for souls might suggest to you." Their suggestions would give rise to an agenda for the Council.

In addition, the Antepreparatory Commission requested the congregations of the Curia to set up internal subcommittees to prepare proposals for the Council. The rectors of the Roman ecclesiastical universities and schools were invited to a meeting on July 3 in which the aims of the Council were specified and their faculties were invited to submit suggestions and recommendations. Tardini told them that the Council would be "practical rather than dogmatic; pastoral rather than theological; concerned with norms rather than with definitions." He also said very directly that the Council was "an internal affair for the good of the Church. Its direct aim is not the return of the dissidents." He was simply stating brusquely what John himself had written in *Ad Petri cathedram,* published the day before. Finally the chairmen of the theological faculties in Rome were invited to a meeting on July 17. Tardini announced that Pope John had decided that the Council would be called the "Second Vatican Council" and set Easter 1960 as the end-date for the Antepreparatory Phase.

Tardini's letter evoked abundant response. Of 2594 bishops solicited, 1998 replied, a 77 percent return. Overall 2812 solicitations brought 2150 responses, a return rate of 76.4 percent. Both the amplitude of the survey and the high percentage of response were unprecedented.

If input from the field was important, so too was the composition of the Antepreparatory Commission. Key men from each of the congregations held seats, making it in effect a miniature Curia! Reportedly John and Tardini did not see eye to eye on this. He was surprised when Tardini suggested the Roman Curia should do the antepreparatory work but accepted his Secretary of State's advice with an insistence that

> the themes should be chosen on the basis of a vast consultation of the whole episcopate of the world. Let antepreparatory commissions be put together with the largest possible participation of bishops and experts.[10]

Tardini's comments at the June 30 meeting did report that "each of the Sacred Congregations is establishing within its own boundaries study committees to which will be called consultors, officials, and scholars from the various languages and nations for the purpose of furnishing concrete proposals for attaining the ends of the Council."[11] The comments of John and Tardini at the June 30 meeting made it clear that while they agreed, John was counting on the bishops while Tardini was counting on the Curia![12]

The process for handling thousands of incoming suggestions made the Antepreparatory Commission crucial. Arriving responses were sorted according to the competence of the respective study committees within each Roman Congregation. They in turn translated the suggestions into concrete proposals the Council might consider. In short, the bishops sent in suggestions, the Curia formulated the issues to be discussed. In synthesizing suggestions from the field, the Antepreparatory Commission and the congregation study commissions did what seemed natural — they coded the material in terms of traditional theological and canonical patterns.

> The general order of the file… began from the vari-
> ous chapters of doctrine according to the usual order
> of theological tracts, and then continued with the
> different aspects of ecclesiastical discipline, for the
> most part according to the order in which the Code
> of Canon Law treats them.[13]

While most of the suggestions came in under such head-
ings, the process made it difficult for any fresh perspective to
gain a foothold. Since a different perspective is ultimately what
emerged from the Council — so different that it led the Council to scrap practically everything prepared for it — the step of
putting only men with a curial mentality in charge of the first
coding was costly. In spite of the broad consultation and the
clear recognition that others of "various languages and nations"
had a role to play, the curial perspective controlled.

Furthermore, Vatican committee work is done according
to the chairman's rules of order, not Robert's![14] The chairman's
rule extends to outcomes. Chairmen expected their committee's
results to reflect the chairman's viewpoint and judgment, whatever others on the committee — even a majority — might think.
Thus the chairmen with the secretaries they named controlled
the whole course of events. Under democratic procedures, this
would violate the very purpose of committee work, but to persons trained in a monarchical and hierarchically authoritarian
tradition, it all seemed proper.

The Vatican approach to committee work is reflected in
conciliar procedures. The pope has the sole and exclusive right
to convoke the Council, determine its arguments, preside over
its workings, intervene authoritatively at any point along the line,
pronounce ultimate and definitive judgments on its decrees,
promulgate them, and execute them. Those whom he appoints
to various positions to assist him in that work share in the pope's
authority by virtue of their appointment. Others may be called
upon to help, but the authority comes from above. In this system, truth and wisdom presumably descend from the top; wis-

dom ascending from below is presumed unlikely. Suggestions from below might be used by the authorities, but at their discretion. The suggestions themselves have no particular right to be heard. In general, that was the working mentality of those responsible for preparing the Council.

Several commentators criticize John for putting Curia officials into key procedural positions in the conciliar process. Hans Küng considers that decision one that the more progressive elements never surmounted. John persisted in this stance even after the Council got under way and he was urged to allow the bishops themselves to select their leaders. Others judge that John was simply doing what seemed to him logical. He took advantage of the offices at hand to help him. He trusted the Italians in the Curia to do the work they best knew how to do. While he wanted the Church from around the world to be involved, there was simply no organized body except the Curia to handle the huge work to be done. Moreover, at this point in his pontificate he relied heavily on Tardini, the master of the Curia.

John's approach risked allowing Roman officials to dominate the process totally. John was aware of this, and from long experience abroad he knew it would be a sore point with the world's local bishops. John took three steps to counterbalance the situation: (1) he derived the issues brought before the Council from a universal consultation; (2) he made the committees which prepared the issues international in membership; and (3) he gave the bishops themselves a free hand in the Council. His first two balancing efforts failed. The third did not.

The Antepreparatory Commission categorized the suggestions coming in and collated them into a 1540 page analytical conspectus, two volumes with 9384 suggestions. Of these 2090 were concerned with the clergy, 1302 with doctrine, 1223 with sacraments and sacramentals, 1464 with liturgy, 547 with seminarians, 558 with religious, 289 with precepts of the Church, 470 with teaching bodies in the Church, 299 with ecumenism, 177 with the missions. The clerical emphasis is striking, as is the limited attention given John's themes of unity (ecumenism) and universality (missions). There was no category dealing with the world and such problems as peace.

In addition to these two volumes, Pope John had all the suggestions, including those of the Curia and the universities, printed in 14 volumes and distributed to the working commissions charged to prepare specific proposals for the Council. The deadline for presenting such proposals to the Antepreparatory Commission was March, 1960. On February 16, 1960 Tardini informed the members that the pope would "follow and direct personally the preparatory labors of the Council." This was the very time when Tardini was threatening to resign. John subsequently relieved him of all responsibility for the conciliar process.

The suggestions that poured in did not challenge the standard Catholic way of thinking and doing business.[15] Little more could be expected. Neither the bishops nor anyone else had ever experienced a Council. Few had given thought to what a Council could or should be. Most thought in terms of their own situation, few in terms of the Church as a whole. Their suggestions now seem petty and small. The bishops were all conservatively trained. Most of them went through the seminary either during or just subsequent to the modernist crisis early in the century. Further, most sent in their suggestions with little or no consultation. They sent them as individuals rather than as members of an episcopal college, so they dealt mainly with the practical problems individual bishops faced in their day-to-day efforts to govern their dioceses. These were the pastoral problems in their view, and since that was what John emphasized, that is what they wrote about. Their suggestions came out of the Church's traditional teaching and practice. The framework itself was not challenged. Only later would questions be raised that demanded a change in old meanings and values.

John read everything submitted — suggestions and summaries — carefully. If there were discrepancies between the suggestions from abroad and John's own intentions for the Council on the one hand, or between the suggestions he was reading and the summaries developed by the congregations on the other,

John didn't say so. In this as in other dimensions of his life, he acted out of a spirit of obedience. "Obedience and Peace" was his motto and in this process he saw the bishops as his superiors. He said nothing.

Actually everyone was trying to figure out what the Council should be, what John wanted, what he felt was needed. There were many ideas in the air — Council for reunion, Council for survival, Council as "internal event," pastoral Council, and so on. Little by little the Vatican worked to clarify the purpose. Tardini held a rare Vatican news conference on October 30, 1959, and he together with Felici appeared on French television (an equally rare use of media) in January, 1960. John himself constantly spoke about the Council. Over and over again he expressed his hopes and desires, each time slightly changing the thought, step by step clarifying his own meaning. Yet however often he spoke, his purpose remained "voluntarily vague."[16] He wanted the Church at large to specify new provisions. His job was to call the bishops together, urging them to take a fresh look at things.

Whatever John's inner thoughts about the Antepreparatory Commission's work, he had nothing but good and encouraging things to say to those doing it. He was satisfied. So when it came time to initiate the second phase of the Council, he made no fundamental changes.

June 1960-1961: Preparatory Period

On May 30, 1960, John reviewed progress toward the Council with the cardinals present in Rome.

> ...no ecumenical Council has been preceded by such a vast consultation of the episcopate, of the Roman Curia and of the Catholic universities as has been this future one. That's a good sign as regards the work which we will now undertake with the help of God.[17]

John then announced that on the following Sunday, Pentecost, he would publish a document (*Superno Dei nutu*) containing general directives for organizing the next phase of the Council. It was John's second Pentecost as pope. John informed the cardinals that they would take part in the preparatory commissions but that bishops and other ecclesiastics, both secular and religious, would also play a role.

> I have… sent a special invitation to my representatives abroad [i.e., papal diplomats] asking that they would send me the names of capable and outstanding theologians and canonists whom I might call to take part in the study commissions. In this way the preparation of the Council will not be the work of the Roman Curia, but together with the illustrious prelates and consultants of the Roman Curia, prelates and experts from the whole world will give their valid contribution. In this as in other things, the catholicity of the Church will shine forth.[18]

Superno Dei nutu's directives were consciously general in order to permit "opportune additions and extensions as this quite vast, complex and multiform work will require."[19] John made at least one such addition even before the document was officially published in the June 4 edition of *Osservatore Romano*. It was the eve of Pentecost.

Superno Dei nutu's opening paragraphs reflect the origin of John's idea for the Council and his hopes for it:

> It is a direct inspiration of the Most High that we have regarded the thought, that flower of an unforeseen spring, which from the first days of our pontificate presented itself to our mind — the summoning of an ecumenical Council.
>
> Indeed, from this solemn gathering of bishops around the Roman Pontiff, the Church, beloved

spouse of Christ, can acquire in these troubled times
a new and yet wider renown.[20]

After highlighting the broad public awareness of the
Church and the stimulus to unity which the Council would
provide, *Superno Dei nutu* restates the Council's main objectives
in the terms of *Ad Petri cathedram* (truth-unity-peace):

> The growth of the Catholic Faith and the renewal
> along right lines of the habits of Christian people, and
> the adapting [*aggiornamento*] of ecclesiastical disci-
> pline to the needs and conditions of the present time
> — that event will surely be a wonderful manifesta-
> tion [*spettacolo*] of truth, unity and charity. It will be
> a manifestation indeed which we hope will be received
> by those who behold it but who are separated from
> this Apostolic See as a gentle invitation to seek and
> find that unity for which Jesus Christ prayed so ar-
> dently to his heavenly Father.[21]

After reviewing the results of the antepreparatory period,
John announced the preparatory commissions and the involvement of many in the new preparatory phase. The function of
the preparatory commissions would be "to study the subjects
selected by us, while keeping before them the wishes expressed
by the bishops and the proposals of the sacred congregations of
the Roman Curia."[22] Each commission was to have a cardinal
as president, a secretary, a "definite number of members... chosen from the ranks of the bishops and distinguished ecclesiastics," and consultors who were to be men with special competence. Each commission had the possibility of being subdivided
according to need. John maintained the right to constitute additional commissions. One article established that "the president
and the members of each of the commissions will be chosen by
us [the pope], and likewise the consultors and the secretary."
Ten commissions were listed. John had mentioned nine of them

on May 30 when he addressed the cardinals. They replicated the most important curial congregations: Theological Commission (Holy Office) "whose task it is to weigh questions touching holy scripture, sacred tradition, the faith and its practices"; Commission of the Bishops and Diocesan Government (Consistorial); Commission for the Discipline of the Clergy and Faithful (Council); Commission of Religious (Religious); Commission of Discipline of the Sacraments (Sacraments); Commission of the Sacred Liturgy (Rites); Commission of Studies and Seminaries (Seminaries and Universities); Commission for the Eastern Churches (Eastern Churches); and Commission for the Missions (Propaganda Fide). The tenth was a surprise, a Commission of the Lay Apostolate "for all questions having reference to Catholic Action in the religious and social fields." John had said nothing of it on May 30. It is clearly an addition intended to give substance to John's concern that the Church deal with the problems of the world and not simply be like a barque tossed about by the sea of world events. In November, 1960 he added an eleventh commission for Ceremonies (Ceremonial), practically completing the match with the Curia.

Superno Dei nutu established also a Central Commission

> over which we ourselves will preside, either in person or through a cardinal especially appointed by us.... The task of the central commission will be to follow the course of the labors of the individual commissions and, where necessary, to coordinate them. It will report their conclusions to us so that we may be able to decide the subjects to be treated in the ecumenical Council. It is also the business of the central commission to propose the rules for the orderly procedure of the future Council.[23]

The work flow was from commissions to Central Commission to pope and then out to the bishops who constituted the membership of the Council proper. With Tardini stepping out of the conciliar process, John himself became the chief co-ordinator, but practically speaking, Archbishop Felici did the work. John was often absent from the deliberations of the Central Commission, but he never named any one individual to substitute for him. Rather he asked the cardinal with the highest rank to chair the discussions. The link was weak — one of many instances of an "inadequate structuring of the line of authority" which some critics see as "one of the great defects of Vatican II."[24]

Superno Dei nutu complemented the commissions with a number of secretariats. One was "to deal with questions touching means of communicating ideas," a second was the Secretariat for Christian Unity, a third was the office of the secretary general to the Central Commission. Others dealt with the economic and technical side of the Council.

The following day, June 5, Pentecost, John delivered an important discourse. As he often did, he started with a balanced reflection on the reasons he saw for both sorrow and joy. The previous Pentecost he had spoken at length about the persecution of the Church in various nations. He touched on that again, but briefly, immediately asserting his reasons for joy. His dominant motive was the "heartening reply" from all over the world regarding his proposed ecumenical Council. He compared what he felt at the moment to an event in scripture — one of his standard rhetorical devices — and then launched into the body of his discourse. It dealt entirely with the Council.

First he presented the four stages of a Council — introduction, preparation, celebration, promulgation. He expressed his pleasure with the antepreparatory phase, announced the beginning of the second and commented on the last two. Then he emphatically made two points:

First, the Ecumenical Council has its own proper structure and organization. It is not to be confused with the ordinary and characteristic function of the various dicasteries or congregations which constitute the Roman Curia. This latter will also continue to function during the Council according to the ordinary course of its usual contributions to the general administration of the Church. These are then precise distinctions: the ordinary government of the Church with which the Roman Curia is occupied is one thing, and the Council another....

Second. The Ecumenical Council will result from the presence and participation of bishops and prelates who will be the living representation of the Catholic Church spread throughout the entire world. A collection of learned and highly competent people from every region and every language will give its contribution to the preparation of the Council. This indeed is a principle already entered into the spirit of every faithful who belongs to the Holy Roman Church: that is to be and to hold oneself, insofar as one is a Catholic, a citizen of the whole world in much the same way as Jesus is the adored Savior of the whole world, *Salvator mundi*. This is a good exercise in true catholicity. All Catholics ought to make themselves aware of it and adopt it as a precept which gives light to their own mentality and a direction to their own conduct in their social and religious dealings.[25]

John then reviewed several steps he had taken in the course of his pontificate to emphasize the catholicity of the Church:

It is fitting to insist on this new furrow, which points in the direction of opening out in yet vaster proportions, and to insist on this cultivation of catholicity, which is a happy promise of noble and bounteous crops.[26]

John drove his points home clearly and forcefully, garnishing them with images drawn from his agricultural past. There was no ambiguity in what he said. He was concerned that the energies "existing also outside of Rome" should be used, "especially to avoid the impression that the Church is completely in the hands of the 'Romans.'" John knew that the press considered his distinguishing the Council from the Curia meaningless when he appointed the curial cardinals who headed various congregations as presidents of the corresponding conciliar commissions!

The rest of John's discourse on Pentecost Sunday 1960 dealt with the supernatural spirit with which Catholics should cooperate with the conciliar effort. He urged that people try to penetrate into doctrine, religious customs, and historical information in order to draw from these an increased ability to "profess the truth in love and grow to the full maturity of Christ." Next John said that:

> it is easy to perceive… the beauty and complete splendor of this great affirmation of the Catholic Church [gathered in] ecumenical Council, in perfect organization, always ready as she is — the Church — for the great developments of the present and of the future. Truth and love: Christ in the lead as the head of his mystical body, which is his Church, a compact and integrated body; Christ in all its joints, each person in his own position, everything for the building up of brotherly love, of holy and blessed peace, and for their progress.[27]

Finally John spoke of the role of the Holy Spirit. The Spirit would give the Council its substance and life. The Holy Spirit makes the Church missionary in its thrust, he said and twice over exclaimed, "Don't believe that the Holy Spirit will abandon the Church to the ruin which is threatened." John closed expressing his own deepest hopes:

Oh, what a prodigious event it would be, and what a flower of human and heavenly love — a decisive beginning of the rejoining of the separated brothers of East and West in the one flock of Christ, the eternal shepherd. This ought to represent one of the most precious fruits of the approaching Second Vatican Council...[28]

John's exuberance on such occasions was balanced by Tardini's terse, lawyerly sobriety, but they were substantially one in intent.[29] Tardini and his aides emphasized the internal dimension of the Council's goals while John and Bea spoke of the ecumenical and missionary dimensions of the whole undertaking, emphasizing the ultimate contribution it might make to Church unity and world peace. John, in fact, emphasized those very points in a special message read by Bishop Bernard Alfrink of Holland over an international radio hookup of several European cathedrals the evening of Pentecost Sunday.

The June 5, 1960 speech was Pope John pure and unalloyed. *Superno Dei nutu* was not. Tardini authored that document, albeit "according to the mind of the Holy Father" and with a preoccupation "that the preparatory work be carried out on the basis of the suggestions of the bishops with ample participation and personalities from the whole Catholic world."[30] The beginning paragraphs of the document seem to breathe John's spirit, but the more technical aspects of it reflect the mentality and background of Tardini. The whole is marked by compromise.

Tardini organized the conciliar work. Its structure was a replica of the Curia he knew so well. John accepted that — collaborating with his collaborators — and yet immediately counterbalanced it. He was willing to bend, but not break, and on Pentecost Sunday he made clear to everyone the points on which he would not be broken. He would accept the involvement of curial personnel and even put them in charge, but they were not to imagine that the Council was to be business as usual. The best persons from everywhere were to be involved. The *Catholic* Church was bigger than the *Roman* Church, and no one was to forget it.

The revolutionary implications of calling the Council manifest themselves at this point. John saw the authority structure of the Church quite clearly and had a keen appreciation of the limitations of the Curia's proper role. He knew that the Curia was an administrative and executive body, not a deliberative one. It was for the pope and the college of bishops to establish Church policy. The Curia was to execute policy, not make it, though it could legitimately influence the making of policy. That distinction had been lost in the consciousness of the Roman Catholic Church, especially in its Roman representatives. John restored it. His speech on Pentecost 1960 provides a clear indication that he fully comprehended what he was doing. The Council would be above the Curia. He would use it to get around the Curia. He did not intend a "palace coup" or a revolution, but there is a foundation for one author's later description:

> At a distance of eight years from what the conservative wing of the Senate of cardinals described as the *coup d'état* of January 25, 1959, the revolutionary character of that event is apparent to all. With it, in fact, Pope John put an end to his predecessors' authoritarian monologue and gave the word to the whole Church, bishops, priests, and laymen included; he dealt a blow at Roman centralization and at the privileges of the curia, opening the way to recognition of the pluralism and federalism of the national and continental churches; he reconsecrated the primacy of the Church's spiritual mission. subordinating to its pastoral ends the legalism of its lawyers and the temporalism of its diplomats; he gave an impulse to the progressive secularization of the ecclesiastical community by extending greater responsibilities to laymen; and finally, he brought the Catholic Church

in a certain sense into the vanguard of ecumenism, thrusting it towards an embrace not only with other Christian communities but often with other faiths.[31]

John clearly staked out his own position as the Council entered its second phase. He also made several organizational moves so he would not be the only agent in the process emphasizing what he felt had to be done. The Commission for the Laity (for which there was no equivalent in the Vatican), the Secretariat for Christian Unity, and the Secretariat for the Media were all potential allies. At least one of these, Bea's Secretariat for Christian Unity, actually served that function. In short, John leavened the dough while ceaselessly talking about the kind of bread he wanted the process to produce.

Having established the structure, John had to staff it. Normally nominations came to John via the Secretariat of State. From the nominations he would select certain individuals and pass these on to General Secretary Felici who in turn would clear the names for theological soundness with the Holy Office. As a result several well-known non-Italian theologians such as Karl Rahner, Jean Danielou, Yves Congar, Henri de Lubac and Marie-Dominique Chenu were rejected in one way or another. Danielou and Rahner, for instance, received no appointment until the French and German hierarchies respectively insisted. John had the power to name who would do what, but in fact he mostly approved lists prepared by those in charge of the various commissions, delegating the power to those with specific competence. Yet according to Felici,

> His work did not limit itself to sovereign approval. He used a detailed report to enable him to know one by one the persons who were presented to him. He knew many of them already and was happy to be able to express his appreciation and esteem of them.[32]

Pavan described him as "having a nose" for appointments: he put a man where he sensed he might do some good. He did not calculate and plot, nor did he count heads in order to make the scales tilt one way or another. Rather he accepted the suggestions of others and made a few himself.

John's general directives led to an impressive assembly of persons. For example, the Central Preparatory Commission had 104 members and 29 consultors. (In contrast, the Central Committee for the First Vatican Council consisted of nine cardinals and eight consultors, all Romans.) Among the members were presidents of national episcopal conferences, among the consultors all the assessors/secretaries of the Roman Congregations, Monsignor Dell'Acqua from the Secretariat of State and Monsignor Cavagna, Pope John's confessor. The Central Committee comprised 60 cardinals, 36 of whom were *in cura animarum* rather than *in curia*. Altogether the preparatory bodies engaged 833 persons, including 652 Europeans, 81 North Americans, 51 South Americans, 33 Asians and 16 Africans. Of the 652 Europeans, 221 were Italian, 97 French, 64 German, 58 Spanish, 40 Belgian, 23 Dutch, 19 Austrian, 18 Yugoslavian, and 16 English.

Balance was the pattern of the day. To be sure, the whole was dominated by men with traditionally conservative mentalities, but within the Church that was considered a strength. It was also an accurate reflection of the situation. Few at that time grasped the widespread and strongly divergent perspectives at play in the Church. Given the state of the Church in those times, even a sprinkling of progressive thinkers constituted a fair balance. Unfortunately John's efforts to give everyone a chance to speak were often frustrated by the arbitrary power of chairmen in the Roman way of doing committee work. John did nothing to correct that.

By November, 1960 the preparatory bodies were staffed up, so on November 14 John assembled them to initiate their labors. He gave copious expression to his hopes and sentiments.

He interpreted the history of past ecumenical Councils as expressions of the pastoral concern of the Church, noting that they always involved "difficulties and conflicts, but [were] always crowned by glorious outcomes." He interpreted the enthusiastic reception given his announcement of a Council as grounds for rejoicing in the "ever flowering youthfulness of... the Catholic Church... [a] masterpiece of the redemptive action of Christ." He observed that most of the previous Councils had been preoccupied with "doctrinal exactitude," but that they also sought to give "affirmation and direction to disturbed consciences in the face of events of a religious and political nature in different nations and settings." The teaching Church was always concerned to exercise its role "in the service of social order, equilibrium and peace."

Turning to the world of 1960, John noted that it was caught up in "an almost exclusive search for material well being." In that context,

> rather than recalling from the pure sources of revelation and tradition one or other point of doctrine or discipline, there is a need to reestablish the value and splendor of the substance of human and Christian thinking and living, of which the Church has been both guardian and teacher through the centuries.
>
> It is certainly a serious duty to deplore the corruption of the human spirit, tempted and tossed as it is toward the sole enjoyment of earthly goods, which modern scientific research easily makes available to the children of our time. But God protect us from exaggerating the proportions of this to the point of making ourselves believe that the heavens of God are already definitively closed up above our heads. We can come to think that in truth "darkness prevails over the whole earth" and be convinced that there is nothing left for us to do except wash our weary way with tears.

To the contrary. We ought to take courage.

No! Christ, the Son of God and our Savior has not left the world he redeemed. And the Church he founded, one, holy, catholic, and apostolic, remains forever his mystical body, of which he is the head.[33]

Moving out from this point John emphasized the "total catholicity" that should mark followers of Christ. He asserted that:

the Council... has a limited function. It is like a city on a mountain, occupying itself first of all exclusively with what concerns our mother the Catholic Church and her current internal organization.[34]

But almost in the same breath he mentioned that he had set up a special Secretariat to keep in touch with "our brothers who are so worthy of our respect, although separated — as the saying goes." Further,

the celebration of a Council of the Catholic Church involves the study of a whole complex of relationships not only with regard to individuals and families, but likewise of all nations on which human life-together [*convivenza*] hinges.... In truth I expect great things from this Council, and I love to repeat it. From it I hope will come an invigorated faith, doctrine, church discipline, and religious and spiritual life. In addition it should make a great contribution to the reaffirmation of those principles of Christian organization which inspire and govern even the developments of civil, economic, political and social life. The law of the Gospel ought to arrive at the point of including and penetrating everything. Everything, even that which derives from the "dew of the heavens and the fertility of the earth" (Genesis 27:28). Yes! it should reach that point, and that implies a conscious, high-minded and sincere participation by all the components of the social order — priesthood and laity, established authorities, intellectual activities, work — the whole social order become preoccupied with the perfectly connecting relationships of heaven and earth, of the present uncertain and perilous life with the future life, eternal and blissful in proportion to our correspondence as human beings and as Christians to the gifts of grace and of mercy which come from the Lord.[35]

John closed by reflecting on the universality of the Church, sad that some churches still experienced persecution and the deprivation of their rightful human and religious freedom.

1961-1962: Final Preparation

In July 1960, the preparatory commissions had received from the antepreparatory study committees suggested themes for the Council. From those they started elaborating conciliar schemata. Until they had something ready to propose, nothing else could be done.

For the next several months, John, with and through Felici, kept himself informed and spoke frequently about the Council. Shortly after Easter 1961 he visited several preparatory commissions. Usually he stayed and listened to the discussion for a while and then said a few words before leaving. Generally these were of an encouraging nature, a reflection on the liturgical celebrations of the day or period of the year, and perhaps some comments on the substance of what the committee was discussing. Pentecost 1961 fell on May 21. Less than a month later, on June 12, John initiated the first week of work of the Central Preparatory Commission,[36] a body which drew its membership from all corners of the Catholic world.

Noting that the echo of Pentecost was still ringing in his ears, John commented on how the members of the Central Preparatory Commission exemplified the universality of the Church. He reviewed the work done previously and told the group that its job was to discuss how the Council itself was to be conducted. It would have to review and revise all of the schemata elaborated by the various preparatory commissions. Theirs was an immense and a weighty work, he said, but it was destined to leave "an indelible mark in the history of the Church" as illustrated by the impact of previous Councils. He then invited the respective heads of the preparatory commissions to give him and all the others progress reports on their labors. At the end of the meeting he talked about the saints whose feasts were being celebrated at that time.

The Central Preparatory Commission met daily from June 12 to 19 discussing who should be invited to the Council, how the actual conciliar commissions (as distinct from the preparatory commissions) should be established and how they should function, voting procedures in the Council, the regulation of debate, the language to be used, and how records were to be kept. On June 20 John addressed the group again, this time at greater length.[37] He again noted the universal aspect of the Church evident in the commission, thanked all who had done the previous work, and noted the interest given the Council by laity and press. He asked journalists to see the Council as something distinct from an academy or a legislature of the people. He closed by identifying the fruits he hoped would derive from the Council, asked prayer for its success, urged "prudence and simplicity of speech," saluted the separated brethren, and thanked all present.

John's behavior in this first session was characteristic of how he conducted himself in the Central Preparatory Commission's next six sessions. He generally said something at the beginning and at the end, usually nothing more than encouraging words and devotional reflections. Though officially president, John missed most of the meetings and left the Central Preparatory Commission to itself during seven plenary sessions (June 12-20 and November 7-17 in 1961; then in 1962 January 15-23, February 20-27, March 26-April 3, May 3-12 and June 12-20).

These meetings constituted a rhythmic march toward the opening of the Council.

During 1961 John attempted to instill a new direction in the Church in other ways. *Mater et magistra* appeared on July 15, 1961, with its authoritative and challenging call for international justice. In September, Russia and the United States were in a state of confrontation because of the construction of the Berlin Wall.[38] Fresh from his August retreat and with Cardinal Cicognani as his Secretary of State, John broadcast a special radio message to the world on September 11. He appealed for concord between peoples and tranquility in the human family.[39] Addressing the leaders, he said:

> I invite the leaders to put themselves before the tremendous responsibilities they carry in the eyes of history and, what counts more, before the judgment of God. And I implore them not to give way to fallacies and deceptive pressures. In fact it depends on wise men that law with free and legal negotiations prevail, not force; that truth and justice be affirmed in safeguarding the essential liberty and the inalienable values of each people, of each man.... My taking note [of these events] ... is intended to be nothing more than a request, a confident appeal to the serene and secure wisdom of those statesmen and governors who preside over each country in the direction of public affairs.[40]

John urged people not to get caught up in "exaggerated nationalism and pernicious rivalries" but to work for the recomposition of a social living-together (*convivenza*) in justice, truth and love.

In the following weeks "Khrushchev backed away from the brink."[41] On November 25, Khrushchev sent special greetings on John's eightieth birthday. It was the first telegram received by a pope from the rulers of Russia since the Communist Revolution in 1917. The telegram, addressed to the Secretary of State, read:

> my congratulations and sincere best wishes for the Pope's good health and for success in his noble aspiration to contribute to the reinforcement and consolidation of peace on earth through a solution of international problems, by means of open treaties.[42]

When John addressed the Central Preparatory Commission on November 7, he mentioned these activities. He noted that "some anxious voice, in an anxious whisper, wonders whether the world is not headed into a tragic situation. I've already expressed my thought in that regard on September 11" (his radio talk). John pointed to his reasons for optimism: the great interest the world was taking in the work of the Church, the response to *Mater et magistra,* the welcome which was given to his September 11 radio message, and the personal recognition bestowed on him by extraordinary diplomatic missions sent by sixty plus nations to help him celebrate the third anniversary of his coronation and his eightieth birthday just a few days earlier (November 4). To John all this was proof that something good was happening and that the work of the Church, and more specifically of the Council, was worth pursuing. Quoting the prophet Ezekiel he admitted that there was much in the world which caused "lamentations, wailing, and woe," but he preferred not to talk about that. It was enough for "each person to have before his eyes his own cares and concerns." John preferred to speak of hope.

Also in November 1961, during the second session of the Central Preparatory Commission, John published his fifth encyclical, *The Eternal Wisdom of God (Aeterna Dei sapientia),* written to commemorate the fifteenth centenary of the death of St. Leo the Great, a pope and doctor of the Church. The encyclical provides an insight into John's conception of the Council. It presents St. Leo at length as "the proclaimer and defender of the unity of the Church both in the fields of doctrine and discipline" and as a promoter of peace in both Church and empire. John praised Leo's style of governing, saying that he "strove to make of himself a faithful copy of the Good Shepherd." In effect, John sketched the profile he sought to fill.

The second part of the encyclical related the work, teaching and life of St. Leo to the Council. It traced the theme of Church unity in St. Leo's thinking, highlighting especially the central role Leo played as the Bishop of Rome in both East and West. John's personal identification with Pope Leo is also evident in the homily he preached on November 4, 1961, the third anniversary of his coronation. John's sweeping vision in the encyclical and his talks stood in stark contrast to the narrow topics being discussed by the Central Preparatory Commission.

John finally convoked the ecumenical Council on Christmas Day, 1961 through *Humanae salutis,* an apostolic constitution having the weight of law. It committed the Church to holding an ecumenical Council and expressed John's vision:

> Today the Church is witnessing a crisis…within society. While humanity is on the edge of a new era, tasks of immense gravity and amplitude await the Church…. It is a question in fact of bringing the modern world into contact with the vivifying and perennial energies of the Gospel, a world which exalts itself with its conquests in the technical and scientific fields but which brings also the consequences of a temporal order which some have wished to reorganize excluding God. This is why modern society is earmarked by great material progress without a corresponding advance in the moral field…. Distrustful souls see only darkness burdening the face of the earth. We, instead, like to reaffirm all our confidence in Our Savior, who has not left the world which He redeemed. Indeed, We make ours the recommendation of Jesus that one should know how to

distinguish the "signs of the times," and we seem to see now, in the midst of so much darkness, a few indications which augur well for the fate of the Church and of humanity.

John pitted his optimism against the pessimism of others, a contrast that would find classic expression when he took on the "prophets of doom" in his opening speech of the Council. John listed several signs of strength in the Church and explained that he was calling the Council "to give the Church the possibility to contribute more efficaciously to the solution of the problems of the modern age." He hoped that the Council would rejuvenate the Church, smooth the way to the unity of all Christians, and "offer a possibility" for men of good will to turn toward peace. He saw the Council in a world context, not an ecclesiastical one.

John's hopes for the Council were clear: renewal of the Church itself (truth), unity with other Christians, peace in the world. Then John reviewed the preparation for the Council and put before all the internal dissonance he felt:

> This [preparatory work done by the commissions] concerns the doctrinal and practical problems which correspond more to the requirements of perfect conformity with Christian teaching, for the edification and in the service of the Mystical Body and of its supernatural mission, and therefore, the sacred books, venerable tradition, the sacraments, prayer, ecclesiastical discipline, charitable and relief activities, the lay apostolate and mission horizons. However, this supernatural order must reflect its efficiency in the other order, the temporal one, which on so many occasions is, unfortunately, ultimately the only one that occupies and worries humankind. In this field also the Church has shown that it wishes to be "Mater et magistra." ... Although the Church does not prima-

rily seek an earthly goal, nevertheless along its way, it
cannot stand aloof from those problems which are of
the temporal order or neglect the concerns which they
generate.... Hence the living presence of the Church
extends... to the international organizations, and to
the working out of its social doctrine regarding the
family, education, civil society and all related problems.... In this way the beneficial influence of the
Council deliberations must, as we sincerely hope,
succeed to the extent of imbuing with Christian light
and penetrating with fervent spiritual energy not only
the intimacy of the soul but the whole collection of
human activities.

Humanae salutis closed by inviting the prayers of all concerned
persons.

John closed the work of the Central Preparatory Commission on June 20, 1962, with words of praise, satisfaction, and
anticipation.[43] This cleared the way for the opening of the Council on October 11, 1962. The date was almost exactly three years
from October 30, 1959 when Cardinal Tardini had indicated
three years would be needed to prepare the Council. It also
matched Felici's projection of an autumn 1962 opening. Two
German cardinals, Josef Frings and Julius Doepfner, actually
asked John in August, 1962 to postpone the opening. They felt
the preparations were insufficient and that problems within the
Central Preparatory Commission required resolution first. John
rejected their advice.

Actually the preparatory bodies had not done their work
badly. Seventy plus documents were in the hopper, ten ready
for conciliar discussion. Subsequent events revealed the inadequacy of these documents, but they served their intended purpose — they got the conciliar debates under way. There were
problems with the texts. They lacked integration. As early as the
summer of 1961 some talked of a special subcommittee to give
all the documents a pastoral and organic character, but that never

happened. Without establishing a formal committee, Pope John encouraged a few persons, including Cardinal Suenens, to think this problem through. Their work eventually had an enormous impact, as we shall see below.

The documents were criticized also for using scholastic, negative, legalistic, abstract and unecumenical language. The contemporary world would not understand them. John was aware of this deficiency. The Council later rejected such language. One story has him examining a particular text with a measuring rod. "Look!" he exclaimed to his visitor, "There are thirty centimeters of condemnations here!" Nonetheless, John approved the documents for discussion and sent them out to the bishops.

In sum, John was thoroughly involved in the preparatory process, prodded others by his example, and steadily but respectfully pointed participants toward the new path he felt the Church had to take. His efforts helped crystallize two distinct approaches that eventually emerged and played themselves out in the Council, as will be discussed below. Two specific aspects of John's preparations for Vatican II deserve consideration: his spiritual preparations, and his attention to making news.

Spiritual Preparation

During the nine months immediately preceding the Council (January to October, 1962) Pope John constantly emphasized its spiritual and religious dimension. He did so through numerous appeals to the members of the Church and by his own example. He intensified his own focus during July and August while in Castel Gandolfo, then undertook a special retreat when he returned to the city in early September. He wrote:

> This time everything is with the intention of preparing the Pope's soul for the Council: everything, including the preparation of the opening speech, which the whole world gathered in Rome awaits, just as it

listened most attentively to the speech which was broadcast this very evening to the whole world.[44]

He refers to a radio message regarding the Council broadcast on September 11, one of numerous events interrupting his retreat. The retreat gave John "courage and a sense of spiritual meaning in everything. And this is what I need in my ministry."[45] John ended his days of recollection satisfied that he had "set a good example.... It was a more intense effort to find union with the Lord, in prayers, thoughts, and a calm and determined will."

His notes from these days close with the famous passages in which John lists the "great graces bestowed on a man who thinks poorly of himself," namely, to have become pope without seeking it, to have accepted the honor simply, and to have accepted without a fuss simple but far reaching ideas such as that of the Council.[46] The final paragraph summarizes John's feelings:

> After three years of preparation, certainly laborious but also joyful and serene, we are now on the slopes of the sacred mountain. May the Lord give us strength to bring everything to a successful conclusion![47]

There was yet one more step in John's spiritual preparation, and that was a devotional pilgrimage he made to Assisi and Loreto on October 4, one week before the Council opened. John explained his journey as a "discreet gesture":

> Today's apostolic pilgrimage to this ancient and venerated sanctuary [Loreto] is intended to seal the prayers which are being raised to God in all the temples of the world, of east and of west, and in the sacred recesses of sorrow and penitence, for the successful conduct of the great ecumenical assembly. This pilgrimage also is intended as a symbol of the road the Church walks toward the victories of that spiritual domination, carried out in the name of Christ,

who is the "light of the nations." It is a domination which is service, fraternal love, a sign for peace, and an ordered and worldwide progress.[48]

Having spiritually prepared himself, the Church, the city of Rome, the Italian people, and, as far as it was in his power, Catholics, other Christians, and persons of good will everywhere for the great event of his pontificate, John waited a week for the realization of his hopes, prayers, and labors to begin. He was ready, and he had taken steps to make sure the Vatican was ready to share that event with the world.

Preparing to Make News

An office to help newsmen cover the Vatican Council was planned for the Council from the very beginning. The unprecedented news conference held by Cardinal Tardini on October 30, 1959, was a part of this new approach within the Vatican. Tardini announced then that there would be a special press office. Given what has already been said about Pope John's sensitivity to this particular dimension of leadership, it is easy to conclude that he was the one promoting the idea. And therein was a problem, for the curial personnel to whom he entrusted the project interpreted John's directives in a way that did not give much help to newsmen.

Pope John spoke explicitly about the press office at least five times: on June 20, 1961 to the Central Preparatory Commission; on October 25, 1961 to the press itself when presenting the man chosen to prepare news releases under Felici's supervision; on November 17, 1961 to the Central Preparatory Commission; on May 12, 1962 to the Central Preparatory Commission, assuring them that a more substantial office was being developed than what existed (there had been complaints!); and on May 28, 1962 to a convention of newspaper editors with whom he shared his own attitude:

> I know well the importance of their [newsmen's] role in the formation of public opinion — I have said it many times — and I appreciate, among other things, the services which they can render in the religious domain by the seriousness and objectivity of the information which they furnish their readers.... To attain the end [of the Council], taking into consideration the conditions of today's world, the cooperation of the press appears not only useful, but in some respects indispensable.[49]

Press headquarters were opened on April 18, 1961 by Monsignor Felici, but the service was not adequate. Hence John's assurances to the Central Preparatory Commission in May, 1962 that the office would be enlarged. John's meeting with the press on October 25, 1961 to present Monsignor Villainc, the newly appointed press representative, was intended to offset the difficulty Felici was giving journalists. Eventually seven language sections were developed within the office, and 1405 newsmen were accredited for the first session. Unfortunately the news they got from the office was so sparse that they had to do precisely what John told a group of editors on May 28, 1962 he hoped they would not do:

> We desire very much, in effect, that journalists not be reduced by a lack of sufficient information to formulating conjectures which are more or less truthful and to launching into public circulation ideas, opinions, and hopes which will later prove to be poorly founded or erroneous.... What counts before everything else in the Church, what demands attention, is the substantial part of her message, the life of faith which she communicates to souls over the ages, the witness she gives, today as in past centuries, the truths she teaches or recalls to the men of each generation.[50]

John emphasized the need for discretion in a general context of being open and communicative. The Vatican officials in charge felt that discretion required that the minimum of information be released and no substantial content. In effect, they subverted John's hopes for an effective press office. Adjustments were made during the first session and after it due to pressures exerted by newsmen and sympathetic ecclesiastics who refused to be "discreet."

John knew he could reach people and the world directly through the media, so that is what he did. He used the radio to reach the world on September 11, and both radio and TV to extend his October 4 pilgrimage to Loreto and Assisi to people everywhere in Italy. In addition, the opening of the Council was televised live throughout Europe and relayed to the Americas a few hours later via Telstar.

John had help from news people in this. If the Vatican was closed and difficult to work with, John was not. He had a positive attitude toward news people, and they knew it. Two incidents dramatize the difference. Cardinal Tardini once invited newsmen to the orphanage where he lived and took them into the children's dining hall. Candles were lit throughout the room. He asked the orphans what they called the room, and they responded, "The Room of Newsmen." Then the Cardinal asked them why it had that name. Their response was, "Because it is full of *bugie*." *Bugie* is an Italian word that means both "candles" and "lies." The newsmen did not miss Tardini's double entendre. On the other hand, when John momentarily ran into a newsman, Curtis Bill Pepper in the sacristy of the shrine at Loreto, he exclaimed, "Well, Mr. Pepper, I presume you are still playing your trombone of truth!"[51]

John liked the press, and they liked him, especially in English-speaking countries. To American journalists he was an Horatio Alger figure. He was friendly, personable, and approachable. For many Europeans those qualities were a liability. They were not characteristic of nobility and aristocracy. Those who favored a different tone and style in the Church knew that John needed the support of the press. After John's September 11 radio message to the world, one cardinal sympathetic to John told a French priest and journalist that newsmen would have to help John make the Council a success.[52] They did.

Two Viewpoints Emerge

When the Central Preparatory Commission concluded its labors in June of 1962, no one expected a great debate in the fall, much less an early confrontation. Yet the Council started with confrontation and by December when the Council's first session ended a great debate had been joined. The two sides have been variously characterized, but fundamentally the division involved two different ways of looking at the Church.

One side approached the Church as a perfect society, the other as a mystical communion. The perfect society conception posits the Church's formulations of doctrine and law to be perfect and ageless. If people want to be part of the society, they must come to it and accept its way of thinking and living. The mystical communion conception believes that the Church's inner reality needs to be explained to people in such a way that they can understand it, glimpse its beauty, and be attracted to its life. The perfect society proponents tended to be conservative, satisfied with the Church's past accomplishments, willing to wait for the world to see the light and come to the Church, resistant to new ways of presenting the gospel and living it. The mystical communion advocates felt that more could be done to reach more people, that the Church's past riches did not suffice in today's world. They were willing to try something new.

This division of outlook had a geographic base. Northern Europeans were generally influenced by the strains of mystical communion. Those closely associated with Rome were trained in the perfect society tradition and tended to stand by it staunchly. The North thought in psychological categories, the South in metaphysical ones.

The difference between these two sides was dramatized in a decision rendered by the Holy Office in 1959. The worker-priest movement had been launched because the Church in France recognized and faced the problem of the dechristianization of the people. People were formally Catholics but they did not live the faith. To reach them, the French hierarchy sent priests with a missionary and evangelizing spirit into the places and the contexts where people lived, including their places of work. In deciding against this pastoral effort, the Holy Office challenged the assumption of dechristianization on the basis that most of the people were still being baptized! For the Roman mentality, the ceremonial formality and its defined metaphysical effect was the critical factor. The northerners focused more on the psychological and social realities.

The two sides thought differently. The Church in northern Europe had experienced the Enlightenment, modern philosophy and social thought, political and industrial revolution. Rome had been somewhat shielded from these influences, as had been Spain, Portugal and therefore Central and South America. As a result northern European Catholics tended to work from experience and observation to conclusions, while the Romans and their Latin colleagues tended to adopt a thesis drawn from their tradition and then line up the data to prove it.

The two different approaches crossed paths in several areas. One was the Bible. Northern European scholars tended to use careful exegesis and historical analysis to grasp the teaching of the scriptures. Romans placed greater emphasis on objective theological categories derived from defined dogmas of the Church, then used scripture to illustrate and support the Church's traditional teachings.

Another area of mutual concern and difference was theology. Rome tended to rely on the scholastic theology developed by St. Thomas and others during the Middle Ages. Northern theologians tended rather to use the principles and theories of modern existentialism, phenomenology, and scientific thought in their quest to better understand the faith.

Finally both approaches had to deal with John's specification that the Council was to be "pastoral." To the Romans the word denoted speaking the truth (=holding to dogma) while for the northerners it meant translating the Church's beliefs into a language people could understand (=adaptation). John's concept comprised both dimensions. The question was which emphasis would prevail at the Council.

One author contrasts the two mentalities as law-centered versus life-centered, defensiveness versus dialogue, and fixed ideas versus historical change.[53] Conflict between the two was aggravated by the fact that the Roman side characteristically felt that theirs was the only proper way of thinking. They argued a tradition reaching back to St. Peter to legitimize their conviction. Because representatives of this Roman tendency held most key positions in the conciliar preparatory commissions, their way of thinking ultimately controlled the schemata presented to the Council for discussion. This was particularly true of the Theological Commission, a complaint voiced publicly by German Cardinal Doepfner during the Council's very first public session. In its extreme, the Roman-based thinkers saw the theologians and experts who came to the Council from the north as revivers of old, presumably discredited, modernist and antiauthoritarian ideas. A pastoral letter issued by the Dutch hierarchy in anticipation of the Council was interpreted in this way and consequently banned in Rome. Similarly, after the publication of *Pacem in terris,* a tract appeared which interpreted it in the context of Pius IX's 1864 *Syllabus of Errors.* Had they been able, the Roman school likely would have banned *Pacem in terris* too.

Given these differences, some contestation was inevitable. The German theologian Karl Rahner wrote later:

> When one realizes what preconceptions many people had in those days — especially in Roman circles — of the course of the Council, one can see that it would have been naive to assume a smooth course. Some participants, for example, believed beforehand that

the Council had as its task merely to codify a little more solemnly than before the old dogmatic assumptions, and that the real job had in effect been finished before the opening of the Council. However, it happened otherwise.[54]

In preparing for the Council, the Roman sympathizers enjoyed a distinct advantage. They enjoyed geographic concentration and a well-organized center of operation while the northern Europeans were dispersed and unorganized. Each bishop was pretty much on his own. He knew what he thought, but he generally had little sense that others thought the same. Some of them gathered together on a national basis, but such meetings were not sufficient to generate a general and united consciousness of their own position. It took the conciliar process itself — the coming together of many persons from many places in one place, extensive dialogue amongst them and public speeches by various intellectual leaders — to help them realize they were of one mind.

These same two tendencies were represented *within* the Vatican as well. They showed in the differences of emphasis between the internal thrust and the outer thrust of the Council, in the tension between John and Tardini, and in disagreements between Cardinals Bea and Ottaviani. There was formal agreement about the goal of the Council, but tension regarding what the goal implied. Likewise there was tension over what "being pastoral" meant. John and Bea saw it as embracing a willingness to revise the expression of doctrine and discipline to help persons, while Romans such as Tardini and Ottaviani saw it as using established doctrine and discipline to keep people's thinking and behavior in line.

But there was more. John and his Council were a definite threat to the integralist mentality in the Curia. They may have liked John personally, but a number of them thought his ideas about the Council mad. A leading curialist once passed a building which was being demolished. He commented to his companion that that was what Pope John was doing to the Church. A prominent Italian cardinal once declared that it would take forty years to undo the damage John had done with his "fifteen minutes of insanity."[55] Others spoke of the Council as a sickness. Even Francis Cardinal Spellman once said, "I do not believe that the pope wanted to convoke a Council, but he was pushed into it by people who had misconstrued what he had said."[56] The coming to Rome of so many foreign bishops at the same time seemed an invasion, a violation, so to speak, of the Curia's territory.[57] The Council did indeed reverse the accustomed flow of things: laws had been made in Rome by Romans for the rest of the world to keep; now laws would be made by foreigners in Rome for the Romans to keep!

The Curia knew how to defend itself.[58] It dominated the preparatory period. More than once John was heard to exclaim, "*Sono in un sacco qui!*" — "I'm in a sack here!" There was opposition to John's plans, and he knew it. As Cardinal Bea put it,

> More than once he [Pope John] spoke to me of his difficulties with various people, difficulties which caused him real suffering.... More than once I had certain knowledge that he fully realized that such opposition was unjustified and had bad effects.... How often have I heard him utter the word "Courage" — for he was not spared opposition and resistance, which he felt acutely, above all when they impeded and planned to obstruct his pastoral efforts.[59]

Bea's words are powerful given his closeness to John, his own profound knowledge of the Curia, and his impeccable discretion. John consistently avoided public complaint and harsh judgment, seeking rather to understand and excuse. According to Bea,

> He never doubted the good faith and good will of the individuals concerned. He excused them, tried to explain their actions and their motives in the best sense

and to treat them with fatherly patience and charity.... He was so large-minded, so tolerant and so forbearing, and yet so strong, so inflexible in his principles and in his purposes.... To a bishop who complained about the difficulties he encountered in his diocese, Pope John answered, very simply and gently: "Excellency, I too have a diocese, and sometimes I too have difficulties. At such times I go to my chapel. And once it seemed to me that Jesus said to me, 'Now, Johnny, don't take these things too hard. There's me, too, still in my Church.'"[60]

John's response was realistic and based on faith. He had come to Rome a neophyte but had learned how the Curia operated. The strategy he adopted for working with it, however, was the one he proposed to the Church in his coronation speech: meekness, gentleness, compassion, patience.

On one occasion John felt that the opposition went too far. In November of 1962 Italy's most respected daily paper, Milan's *Corriere della Sera,* published three articles which accused him of Modernism.[61] The author was a journalist to whom John had granted an interview in the spring of 1959. He determined who in the Curia was behind the articles and on November 26, 1962 wrote this note to himself: "See whether this case doesn't call for a response to such intended and pernicious maligning."[62] But even then he opted to be the "good pope." He stuck with his style of visiting people in their offices, having his picture taken with them and sending it to them, talking and talking, being meek, gentle, patient.

John was able to run through the personnel of the Curia, characterizing the stance of each relative to his program. Yet he seldom if ever reproved those who were blocking him. When a famous Jesuit orator (Fr. Riccardo Lombardi) attacked the Curia early in 1962, he even defended it. Bea connects this aspect of John with his enormous respect for the freedom of others:

> Those who were in a position to be aware of the way
> in which he observed the work of the Congregations
> … know how careful he was to respect the just free-
> dom of initiative and of action in those positions of
> responsibility — even in cases where he would per-
> sonally have preferred different methods, and where
> certain action caused him, with his inclination toward
> kindness, very deep suffering. His forbearance sprang
> from his sincere respect for human persons and their
> freedom.[63]

John's stance could thus seem ambiguous, his intentions confused and uncertain. At times he spoke forcefully about hopes which on other occasions he and his top aides flatly affirmed were goals intended only for after the Council. To the bishops gathering in Rome in the fall of 1962, John seemed a mixture of opposites. No one knew for sure where he stood. His efforts to balance things out and the freedom he allowed others seemed to lack firmness.

To summarize, the elements of a contest were present, but latent. If there was to be a debate at the Council, something had to bring the sides out into the open. In fact, that happened and John played an important role in the three developments that made it happen: (1) a controversy over the Pontifical Biblical Institute; (2) the prominence of the Secretariat for Christian Unity; and (3) John's opening speeches to the Council.

Controversy over the Pontifical Biblical Institute

John's election to the papacy lowered the profile of the Jesuits in Rome.[64] Pius XII had entrusted many key responsibilities to Jesuits; Pope John gave the secular clergy more prominence. His choices were often alumni of the Lateran or Roman seminary, John's own alma mater. John's election gave the Lateran, at the time not even an ecclesiastical university, an opportunity to strengthen its position. Indeed, the only pontifical university in the city was the Jesuit-run Gregorian. A Pontifical Biblical Institute (Biblicum for short) was attached to the Gregorian. Cardinal Bea had been its rector for nearly twenty years and had raised its prestige considerably under Pius XI and Pius XII.

From the beginning, John went often to the Lateran both as Bishop of Rome and as friend of many persons there. In 1959 he raised the Lateran to the rank of a university. This played into the hands of curial forces that wanted to consolidate control of teaching in all Catholic seminaries and universities through the Lateran.[65] A major target of these forces was biblical research and the new ways of thinking about the scriptures spurred by Pius XII's 1943 encyclical *Divino afflante Spiritu.* The degree to which its teaching was not accepted by prominent persons, even twenty years later, is reflected in an article published on page one of the *Osservatore Romano* in June, 1961. The author was Cardinal Ruffini of Palermo, a staunch and influential integralist. His thought directly contradicted Pius XII's teaching.[66]

Ruffini's article fit into a pattern of activities that unfolded in the last year of Pius XII and the early years of Pope John. Vatican offices banned books, issued warnings, attacked professors, and finally just a few months before the Council started in 1962, suspended from teaching two Biblicum professors. This final step accompanied the nomination of a new secretary for the Pontifical Biblical Commission. The previous one had died. Many pressures regarding the nomination were brought to bear upon Pope John. Counsel was divided and John was inclined to give some credence to all: " *Sono tutti buona gente*" — "They're all good people," he said.[67] His solution was a unique compromise. He allowed the suspension of the two Biblicum professors, but insisted that one of them, Fr. Stanislaus Lyonnet, maintain his position as dean of the New Testament faculty! The other censured man, Fr. Maximilian Zerwick, could continue to teach biblical Greek but had to stop teaching exegesis. In return, Pope John appointed an exegete well acquainted with modern methods as the new secretary to the Biblical Commission, and simultaneously appointed many consultors who shared the same orientation. He did this against the objections of many cardinals on the Biblical Commission.

John's exasperation with the whole situation is reflected in a document he addressed to Cardinal Tisserant, the then President of the Biblical Commission:

> Either the Biblical Commission intends to get itself moving, to work and to provide, preparing for the Holy Father's considerations, suggestions which respond to the needs of the present time, or it would seem worthwhile for it to dissolve and higher authority in the Lord will see to its reconstitution. But the impressions of indecision which circulate here and there must absolutely be taken away. They do honor to no one. Uncertainty arising from fears over clear positions which need to be taken concerning the directions of persons and schools [must be eliminated]. … It would be a motive of great consolation if together with the preparation of the Ecumenical Council we could succeed in developing a biblical commission of such repute and dignity as to become a point of reference and respect for all our separated brothers. Having left the Catholic Church they seek safety and salvation in the shades of Sacred Scripture, variously read and interpreted.[68]

Apart from his compromise decision, John did nothing public to resolve this conflict. He never rescinded the suspension of Frs. Zerwick and Lyonnet. Pope Paul VI subsequently resolved their situation, favorably and decisively.

John's handling of this affair was severely criticized by scripture scholars in the Church, and deservedly so. Some felt he was fiddling with his Council while the very foundation of Catholic belief and practice was under attack. Others accepted his compromise as the best that could be expected under the circumstances. In 1963 when the Biblicum needed a new rector this conflict surfaced again. The nominating process included maneuvering for an appointment favorable to the effort to subject all ecclesiastical institutions in Rome to the Lateran. In the end, John appointed a man fully consistent with the tradition of the Biblicum. Cardinal Bea certainly played a key role in these matters.

Actually these attacks on biblical scholarship and the Biblicum were veiled attacks on Bea. Bea had led the Biblicum to international respect and made it the highly disciplined scholarly community it was. Bea had convinced Pius XII to endorse a scientific approach to scriptural studies in the Church. Bea was using biblical scholarship to alter Catholic self-understanding and Catholic thought on issues such as Church unity and religious freedom. Integralist security required that Bea be stopped! To state the matter simply and without nuance, the argument was one between the Lateran and the Biblicum, a group of secular priests and a group of Jesuits, the Holy Office and the Secretariat for Christian Unity, Cardinal Ottaviani and Cardinal Bea. Others became involved on both sides. These incidents drew lines along which conciliar tendencies would crystallize.

Though these events stretched over several years, they crashed into the consciousness of the conciliar fathers only when they got to Rome in early October 1962. Upon arriving they received several Italian articles published as part of the attack on the Biblicum. Soon after the Biblicum distributed a pamphlet outlining its position. English-speaking bishops especially learned of the matter through Xavier Rynne's explosive "Report from Rome" in *The New Yorker.* It appeared as the first session of the Council started and presented in unvarnished terms the plot to gain control of the intellectual life of the Church through a unification of Roman institutions. Rome's newsstands sold out immediately.

The bishops were alerted. Their collective consciousness began to crystallize.

Role of the Secretariat for Christian Unity

The second factor clarifying the tendencies at play in the minds of the Council fathers was institutional. Besides individuals sharing a way of thought, movements need an organizational embodiment. During the preparatory period, persons favoring significant change in the Church perceived that the Secretariat for Christian Unity served that purpose. Many factors supported their perception. The dispute over the Biblicum surfaced a fundamental point of divergence between traditional Roman theology and newer scriptural exegesis. Cardinal Bea was one of the best of the "new exegetes." Further, Bea's staff in the Secretariat had been drawn from nations where modern history produced fresher patterns of thought and style. Bea's extensive efforts to publicize John's hopes for the Council had given the Secretariat international visibility. Finally, the highly visible presence of the observers at the opening ceremonies of the Council dramatized the work and importance of the Secretariat.

As the opening of the Council approached, then, two contrasting ideological positions with parallel organizational structures were on the field. They needed only an authoritative voice to point them out and an issue to bring them into open conflict. John provided the voice.

John's Opening Speeches, September 11 and October 11

The situation demanded leadership from the man who had called the Council. Unless he resolved his ambiguous stand, either someone else would have to provide a clear lead or those with official responsibilities — that is, the Curia — would direct the Council by default. If John did not act, the first alternative was improbable given the hierarchical structure of the Roman Catholic Church. The second seemed the likely course of events. Happily John did resolve the ambiguity which surrounded him, pointed in the direction to take and legitimated the protest of those dismayed with what they were getting from the Council's preparatory commissions.

He did so with two speeches, one on September 11 and the other on October 11. Together they articulated a unifying vision lacking in the discussion documents. In effect, they invited the assembled bishops to be more than a rubber stamp.

The September 11 speech was a radio message to the world dealing entirely with the Council's intended contribution to contemporary humankind. Its theme was Christ the Light of the Nations. Given the manifest struggle between good and evil, John said that:

> the world has need of Christ and it is the Church which must bring Christ to the world.... [The Council's] reason for existence is the continuation, or better still the most energetic revival, of the response of the entire world, of the modern world, to the testament of the Lord... which he pronounced... with hands stretched out toward the farthest ends of the world: "Go, therefore and make disciples of all nations."[69]

The Church entering Council hoped to present "in clear language, solutions to current problems which are demanded by the dignity of man and his vocation as a Christian." The Council intended to serve as a model of that *convivenza* for which all mankind yearned.

The speech was a real surprise. It stood in stark contrast with the inward concentration of the preparatory documents. In his discretion, John said nothing negative about the work done. In fact, he praised it. Yet the very difference of perspective and horizon between John's September 11 talk and the documents which the bishops were reading as they came to Rome raised questions. The documents led them to expect business as usual at the Council; the speech made them feel they were about to take part in something truly significant for the whole world.

The better known of the two speeches is the one which

John delivered on October 11.[70] This one, truly, was a trumpet blast. When Pope Paul VI opened the second session of the Council in 1963, he said of John's October 11 words:

> that speech which appeared like a prophetic voice to the Church and to the world — a speech which still echoes in our memory and in our consciousness — in order to mark out to the Council the path it was to follow, and in order to free our minds from every doubt, from every weariness that might overtake us.[71]

John's speech was lengthy. It stated his real feelings about what the Council should do and the spirit in which it should be done. It heartened those who felt there had to be a change, for Pope John indicated that his own outlook differed from that of the people who surrounded him in the daily exercise of his office. Those who felt misgivings about the control they had so long accepted from Roman officials felt supported in their desire to change the way the system worked.

John opened with a reference to the Church's teaching authority. In calling the Council, he:

> intended to assert once again the Church's magisterium, which is unfailing and perdures until the end of time, in order that this magisterium, taking into account the errors, the requirements and the opportunities of our time, might be presented in exceptional form to all men throughout the world.[72]

This theme engaged both the most conservative elements (whose concern was the preservation of the teaching authority of the Church) and the more progressive elements (who strained to present effectively the Church's teaching to people today). John recalled his motives for both joy and sorrow, reviewed his original inspiration for the Council, and recalled its preparatory steps. He presented the Council as an internal event but one intended to serve as a light of organization and cooperation bringing humankind and Christ closer together.

John characterized the circumstances under which the Council was beginning as happy. Then, politely but directly, he dissociated himself from the negative and pessimistic outlook of the curialists and integralists:

> In the daily exercise of our pastoral office, we sometimes have to listen, much to our regret, to voices of persons who, though burning with zeal, are not endowed with too much sense of discretion or measure. In these modern times they can see nothing but prevarication and ruin. They say that our era, in comparison with past eras, is getting worse and they behave as though they had learned nothing from history which is, nonetheless, the teacher of life.
>
> We feel we must disagree with those prophets of gloom, who are always forecasting disaster, as though the end of the world was at hand. In the present order of things, Divine Providence is leading us to a new order of human relations.[73]

John then identified several contemporary factors offering distinct advantages to the Church in her efforts to fulfill her mission.

These preliminary remarks served as a backdrop to the substance of John's speech. He outlined the principal aims of the Council, using the same categories found in his first encyclical — truth, unity and peace. He started with truth, appealing to both conservatives and progressives by asserting that the Council's greatest concern was that doctrine be both "guarded" and "taught more efficaciously." But then John proceeded to a crucial and delicately phrased portion of his speech in which he revealed his own expectations:

> Our duty is not only to guard this precious treasure,

as if we were concerned only with antiquity, but to dedicate ourselves with an earnest will and without fear to that work which our era demands of us.

The salient point of this Council is not, therefore, a discussion of one article or another of the fundamental doctrine of the Church... which is presumed to be well known and familiar to all. For this a Council was not necessary. But from the renewed, serene and tranquil adherence to all the teaching of the Church in its entirety and preciseness... the Christian, Catholic and apostolic spirit of the whole world expects a step forward toward a doctrinal penetration and a formation of consciences in faithful and perfect conformity to the authentic doctrine which, however, should be studied and expounded through the methods of research and through the literary forms of modern thought. The substance of the ancient doctrine of the Deposit of Faith is one thing, and the way in which it is presented is another. And it is the latter that must be taken into great consideration, with patience if necessary, everything being measured in the forms and proportions of a magisterium which is predominantly pastoral in character.[74]

John's stance was clear. The integralist concern with preserving doctrine was legitimate. He both recognized and embraced it. But it was an insufficient concern in itself. He expanded the horizon. The need was not for new doctrines or hearty reaffirmations of old ones, but for digesting them and going on to another step in the process. In saying this John was holding up a standard to which the progressive fathers in the Council could rally, and when they gathered around the pole, they discovered that they were many.

John said more. Not only was it important to do more than simply reaffirm old doctrines in old ways, but the manner of handling errors also had to be revised. Apart from the fact that in the course of time erroneous opinions "vanish as quickly as they arise, like fog before the sun," it was nonetheless true that the Church always made it a point to oppose them. At times the Church did so through severity and condemnation, but to-day "the spouse of Christ prefers to make use of the medicine of mercy rather than that of severity. She considers that she meets the needs of the present day by demonstrating the validity of her teaching rather than by condemnations." In John's view, errors make their weaknesses manifest. Contemporary man is wise enough to see them for what they are and abandon them. The Church's role was "to show herself to be the loving mother of all, benign, patient, full of mercy and goodness toward the children separated from her."[75]

Finally John dealt with "peace and the brotherly unity of all." His perspective embraced the entire human family. The unity of Catholics, then of Christians, then of all religious people, and finally of the whole human race had to be the perspective in which the entire work of the Council was seen and carried out.

> Venerable brothers, such is the aim of the Second Vatican Ecumenical Council, which, while bringing together the Church's best energies and striving to have men welcome more favorably the good tidings of salvation, prepares, as it were, and consolidates the path toward that unity of mankind which is required as a necessary foundation in order that the earthly city may be brought to the resemblance of that heavenly city where truth reigns, charity is the law, and whose extent is eternity [citing St. Augustine].[76]

He exhorted the fathers to work hard and to do so in a spirit of faith "in order that the work of all may correspond to the modern expectations and needs of the various peoples of the world. This requires of you serenity of mind, brotherly concord, moderation in proposals, dignity in discussion and wisdom of deliberation." Pope John closed with a prayer, then left.

It was an historic act of leadership, a great act of courage. John stepped out in front of the body as he had done when he called for the Council. He took a stand which few were expecting.

John wrote the speech himself and directed publication of his original Italian text together with the official Latin translation "to make clear whose responsibility it was, that it was the Pope's."[77] John surely consulted with Cardinal Bea and Msgr. Capovilla in preparing the text. Its central concepts appear in various places in their many speeches and writings preceding the Council.[78] The two speeches also used a distinction of the Church *ad intra* and *ad extra* developed by Belgium's Cardinal Suenens, about whose role more below.

In effect, John's two speeches started the Council by making all of the prepared documents obsolete. The first session merely acted out the implications of his words, rejecting all documents except one on liturgy. The bishops decided that new documents should be based on John's opening speech. Viewed historically, John's October speech was a strong denunciation of Integralism and a clear effort to lay to rest forever the "ghost of Modernism."[79] It signaled the end of an era.

The stage was set. The elements of contrasting sides were in the air, an institutional arm was ready to serve as a center of unity for the forces contesting the established order, and the leader had spoken in a way which not only left room for contestation but even specified some issues over which sides could be taken. He left no doubt about his own sentiments. He appealed to non-curial forces to bring their ideas to bear on the Council's deliberations. They heard him and were heartened.

Having spoken, John retired from the conciliar assembly and attended to other duties. Councils were something for bishops to run. As usual he followed developments and did his duty in its regard, but he left the assembled bishops alone to conduct their own affairs. His opening speech gave the Council a charter if not an agenda, a license to be open as well as faithful, a direction and tone. The three and a half years of preparation were ended. The Council had begun.

Two Viewpoints Clash

October-December 1962: The Dramatic First Session

On September 6, 1962 the Vatican released *Appropinquante concilio,* a document defining the organization and rules of procedure for the Council. It patterned the conciliar structure on the preparatory organism (which in turn copied the Curia): ten commissions, five secretariats (including Bea's Secretariat for Christian Unity and Felici's General Secretariat), an Administrative Tribunal and a Council of Ten Presidents. The ten presidents would rotate daily in presiding over the sessions. Together they would control the overall conciliar process. The ten presidents were distinct from the presidents of the ten commissions. All twenty were cardinals and all were appointed by the pope.

The presidents of commissions had considerable power in their own area of concern but did not have the authority to run the entire process. Each commission president had the right to hand-pick his team, selecting one or two vice presidents from among the members of the commission and a secretary from among the theologians or canonists (experts or *periti*) of the Council. Since all the presidents proved to be the same heads of curial congregations who had presided over the preparatory commissions, and given the Vatican's procedures for committee work, the prospects for an open process within the commissions were not bright.

There was one hope — the committee members were to be selected through a twofold process. The bishops were to elect 16 of the 24 members with the pope naming the remaining eight. All committee members had to be members of the Council, that is, bishops.

John announced his appointments to key positions the same day the Vatican released *Appropinquante concilio*. He named cardinals from the Curia as presidents of the commissions, but mostly cardinals *in cura animarum* from all over the world to the Council of Ten Presidents. A Secretariat for Extraordinary Affairs balanced curial and non-curial cardinals with a slight non-curial tilt. That tilt was counterbalanced by the appointment of Archbishop Felici, a thorough curialist, as General (i.e., executive) Secretary of the Council. Felici had managed all the preparations for the Council.

The conciliar process is unique.[80] A Council is a religious assembly in which bishops come together to discern as a group the intentions of the Spirit of God active in contemporary human history. Councils seek a consensus approaching unanimity rather than a mere majority. The goal is prayerful certainty among the members that what the Council says to the rest of the Church and to the world is the most accurate possible reflection of the will of God. Through Councils the Church takes stock of herself and her meaning in the contemporary world. The process involves deliberation on the proposed documents or schemata. Through such deliberation common thoughts and attitudes surface, common formulations are developed and common conclusions are reached.

The conciliar process is not political but it has political dimensions. The decisions made are collegial and involve compromise, yet the compromise is of a different nature from that associated with politics. All in the Council are concerned with the universal common good as best they perceive it. That may at times get mixed up with special or self-interests, but the goal is not directly the protection of such interests, as is usually the case in political processes. For this reason the Council is best interpreted in terms of distinct tendencies, approaches and mentalities rather than "parties." Speakers, for example, normally talk on their own behalf, not as representatives of a party, and each bishop votes as an individual, not as a partisan. Councils involve a high degree of equality and individual freedom.

The first item of business at Vatican II was the election of members for the conciliar commissions. Balloting was scheduled for October 13, the first general session. As soon as the opening ceremonies ended, Secretary General Felici asked the Fathers to fill in the electoral ballots. Before they could, Achille Cardinal Lienart of France, a Council President, took a microphone and asked that the voting be delayed to give the bishops a chance to get acquainted with one another. He suggested that electoral lists be developed by the national episcopal conferences as an alternative to the lists prepared by the Curia. Two German cardinals, Frings and Doepfner, as well as the Austrian Cardinal Koenig, seconded Lienart's suggestion. The full body of bishops applauded their consent. It was an obviously prepared and coordinated move to break the fear of the Curia and to lay a basis for eventual revision of the texts that had been prepared.

Though many persons who had served on the preparatory commissions were reelected to conciliar commissions, the open elections produced a better balance. This was true in the most important Commission headed by Cardinal Ottaviani. Where the Preparatory Theological Commission had a clear conservative majority, the conciliar commission had a clear, but not lopsided, progressive majority. Unilateral control, whether by one side or the other, invited disaster.

Pope John had not expected the quick lead taken by Lienart and Frings but was not dismayed and allowed events to run their course. When the bishops' votes were in, John had to appoint his eight members. He decided to appoint nine instead and named many conservative Italian curialists. His choices seemed one-sided to many. In the end, the commissions had twenty-seven representatives from the Curia, all appointed by the pope; forty-four Italians, twenty-four nominated by the pope; twenty-two Americans, three named by the pope; twenty French, four appointed by the pope; eighteen Spaniards, eight appointed by the pope; twelve Germans, one appointed by the pope and so it went. In the elections themselves the two names at the top of the various lists included six Germans, six Frenchmen and two

Italians, while at the bottom of the list there were no Germans, one Frenchman and four Italians. At first there was grumbling. Eventually the bishops understood that, as Bernard Häring put it, "John wanted no one on their knees."

The Council started with neither fixed agenda nor established method. To remedy the situation, the Council of Presidents met on October 15 and selected the document on liturgy to begin deliberations. They judged it would be the easiest to discuss. The northern Europeans again took the lead. John approved the decision. This choice pleased those bishops bent on reform because the preparatory Liturgical Commission had been uniquely well-organized, competent and open to modern developments. It had done exceptionally progressive work for a committee dominated by the Curia. Its document was the only preparatory schema to survive conciliar debate more or less intact.

The liturgy schema was a good first choice also because liturgy is a practical and pastoral concern that all bishops could address, a quality less true of the more technical theological schemata. Also, liturgy directly raised two sensitive questions: local initiative and vernacular language. The liturgical schema had the potential to challenge the established order, at least symbolically. Change here would signal change elsewhere. Further, the liturgical schema used biblical, patristic and pastoral language rather than the abstract scholastic and legal expressions that marked the other prepared schemata. Implicitly it involved a theology calling for revision of formulas, greater local autonomy and, ultimately, episcopal collegiality. It did all this without immediately raising these issues on a thematic level. That would have provoked rigid defenses.

In the third general assembly of the Council, prelates from northern Europe proposed the release of a "Message to Mankind." The document was accepted, so the Council's first substantial act associated it with John's spirit and direction.

That done, the Council took up discussion successively of the schemata prepared on liturgy, revelation, communication,

Church unity, and the Church. By moving through this agenda the Council slowly found itself. Central issues began to surface. A crisis came during the debate over the schema on revelation (November 14 to 21). The two latent tendencies sketched above exploded into open confrontation. Ottaviani's Theological Commission and Bea's Secretariat for Christian Unity played important roles in crystallizing the matter. When it took up the last schema considered in the first session, that on the Church, the Council found its central theme.

John's Role and How He Managed It

John presided from a distance, allowing the Council to find its own way while making sure it did not get stuck on any one issue. He was active on three fronts: work with conciliar bodies, interventions in the Council itself, and audiences, that is, meetings with various individuals and groups. He regularly worked with the intermediary organs set up between himself and the body of bishops, the Secretariat for Extraordinary Affairs, the General Secretariat, and the Council of Presidents. But he generally left these bodies to manage their own affairs, responding as needed to their requests for decision or support.

John made 25 public interventions of one sort or another, including his responses to the intermediary bodies, but he made many more unofficial interventions. For instance, when the elections were being conducted, John told an American bishop to vote freely without feeling bound to the lists handed out. He assured the prelate that such a vote would not betray the Pope. News like that travels fast!

Finally, Pope John gave audiences to many groups, especially of bishops. Between October 8 and November 27 (when he became ill), John met with the bishops of 41 nations. He started with the bishops from Eastern European countries, many from behind the Iron Curtain. He encouraged the bishops, sharing his own spirit and optimism. For example, he saw the French bishops just when debate in the Council was deadlocked over the question of revelation. He told them that debate was necessary and that he felt like the patriarch Jacob watching in silence as his sons argued.

Silence and nonintervention were central to John's leadership in the first session. He allowed things to develop. He did not panic — not when Cardinals Lienart and Frings introduced an unforeseen voting procedure on the first day, not when the debate over vernacular languages in the liturgy dragged on, not when the debate over revelation got hot. He intervened only when necessary — in the words of Cardinal Tisserant, "whenever the interpretation of rules or the aims and goals of the Council required a loving word of guidance from the venerable Head of the Church."[81] In short, he intervened to keep the process moving and to preserve the freedom of the bishops, not to force a direction.

John's most famous intervention regarded a vote on the schema dealing with revelation. The conflicting tendencies fully revealed themselves in this debate. When the schema presented by the Theological Commission was vigorously attacked, the Secretariat for Christian Unity emerged as its symbolic and real opponent. Debate came to a vote whether to send the schema back for revision or to continue discussing the text presented. A parliamentary maneuver by forces supporting the Theological Commission's document formulated the vote in such a way that those wanting to send it back for revision had to muster a two thirds vote. Normal procedures would have required the text itself to receive two thirds of the vote to remain under consideration. The instructions for the vote were confusing: the Fathers were to vote "Yes" if they did not want continued consideration of the schema and "No" if they did. The results were equally confusing: 1368 Yes votes, which meant that they rejected the schema as it was; and 822 No votes, meaning they wanted consideration of the text to continue. The Yes votes constituted a clear majority, but not a two thirds majority. So Council officials announced that discussion of the Theological Commission's schema would continue the following day.

Dismay greeted the announcement, so the issue went to Pope John. He decided not only to withdraw the schema but to submit it for revision to a new commission composed of members from both the Theological Commission and the Secretariat for Christian Unity. The job of the commission was to amend the document and shorten it, "for everyone knows," claimed the Secretariat of State, "that this same doctrine has already been expounded by the Council of Trent, and the First Vatican Council."[82]

The problem was that the previous two Councils had left certain ends loose, such as the relationship between scripture and Church tradition. It was over those loose ends that sides had been formed: the Curia and Lateran emphasized tradition, while the Northerners and the Biblicum emphasized scripture. Three days later the composition of the mixed commission was named. Bea and Ottaviani were co-presidents, Lienart and Michael Browne (a strongly conservative Dominican cardinal in the Curia) were the vice presidents, while Sebastian Tromp from the Theological Commission and Willebrands from the Secretariat for Christian Unity were co-secretaries. Several members came from each of the two conciliar bodies already mentioned, and six members were added through papal appointments, including Lienart, Frings and Cardinals Meyer of Chicago and Ruffini, both former professors of scripture. Ruffini held an integralist perspective while Albert Meyer was open-minded.

Three qualities mark John's decision here: balance, swiftness, and clarity. John adopted a suggestion made on the Council floor by Archbishop Gabriel-Marie Garrone of France and made it his own through his nominations. The balance was decidedly on the side of change, one observer estimating that Ottaviani could count on only 18 votes from the more than 45 members of the commission. John made his decision quickly. The conservatives, delighted with the vote the day before, were not so happy with John's resolution of the impasse. The progressives and moderates rejoiced. One American bishop commented:

The action of the Holy Father has saved the Council. After the method employed yesterday the resentment became bitter, and there is no doubt but what the debate would have been endless on the present schema.[83]

John's intervention broke curial control of the Council's documents. According to Bea,

He overrode the letter of procedural rules; but he did so only after the Council Fathers had discussed freely and fully, and he intervened in a way which enabled free expression of opinion to be more effective.[84]

John's decision on the revelation issue set the momentum of the first session in favor of the more open-minded prelates and their leader, Cardinal Bea. It enhanced the prestige of the Secretariat for Christian Unity. It broke, at least for the moment, the dominance of that mentality which was closed to the horizons John had been promoting for three long years. It freed the Council and pointed a way without imposing a direction. John wanted the Council to do that on its own.

After the suspension of debate on revelation, a different air prevailed in the Council. The bishops quickly discussed two minor schemata (Communication and Church Unity) then began debate on the Church. This document too had been developed by the Theological Commission. The divisions which had marked the debate over revelation reappeared immediately. The two sides did battle for three days. On the fourth day (December 4), Cardinal Suenens of Belgium called not only for a redrafting of the schema on an entirely new basis but as well for a reconceptualization and unification of the entire work of the Council. He proposed the *ad extra, ad intra* distinction Pope John had used in his two opening speeches and John's September theme of "Christ the Light of the Nations." Suenens' talk revealed a plan that he and Pope John had developed during the previous nine months. It is an episode that once again illustrates well John's genius for leadership.

Cardinal Suenens' Role

A one-time vice rector of Louvain University in Belgium, Léon-Joseph Suenens had been appointed to one of the Preparatory Commissions for the Council as early as 1960. Soon afterwards he became Archbishop of Malines-Brussels and in the spring of 1962 wrote a Lenten pastoral letter to his diocese concerning the Council. That was just before that year's March consistory in which John named Suenens a cardinal. Soon after the consistory John named Cardinal Suenens to the Central Preparatory Commission of the Council. Sometime during this period he read Suenens' pastoral letter, was pleased with it, and asked Suenens to develop his thoughts further.

Suenens was concerned that the seventy-plus documents being generated for the Council lacked unity and integration. His pastoral letter had been structured in terms of what the Council should not be and what the Council should be. In the memo he prepared for John he suggested a distinction of the Church *ad extra* (in its relations to the outside world) and the Church *ad intra* (in its internal affairs). John used this document in his September-October speeches, acknowledging Suenens' contribution by sending a copy of the September speech to the cardinal together with a note and a set of John's five-volume study of St. Charles Borromeo with a dedication dated September 12 (the day after his talk).

When the Council finally got under way, the bishops quickly recognized the problem of too many uncoordinated documents, but no one offered a solution. In fact however, John had photocopied Suenens' memo and asked him to meet with a number of other leading cardinals — Montini, Doepfner, Siri, and Lienart among them — to discuss it. In substance, they accepted Suenens' plan. John told Suenens that he had not forgotten about the problem, that he wanted to support efforts to address it, but he wanted to allow the Council to find its own way. He told Suenens that he would signal when to make the plan known.

At the end of November, 1962 John became seriously ill. He was reported to be dying. Suenens became alarmed and decided to take the plan to the Council. He sent the text to the pope to advise him of his intentions. The pope got back to Suenens through Monsignor Dell'Acqua with several written observations and suggestions. Then Suenens made his December 4 intervention. Bea, Montini, Lercaro and most of the bishops endorsed Suenens' plan. A consensus was emerging.

On December 5, Pope John approved a plan to "facilitate and accelerate" the work on the schemata between sessions (the second session was slated to begin the following September 8). Norms for reworking the documents were derived from John's October 11 speech, specifically from a passage, cited verbatim, which stated that the "main point" of the Council was not the discussion of one or the other doctrine, but a "step forward toward the doctrinal penetration and a formation of consciences. … The substance of the ancient doctrine of the Deposit of Faith is one thing, and the way in which it is presented is another." General principles regarding the universal Church were to be considered while particular problems and questions were to be referred to a future revision of the Code of Canon Law.

John established a special Coordinating Commission headed by Secretary of State Cicognani. He charged it to coordinate the labors of the commissions, follow them, and deal with the presidents of the same commissions not only with regard to problems of competence, but with regard to assuring conformity of the schemata with the purpose of the Council. John strongly encouraged consultation with experts. The revised documents would be reviewed by the pope and sent to all the bishops for examination and comment. Where possible, the documents would arrive through the presidents of national episcopal conferences. That strengthened their status.

On December 17, the Vatican announced the composition of the Coordinating Commission. Cardinal Cicognani chaired the group with Cardinals Lienart, Doepfner, Suenens, Spellman, Urbani and Confalonieri included as members. It appointed General Secretary Felici and five sub-secretaries to help. The group was balanced in favor of reform.

The Coordinating Commission used Suenens' plan to reduce the nearly seventy preparatory schemata to less than twenty. Each of the cardinal members took responsibility for specific documents. Suenens supervised one on the Church and one on the Church in the Modern World. Cardinal Lienart supervised the document on Revelation. Thus of the four most influential documents eventually issued by the Council (those dealing with the Church, Revelation, Liturgy, and the Church in the Modern World), three were under the supervision of proven spokesmen for a changed point of view. The fourth (Liturgy) already had that thrust and was basically approved during the first session. The commissions continued to carry the burden of the work, but as the Council emerged from the first session, the Fathers of the Council were in control, not the Curia.

The emerging consensus centered around a new vision, new values, new meanings. It was inspired by Pope John, but the Council had made it its own. John had given the lead and had left the Council free to decide whether it wanted to follow. In the vote on Revelation he had preserved the freedom of the assembly from domination by a minority. At the end of the first session he confirmed the emerging consensus. In short, he provided effective leadership without compromising the legitimate independence of an assembly that was entitled to formulate policy for the Church and, with the pope, adopt it as law.

On December 8, barely recovered from cancerous internal hemorrhaging that had momentarily threatened his life, Pope John reentered St. Peter's Basilica and addressed the Council for the last time. His speech was typically Joannine: a contented review of the past, a sober awareness of the present, an optimistic look toward the future. He reflected on the ups and downs the bishops had experienced and expressed his satisfaction. Good had been accomplished. He was hopeful that the "good beginning" would be extended to "all departments of the life of the Church, social questions included" and saw coming from the work a "new Pentecost." He reminded the bishops that the work of the Council would go on "unflaggingly" in the coming months, and asked them to "continue to study and investigate the schemata provided and whatever else may be sent later." John left the Council that day, pale and drawn. The bishops felt they would never see him again. Most did not.

Having structured the Council anew to do the work that needed to be done, John reverted to style and left others to do their work. He did his part, examining the documents as they came in, and quickly dispatching them to the bishops. He with Cavagna spent an astonishing amount of time reviewing conciliar documents even during the last month and a half of his life.[85] He also visited the Coordinating Commission when it was in session and met with cardinals, bishops, and other prelates who came to Rome and wanted to see him. He led to the end.

John was deeply concerned that the bishops not lose the momentum of the Council. He personally wrote them a long letter dated January 6, 1963 asking that they keep the Council as the "apple of their eye." John emphasized their role as bishops, reminded them that the Council was of interest to all humankind and told them that they were responsible for the salvation of the whole world.

On March 29, 1963 John instituted a Commission for the Reform of the Code of Canon Law, composed of 28 cardinals, twenty from the Curia and eight heads of dioceses. It was, perhaps, a parting effort to win the cooperation of the Curia and to prevent an excessive hardening of sides without sacrificing the substance of the Council. John knew he was dying. Since the Code would be updated only after the Council, the composition of this commission could be changed before important decisions were made. At the same time, curial forces could feel that they would control the outcome of the Council in its legal form. Creating the commission brought literal and symbolic completion to John's program, announced at St. Paul's Outside the Walls on January 25, 1959 — Synod, Council, Updating of the Code of Canon Law.

Summary

This lengthy recap of the Council shows John providing managerial leadership without dominating, convincing without controlling. He spoke and acted forcefully, but always with respect for others. He gave others the freedom necessary to make their own moves, even to oppose him, though not to oppress others. He relied on persuasion, not on brute power or formal authority.

John set clear goals for the Council — truth, unity and peace; doctrinal penetration and the formation of consciences; renewal of the Church and an improved way of relating to other believers and to the world at large. Believing as he did that the spirit in which things were done was more important than the deeds themselves, he established a tone of freedom and respect in the Council's work. John's goals were open and John consistently refused to fill in the details. That was for the Council to do.

In calling a Council, John started a unique process. Having set it up, he respected its nature and its autonomy. When conflict emerged, he stayed true to his fundamental propositions, insisted on fair play among those involved, remained optimistic about the outcome and sought to instill that spirit in those who were engaged in debate. He did not seek to destroy the old. He merely wanted to point a way to the new and open it.

Through and with the Council, John infused the entire Church with fresh air — a new sense of meaning and movement in a new direction. By the end of the first session he was sick unto death with cancer. The whole world knew he did not have much longer to live. Yet ill as he was, John spent six more months in an energetic and determined pursuit of his third goal, peace.

Questions for You from John's Model

1. How broadly are you willing to consult when you undertake major projects?
2. Are you skilled at setting up structures that enable others to participate in decision-making processes? Are you willing to let others set them up for you?
3. Do you think through the long-range implications of your choices of personnel for controlling positions?
4. Do you take care to establish adequate lines of authority when you set up complex structures?
5. Do you collaborate with your collaborators?
6. Can you refrain from dominating processes under your supervision and maintain a constant rhetoric about the way you want things to unfold while "leavening the organizational dough" with likely allies who will actually move the organization in that direction?
7. Do you approach your work with spiritual intensity?
8. Do you consider public opinion, inside and outside your organization, an important factor?
9. Do you cultivate good relations with the press?
10. Could you characterize your style as one of meekness, gentleness, compassion, patience?
11. When you create committees, do you seek balance, or do you stack the deck in a one-sided way?
12. Are you careful about the starting point of deliberative bodies?
13. Are you comfortable allowing serious debate within your organization over serious matters?
14. Can you lead by silence and non-intervention?

Chapter 3

Execution Three: Toward World Peace

All organizations, from parishes to the White House, operate within some internal context, but what happens there has implications for, and an impact on, the external world. Leaders at every level need to be aware of that and work to have the impact intended. Indeed, for most organizations an impact beyond their own well-being is the larger part of the mandate and mission entrusted to managerial leaders.

The Second Vatican Council was an internal event with an external horizon. It had unprecedented external impact. The leadership John exercised internally has been reviewed in some detail. But he exercised also a leadership on behalf of peace focused directly on the world at large. He was surprisingly effective there as well.

This chapter studies John's strategy and technique for contributing to the peace of humankind. It is offered with the hope that other managers will find in it a model of how their skills in managing their own domain can be extended to impact the larger world in which they live to the benefit of people they may never know — indeed of all humankind.

John's Way to Peace

Like his ecumenical effort, Pope John's drive for peace started slowly and built to a climax. His overall diplomatic record provides the background for interpreting his "death march for peace."

Angelo Roncalli's longest and deepest experience was as a Church diplomat. He approached diplomacy (as everything else) with a pastoral spirit, as evidenced by an entry in his *Journal* shortly after arriving in Venice as the new patriarch:

> To tell the truth, I have always believed that, for an ecclesiastic, diplomacy so-called must be imbued with the pastoral spirit; otherwise it is of no use and makes a sacred mission look ridiculous. Now I am confronted with the Church's real interests, relating to her final purpose, which is to save souls and guide them to heaven.[1]

For John the essential element in his relations with others — even with nations — was good will, not ideology or diplomatic standing.[2] John's goal in diplomacy was his goal as a pastor: "to be good to everyone, always!"

The Vatican is an internationally recognized sovereign state capable of entering diplomatic relations with other sovereign states. When John became pope, the Vatican's formal diplomatic network was well-established and respected, comprising nearly fifty nations. Other nations were increasingly disposed to recognize the role of the Holy See in international matters.

John's attractive personality and global vision raised papal diplomacy to a new high in a number of ways. More nations sought formal diplomatic relations with the Vatican and nations without formal ties sent special diplomatic delegations to important events. Sixty-two nations had representatives at John's coronation in 1958, 68 at his eightieth birthday observance in 1961, and 72 at his funeral in 1963 (plus nine delegations from major international organizations). Eighty-six special diplomatic missions attended the opening of the Second Vatican Council in the fall of 1962. At this writing in 2002, 176 nations have formal ties with the Vatican, including now the United States.

Another indicator of the growth in both recognition and activity of the Holy See during John's reign is in the number of official visits paid to him by sovereigns, members of reigning royal families, and heads of government or state. Pius XI received 13 such visits in 17 years and Pius XII received 21 in 19 years. Pope John received 29 in his first four years and at least one more before he died![3] These totals do not include the unofficial visits of heads of state, such as that of Eisenhower in 1959, nor those of many important personalities of lesser rank in governments around the world.

John handled his diplomatic responsibilities in a natural and personal way. He was at home with diplomats and had a high regard for their contribution to world peace. Yet John did not limit himself to formal and official diplomacy. He used every channel he could. He worked through Cardinal Koenig of Vienna to contact Cardinal Mindszenty in neighboring Hungary, where he was living in the American embassy, a prisoner of the Hungarian communist government, and he went through American editor Norman Cousins to communicate with Russian Premier Nikita Khrushchev.

The Vatican's diplomatic policy evidenced only modest change during John's pontificate. As time passed John's references to communist nations were softened, but official policy did not change. However one step early in John's pontificate signaled things to come: the Vatican withdrew diplomatic recognition from two governments in exile — those of Poland and Lithuania. This cleared the way for dealing with the communist governments ruling those lands and with Russia.

New Diplomatic and Political Direction

John desired to disengage the Church from political involvement as much as possible. He expressed this attitude during his August, 1961 retreat as he was changing Secretaries of State (Tardini to Cicognani). Reflecting on the role of bishops, he wrote:

> The sublime work, holy and divine, which the Pope must do for the whole Church, and which the Bishops must do each in his own diocese, is to preach the Gospel and guide men to their eternal salvation, and all must take care not to let any other earthly business prevent or impede or disturb this primary task. The impediment may most easily arise from human judgments in the political sphere.... The Gospel is far above these opinions and parties.... May the Pope's example be a lesson and an encouragement to them all. The Bishops are more exposed to the temptation of meddling immoderately... and it is for this reason that the Pope must admonish them not to take part in any political or controversial question and to declare for one section or faction rather than another. They are to preach to all alike... courteously defending the rights of the Church when these are violated or compromised.[4]

As usual John acted forthrightly to provide an example. He took several steps to disengage the Vatican from Italian politics. He removed Italian Catholic Action, the Church's political arm in Italy, from the Vatican and entrusted it to the Italian Episcopal Conference. He met with the leaders of various parties in Italian politics, breaking the Christian Democrats' near monopoly over papal support. He reprimanded Cardinal Ottaviani for continuing to act as though the Church should control Italian politics and had the right to sit in judgment on the activities of leading politicians. Finally, in the spring of 1963, he met with communist editor Alexei Adzhubei of Russia.

Establishing communications with countries under communist governments constituted the greatest change John introduced in Vatican diplomacy. As early as 1956 Khrushchev is reported to have sought contact with the Vatican through the Russian Embassy in Rome, but Pius XII rejected it. The Vatican's anticommunist, pro-Western position under Pius XII was dramatically confirmed that same year when Russia invaded Hungary. Pius XII vigorously and frequently condemned the Russian intervention. In January 1958, Wladyslaw Gomulka, the communist leader of Poland, indicated that the Soviets wanted to work with the Vatican on issues of peace and the use of atomic energy. Pius XII's Vatican again rejected the offer.

This anticommunist, anti-East, stance of the Vatican continued under Pope John in his early days. Here too he bided his time, waiting for an opportune occasion to take a step that would effectively improve the situation. His goal was active neutrality building positive and effective relations with all nations. He allowed events to take their course but read the signs of the times to know when to sow a seed, when to reap a harvest.

Contacting Russia

The occasion for a breakthrough came three full years into his pontificate. On November 4, 1961 John celebrated his eightieth birthday and his third anniversary as pope. Sixty-eight countries sent delegations to honor Pope John. As usual, the Russians did not. But on November 25, the actual day of John's birthday, Russian Premier Khrushchev sent a telegram wishing Pope John good health and success in his efforts on behalf of peace. The reference was to John's September 10, 1961 intervention regarding Berlin. This historic telegram was the first official communique from Russia to the Vatican since 1917.

Cautious but thinking this might be a "thread of Providence" which he should not cut, John thanked Khrushchev and expressed "to the whole Russian people the pope's cordial wishes for the development and consolidation of universal peace thanks to happy understandings of human brotherhood."[5]

That exchange of telegrams was one of the first signs that John's strategy of appealing to the good will of all people, whatever their ideological and political commitments, was beginning to bear fruit. He made such appeals on September 10, 1961 over the Berlin problem; on June 3, 1962 over the Algerian situation; and on October 25, 1962 over the Cuban missile crisis. All three were steps taken after Tardini's death and the beginning of Cicognani's service as Secretary of State. They embodied John's basic principle of respect for all persons. He spoke to people's consciences, confident that the "balm of sweetness" would do more to heal the "wounds of mankind" than threats, vehemence, and force. He believed that bishops, including the pope,

> must beware of making any rash judgment or uttering any abusive words about anyone, or letting himself be betrayed into flattery by threats, or in any way conniving with evil in the hope that by so doing he may be useful to someone; his manner must be grave, reserved and firm, while in his relations with others he must always be gentle and loving, yet at the same time always ready to point out what is good and what is evil, with the help of sacred doctrine but without any vehemence.[6]

John's open and trusting willingness to deal with the Soviets was rewarded when Moscow permitted two delegates from the Russian Orthodox Church to attend the Council as observers. As it turned out, they were the only representatives of Orthodoxy present, and they came only after delicate negotiations with the Kremlin by Monsignor Willebrands of the Secretariat for Christian Unity. Willebrands had to assure the Russians that the Council would not be an anticommunist harangue. It wasn't.

The 1962 Cuban Missile Crisis

John's September 1961 intervention to ease the tension between Russia and the United States over the Berlin wall had not resolved the conflict. One year later, in October 1962, the world's two superpowers were sailing toward atomic confrontation. Russia was shipping nuclear-capable missiles to Cuba. The U.S. established a defensive flotilla around that island. If neither side backed down, war was probable and no one knew where it would end.[7]

During the very days this crisis came to a head, a group of American and Soviet scholars were meeting in America. Persons at the meeting suggested having Pope John invite both sides to back down so neither would lose face. The proposal was cleared with both governments and John happily played the small but crucial role suggested. On October 25 he broadcast a radio message calling the leaders of nations to seek peace. Many factors were at play and no one knows exactly which of them determined the course of events, but history does show that the Soviet ships turned around, the confrontation was avoided, and the two countries found a non-violent way of resolving their differences. Pope John played some role.

John's successful intervention over Cuba deeply impressed him. He spoke of it in his Christmas message. More importantly, he initiated the composition of *Pacem in terris,* reasoning that if a radio appeal for peace had such good effect, how much more might an encyclical on the topic accomplish.

Respectful appeal to persons of good will on both sides of the ideological wall dividing the world also impressed others. Norman Cousins, editor of *The Saturday Review,* had worked behind the scenes to arrange for the papal intervention over

Cuba. He felt the Holy See could exert still more influence to bring the governments of Russia and the United States together. Between December of 1962 and April of 1963 Cousins journeyed often from the U.S. to Rome to Moscow and back again. He met personally with the leaders involved — Kennedy, Khrushchev, and Pope John — carrying gifts and messages, conveying the concerns of each party, developing a network for peace.

Pope John's particular Church concern at the time was to alleviate the situation of churchmen in jail behind the Iron Curtain. Helping them would be a first step toward improving the situation of the churches themselves. Cousins carried to Khrushchev John's concern for detained Archbishop Josef Slipyi, the one-time leader of Catholics in the Ukraine. Khrushchev told Cousins that he would do what he could. On February 10, 1963 Pope John received the freed Slipyi in the Vatican. John's international "opening to the left" was bearing fruit.

In March, Khrushchev's son-in-law editor of *Izvestia,* Alexei Adzhubei, visited Italy. Adzhubei wanted to visit Pope John, and John welcomed the opportunity to meet him: "I would condemn all of my previous conduct if I refused to see a man who courteously and without any pretext asked to see me to bring me greetings and a gift." He recalled that the Russians had made several gestures of courtesy toward the pope with no strings attached.[8]

John received Adzhubei in as inconspicuous a manner as possible and talked with him about inconsequential matters. Nonetheless the meeting was important. It manifested the change of style and direction John had introduced into Vatican affairs. Early in his pontificate the Vatican had prohibited voting for or being a member of the Communist Party. Now here was the pope meeting with leading communist figures and collaborating with them to get certain things done. John's stance started Western detente.

Pacem in terris

If John's actions in his waning months spoke loudly of a new relationship between the Vatican and the communist world, his final encyclical, *Pacem in terris,* interpreted those actions.

The document's most significant passage came in a fifth and final section, "Pastoral Exhortations." It asserts the importance of Catholics taking part in public life, and calls on them to bring their faith and spiritual values to bear on the problems of the world. Realistically John recognized that this would involve collaboration with persons who did not profess the Catholic faith, perhaps no faith at all. Believers needed to preserve their integrity while at the same time respecting all persons, even those whom Catholics considered to be in error.

> One must never confuse error and the person who errs, not even when there is question of error or inadequate knowledge of truth in the moral or religious field. The person who errs is always and above all a human being, and he retains in every case his dignity as a human person; and he must always be regarded and treated in accordance with that lofty dignity. Besides, in every human being, there is a need that is congenital to his nature and never becomes extinguished, compelling him to break through the web of error and open his mind to the knowledge of truth. And God will never fail to act on his interior being.... Meetings and agreements, in the various sectors of daily life, between believers and those who do not believe or believe insufficiently because they adhere to error can be occasions for discovering truth and paying homage to it.[9]

Pacem in terris also distinguished between false philosophical teachings and the historical movements deriving from them.

Teachings change in the course of time as they get applied practically. John went further, admitting even that such movements "contain elements that are positive and deserving of approval."

> It can happen that a drawing nearer together or a meeting for the attainment of some practical end, which was formerly deemed inopportune or unproductive, might now or in the future be considered opportune and useful.[10]

Thus did John explain his "opening to the left" both in Italy and internationally. He looked upon each individual as a fellow human being struggling to find the truth. He dealt with nations in the same spirit. Ultimately, John believed, truth would prevail over error on its own merits.

The foundation of the entire encyclical is the concept of human beings as persons who have certain rights and duties. Its teaching is grounded in natural values. It begins with the person and illustrates the natural building up of human relationships from the level of persons to that of communities to that of states to that of international relations between states. At each step John illuminates a *natural order* which the believer accepts as "laid down by God." By respecting this order and acting according to its nature, believers and unbelievers alike can achieve peace on earth.

John's encyclical synthesized previous papal teaching but added new and powerful concerns. The encyclical addressed "all men of good will," most of whom were drawn by John's personality and work. *Pacem in terris* was received like no other encyclical in history. It was translated, published and distributed in practically all the languages of the world. John sent a personal copy to Khrushchev via Cousins. Statesmen throughout the world listened. President John F. Kennedy, who insisted on his independence from the pope in matters of state during his campaign for the presidency, said publicly that he was proud of the encyclical as a Catholic and that he had learned from it as a statesman. The encyclical occasioned "Pacem in Terris" convocations sponsored by the Center for the Study of Democratic Institutions with participation of leading scholars and statesmen from around the world. The encyclical had unprecedented impact.

Pacem in terris was part of Pope John's effort to direct the work of the Council outward toward the world without being authoritarian and arbitrary. It was his last encyclical. He spoke clearly and forcefully about a matter of substance the Council needed to address, but did so in a context apart from the Council itself. That left the Council fathers free to pick up John's lead and act upon it or to let it pass. Eventually the Council made John's concern for justice and peace its own in a major conciliar document, *The Church in the Modern World.*

The reaction to *Pacem in terris* was not universally favorable. Its teaching disconcerted many both within and outside the Church. Pope John received some heavy and hurtful criticism. He accepted it:

> The world has awakened. Slowly, slowly the pure doctrine of the encyclical will find its way into consciences. No, I am not grieved by what is written and said about me. It is all too little when compared with the sufferings of Jesus, Son of God, during His life and on the Cross.[11]

John trusted in the power of persuasion and exemplary faith to the end. A week after John's death, this approach was exemplified by President Kennedy's important address at the American University in Washington, D.C., on June 10, 1963. Kennedy made a dramatic appeal for the end of the Cold War and for a new U.S. collaboration with Russia for peace. He urged the signing of a limited test ban treaty,[12] the forerunner of later SALT (Strategic Arms Limitation Talks) agreements.

John did experience some international recognition for his efforts when he was awarded the 1963 Balzan Peace Prize.[13] The announcement was made in early March, but the prize was not conferred until May 10-11. By then John was very ill, within two weeks of being confined to bed. Yet he pushed himself to go through the public conferral ceremonies, a final service to Church and world.

Ironically, John's prize had nothing directly to do with either his openness to communist leaders or his encyclical on peace. Rather it honored the contribution of his Council to peace. It recognized John for inviting representatives of other Christian denominations to the Council, for promoting greater mutual understanding among Christians, and for establishing contacts that reached well beyond the Christian community. In fact, public evidence of John's contacts with the Soviet bloc emerged only after the award was granted. Indeed, John received Adzhubei on the occasion of a meeting with journalists prompted by the announcement that John would receive the prize. The occurrence of the official conferral after the release of *Pacem in terris* was a happy but fitting accident.

Pacem in terris was truly the crown of Pope John's pontificate. It summarized what John had worked to bring about. His purpose had been to use truth to unite Christians with one another and with others of good will so as to help build peace in the world. *Pacem in terris* summarized Christian thought on the question of peace. It brought persons of many persuasions together in a more urgent search for peace.

As John neared death, he saw things in long perspective. When receiving the Balzan Prize, he insisted that it was a recognition of the entire line of 20th-century pontiffs. His exhausting journey across town from the Vatican to the Quirinal Palace to meet with the other Balzan Prize winners and the president of Italy was a final effort to heal the century-long rift between the Vatican and the Italian state. The Quirinal, official residence of the President of Italy, had formerly been the pope's residence. John went without jealousy, hostility or regret.

Four days later, on May 15, John held his last general audience in St. Peter's. On May 17 he said his last Mass. On May

20 he left his apartment for the last time to greet Cardinal Wyszynski of Poland in his private library — a dying courtesy to a man who had long dealt courageously with a communist government. On May 23 he stood for the last time at the balcony of his apartment to bless the crowds in St. Peter's square.

Then began his eleven day death vigil. Radio and television enabled all the world to join the praying crowd in St. Peter's square. On May 31 John met for the last time with Secretary of State Cicognani. He offered his life for the Church, the Council, the union of Christians, the sanctification of bishops and priests, and for the peace of the world. A week earlier John had told Cicognani that it was time for the Church to "recognize the signs of the times, to take advantage of the opportunities offered, and to look toward distant horizons." Catholics, he said, had to be concerned with defending "above all and everywhere the rights of the human person and not only those of the Catholic Church.... It's not the Gospel that is changing; we are. We are beginning to understand it better."[14]

John spent his final three days in a semi-coma. He died on June 3 as the crowds at a special Mass in St. Peter's square heard the celebration's concluding words, "The Mass is ended. Go in peace!" It was the day after Pentecost. John's pentecostal pontificate was accomplished.

Questions for You from John's Model

1. Do you key off of successes to pursue new projects that will extend your success?
2. Are the principles underlying your actions clear enough to you to sustain you through criticism of the directions you take?
3. Are you willing to push on through rejection, opposition, public criticism, pain and suffering in pursuit of your objectives?

4. Do you understand the power and importance of clear and repeated statements of your vision?

5. Do you take advantage of ceremonial occasions to make symbolic statements?

6. Do you direct the mission of your organization to the well-being of the larger community, even of all humankind?

7. Are you willing to sacrifice your life for the mission of your organization? Is its mission worth such sacrifice?

The Leadership Wisdom of John XXIII

A leadership formula and manual such as we have developed in this study of Pope John XXIII is instructive in an important but limited way. In the end, it is a person who leads, and each successful leader has a wisdom so personal that it becomes, in many respects, inimitable. Yet even to know that is to know something worthwhile.

This chapter identifies three dimensions of Pope John's leadership wisdom. We have already studied one of them in some detail, having a strategy. The other two — his tactics and his personal spirituality — are largely idiosyncratic, but we can learn from them too. Happily, John articulated many points of his tactical wisdom in nugget form. To know them is to have the possibility of acting on them. Finally, John kept a spiritual journal all his life, published posthumously as his *Journal of a Soul.* Looking through that into his soul is to know some of the possibilities of our own.

Every leader has personal secrets to success, a personal leadership wisdom. So do you. This chapter may help you get in touch with your personal leadership wisdom. Doing that is critical to your eventual success.

Strategy, Tactics, Spirituality

One can assess the effectiveness of John XXIII's leadership by reviewing the present state of the Catholic Church and Catholicism in relation to his three goals — truth, unity, and peace. Without doubt, Roman Catholicism has changed since 1958 along the broad lines intended by John.

With regard to truth, the dominance of a scholastic and legalistic way of thinking about and within the Church has been broken, the Church is coming to terms with modernity, and Catholics are addressing the claims of other traditions and religions. With regard to unity, the Church has abandoned its onetime aloofness toward other Christians, has entered into respectful dialogue with them on an organized and sustained basis, and is actively collaborating with other churches in many different ways. Pope John Paul II's 1995 encyclical *Ut unum sint* went so far as to ask other Christians to help the papacy think through the way it serves Christ's Church as a whole. With regard to peace, the Church has truly become global, strengthening its presence in formerly communist and colonial nations and playing an active role in pressing for peace and justice throughout the world. Again, Pope John Paul II admirably embodied these dimensions of John's program, as he closed the second millennium and opened the third.

Pope John's goals have not been fully attained, nor has movement toward them been a matter of uninterrupted progress. Some of the change has weakened the Church and confused the meaning of Catholicism for members and nonmembers alike. Nonetheless when Pope John Paul II called an Extraordinary Synod in 1987 to assess the impact of the Council on the 25th anniversary of its start, the representative bishops gathered from all around the world affirmed the work of the Council and called for its fuller implementation. John's work was good!

The leadership of Pope John alone does not explain all the change that has occurred. His leadership did not directly cause all subsequent developments in the Church, but the Church has been moving in the overall direction of John's purposes. Without doubt, he pointed the way and started the Church on a journey in that direction. We have examined how he did it and how he succeeded. Now we look at the leadership wisdom that guided him, the secrets of his success.

Strategy

Pope John's strategy was outlined in Part I, Chapter 3. That was a major part of his wisdom. While seeming somewhat purposeless and undisciplined, we saw that John was in fact intensely purposeful and disciplined in the way he went about his role. The fivefold strategy of Person-Program-Symbolic Communication-Institutional Ally-Consistency goes far to explain why his elderly aspirations restored youthful vigor to the ancient institution he led. His strategy recommends that leaders identify fully with the nature and character of the organization they lead and then embody in themselves what it is all about. Leaders must design a program of action with clear goals that can enable all involved in the organization to buy into them and become part of moving the organization toward them. Effective leaders communicate their vision not only in words and dry plans but in symbolic forms that capture the imagination and engage the energies of those who need to be involved.

John's model suggests that to lead by example and persuasion with full respect for the dignity, freedom and responsibilities of others, leaders must have an Ally within the organization. Such an Ally must be strong enough, talented enough, and strategically positioned enough to influence the organization effectively in the direction the leader points. Finally, the leader's way of working these four factors must tie them all together. Consistency of behavior is necessary. The Program must reflect the Person to be credible, and the Person must embody the Program to be persuasive. The Symbolism must reflect the Person and the Program so others can grasp the leader's intent and direction. The Ally must be loyal to the Person, devoted to the Program and imbued with the Symbolism. Take any one of these factors out of the mix, and whether John's short papacy would have made any significant difference in the life of the Catholic Church and of the world would be a very open question.

Pope John XXIII was strategically wise. Leaders who seek to imitate John will not fail to have a strategy, conscious or unconscious, and to make that strategy operative. John's success was not an accident. It was an effect, a work of wisdom.

Tactics

Brilliant strategy often lacks appropriate and effective tactics and so goes awry. Here again the principle of Consistency is critical. John XXIII was not only a masterful if unassuming strategist. He was a disarmingly efficient tactician, as seen in the detailed study of how he made the Council happen and the way he pursued peace in the world. John plotted, plodded and prodded every year — pentecostally. He refused to force things but recognized opportune moments when they came and acted on them promptly. He knew when and how to intervene. He kept his distance from the organization he set in motion, respecting others, but he did what he needed to when he had to make the organization respond. He kept the enterprise moving in the directions he wanted it to go. He was shrewd, astute, clever. At the same time he was unfailingly good, holy and lovable.

The above record portrayed John using the following tactics among others:

- respecting all persons and participative processes
- respecting tradition even while changing it
- taking balanced stands and communicating them clearly
- intervening with restraint, but clearly, swiftly and in a timely and balanced manner when doing so
- asserting vision, values, meanings which are not new to

the organization but new in their accent and emphasis
- being forceful, yet respectful: leading without dominating, convincing without being controlling, persuading rather than commanding
- being open to all factions and factors: being actively neutral rather than ideologically one-sided
- biding one's time and waiting for the opportune occasion rather than forcing the situation
- reading the signs of the times
- taking small, manageable, opportune steps which, if successful, can occasion bigger steps
- knowing the mindset(s) that operate within and dominate the organization: respecting them all, using their strengths, offsetting their limitations
- realizing the power of symbolism and using it
- defining a clear program and throwing one's energy behind it
- combining lovableness with courage, optimism and a willingness to try something new in pursuing a clear program
- "bending but not breaking"
- "seeing everything, overlooking much, correcting a little" (that is, one thing at a time)
- "in essentials, unity; in questionable matters, freedom; in all things, charity"
- observing, judging, acting
- entrusting each collaborator to his own distinct post and honoring the work the person does from that post
- giving to fellow-workers everything that is due: respect, a share of the responsibility, and confidence — always confidence, even after they mess things up
- not losing oneself in administrative trivia
- attending to people with a sincere heart and, with the prudence of experience, leading them

- ordering to be done only what one has some grounds for believing will be done
- watching, correcting, supporting
- making happen, knowing how to make happen, letting happen, and charging others to make happen
- doing some things oneself, making others do some things, and leaving certain things alone
- avoiding many laws and directives, which make bad government

John's tactical wisdom, like all wisdom, is not novel. It merely captures the common sense that so often eludes most of us. Formulating it, stating it, awakens and confirms our best instincts. John's tactics were a fruit of his native intelligence, organizational shrewdness, and experience. But they arose primarily from his deep spirituality, the final and most important dimension of his leadership wisdom.

Spirituality

John XXIII's spirituality was the most important component of his leadership wisdom. It was more personal than either his strategy or his tactics. John's spirituality is ultimately the secret of his success. It was the source of his vision, his style, his mode of expression, his discernment, his approach to decision-making, and his manner of execution. He was an amazingly effective executive leader, but he was more than that. He was a startlingly integrated person, a saint. Already formally declared a "blessed" person, he will surely be declared a saint soon.

Our review of Pope John's record demonstrates that he was in fact a capable and resourceful manager and leader. But that does not reverse the fact that he was chosen for his personal qualities, not for his executive abilities. Indeed, John's personal charm and goodness made him a highly popular pope. Beneath all his attractiveness and accomplishment lay his spirituality. What was it?

Spirituality is defined in many ways. Common to all is a mixing of the human and the divine, an interpenetration of God and the individual personality, of spirit and Holy Spirit. Spirituality is the human result of this mixing. Spirituality is the tone or style of life that emerges when God mixes with man — indeed, with this particular person.

Pope John's spirituality was so thorough a blend of the elements that go into a godly human life that one could no longer distinguish the elements. John was so profoundly spiritual that one never thought to describe him as "otherworldly" or "supernatural" or "ascetic" or even "holy." Rather he was considered "human," "good," "down to earth." He had "integrity." Angelo Roncalli was an exceptionally integrated human being. He was complex, but he impressed those who met him as simple. He held an office that was "supernatural" by definition, yet he held it most naturally.

Three descriptions of Pope John illustrate this integrity. Cardinal Suenens' commemorative sermon at the second session of the Second Vatican Council in October of 1963 put it this way:

> If one had to express it all in one word, it seems to me that one could say that John XXIII was a man surprisingly natural and at the same time supernatural. Nature and grace produced in him a living unity filled with charm and surprises. Everything about him sprang from a single source. In a completely natural way he was supernatural. He was natural with such a supernatural spirit that no one detected a distinction between the two. Filling his lungs, as it were, he breathed the faith just as he breathed physical and natural health. "He lived in the presence of God," one wrote, "with the simplicity of one who takes a walk through the streets of his native town." [1]

Cardinal Lercaro of Bologna also spoke of John's integrity in terms of simplicity. John was unstudied, direct, and spontaneously human. But in fact his thoughts and sentiments were rich and profound. The simplicity of his personality integrated many diverse factors. An Italian author who knew Roncalli well, Rev. Giuseppe DeLuca, attests to this same quality:

> While in appearance no one is more open, easy, and approachable than he is, in fact no one is more hidden, slower and more laborious in maturing his sentiments, judgments, and actions. Above all, no one reveals himself more inimical to simple-mindedness.[2]

Cardinal Lercaro affirmed John's integrity in another way[3] when he addressed the accusation that John was uncultured, a simpleton who acted rashly and thoughtlessly during his pontificate because he did not adequately grasp what was at stake. John appeared simple, concluded Lercaro, perhaps uncultured, because he neither consumed nor displayed culture in a conspicuous manner. His culture was something deeper. He *created* culture. He was an individual who drank so deeply of the sources and who integrated them in himself to such an eminent degree that he was fresh and creative in a profoundly cultural sense simply by being himself and following his own inspirations. "Simple" Angelo Roncalli was, in Lercaro's view, but "simpleton" he certainly was not.

Msgr. Pietro Pavan, John's chief collaborator in the composition of both *Mater et magistra* and *Pacem in terris,* offers a third view of Pope John's integrity. Pavan spoke of Pope John's goodness. He distinguished between "a good man" and "a man who is good." "A man who is good" is virtuous, but he makes you aware of his virtue. His goodness obviously costs him something; he must make a conscious effort to be good. "A good man" on the other hand has so integrated goodness into his basic personality that he seems naturally and effortlessly good. To Pavan, Roncalli was "a good man." Even popular terminology reflected this in Italy where John was commonly called not *il papa buono* (the pope who is good), but *il buon papa* (the good pope).

Suenens, Lercaro and Pavan all testify to the same quality — the thorough integration that marked John's personality, his spirituality. John's integrity embraced factors central to the nature and purpose of the Church, namely the supernatural, religious piety, and godly goodness. Interestingly, Angelo Roncalli consciously sought that quality in the course of his life. He sought to be holy:

> Everyone calls me "Holy Father," and holy I must and will be. I am very far from attaining this holiness intact, although my desire and will to succeed in this are wholehearted and determined.[4]

One of John's mottos was "to be good always to everyone." He sought simplicity in religious bearing and conduct:

> I leave to everyone else the superabundant cunning and so-called skill of the diplomat, and continue to be satisfied with my own *bonhomie* and simplicity of feeling, word and behavior. In the end all turns out for the good of those who are faithful to the teaching and example of the Lord.[5]

Convinced that the divine was in the natural and the natural in the simple, John resolved

> to simplify all that is complicated and to treat everything with the greatest naturalness and clarity, without wrapping things up in trimmings and artificial turns of thought and phrase. "To be simple with prudence" — the motto is St. John Chrysostom's. What a wealth of doctrine in those two phrases.[6]

Integrity and personal integration distinguish Pope John's

spirituality. The elements he integrated were his own humanity on the one hand and essential values of the Church (holiness and goodness) on the other. This unique combination constituted Pope John's integrity, his simplicity, his spirituality and his wisdom. This spirituality was the secret of his person and the secret of his success.

Pope John's human touch is legendary. Others constantly commented on his ability to be himself and to put those in his presence at ease. Cardinal Koenig of Vienna counts the restoration of a human dimension to Church office as one of John's great accomplishments. His humanness flowed largely from his ever-cherished roots in the humble Roncalli family of Sotto il Monte. The first time he used the *sedia gestatoria* (the chair on which the pope used to sit when lifted above crowds and carried through them), he thought of an occasion in his youth when his father hoisted him up to his shoulders so he could see the pope. The recollection is typical. John's papal speeches and remarks regularly referred to his family, his home, and other life experiences with his brothers and sisters throughout the world. Integrated experience, not abstraction, was the well from which he drew life-giving water.

Pope John viewed himself as one with others rather than above them. He sought what united him with others. He left aside what set him (or them) apart. Once John told a portly employee of the Vatican, "You and I belong to the same party." The man was stupefied and replied, "But your holiness, I don't belong to any party." "Yes, you do," said John, pointing to his stomach, "We belong to the fat man's party!"

When Pope John received Brooks Hays, a U.S. Congressman from the Baptist South, Hays somewhat anxiously told John. "I'm a Baptist!" The pope replied, "Well, I'm John!" indicating that he was a Baptist too! John then promised to remember the Hays' daughter in his rosary, an unusual gift to a Baptist but a natural one from Pope John. Many are the instances of John's identifying with those to whom he spoke: "Are you a theologian?" "No." "Good, I'm not either!" "I'm a member of PIME too!" (PIME is a missionary order of priests.)

The most famous such incident occurred when John visited prisoners in Rome's Regina Coeli prison during his first Christmas as pope. Not only did he go to them and insist on going through the jail to see them all, but he shared with them a family secret: an uncle of his had once been in jail. Pope John shared this to establish a fellow feeling with the prisoners. Before leaving them that day he told them:

> Okay now. I have come and you have seen me. I have used my eyes to look into your eyes. I have put my heart next to your heart. This visit will remain deep in my soul, you can be sure of that. At the beginning of this new year, the first year of what they call my pontificate, I will have the pleasure of knowing that this work of mercy toward you will call forth all the others, will give the tone to the others.[7]

John showed his solidarity with others also through unfailing courtesy, both in private audiences and in official ceremonies.

> His getting to his feet and uncovering his head when he greeted a visitor — his overcoming the rigidity of protocol by the warmth of his gestures; his introductory words and the gentle look around he would give so as to stimulate an atmosphere of sympathetic participation and exchange before he began solemn actions — all of this was not a renunciation of the majesty of the job he had assumed. Far less was it a nonchalance about ceremony. It was simply that in every man, even through the veil of faults and errors, he saw the image of God.[8]

Most of the stories about Pope John concerned how he affirmed and manifested his kinship with the human race. Physically he was a "tubby pontiff with the head of an overgrown elf," but he did everything with a dignity so much his own that it all seemed acceptable.[9] In an audience with newsmen on October 13, 1962, two days after the opening of the Council, he remarked on the journalists' temptation to be sensational. Then, departing from his text, he looked up over his glasses and said, "I know you have many other temptations, but now I am speaking only about this one!" He quickly added that he was confident they would not fall.[10]

John frequently related to the family of his visitors as something every human being has in common and holds dear. He asked Alexei Adzhubei, the editor of *Izvestia* and his wife Rada, the daughter of Russian Premier Nikita Khrushchev, about their children, Nikita, Alexei, and Ivan. He sent a blessing for them with Rada, including a special one for Ivan because he shared John's name. He gave Rada a rosary, saying it was a prayer he had learned from his own mother. By such familial touches, John entered the world of others and allowed them to enter his.[11]

Pope John looked on himself as a brother to the entire human family. He was their fellow, not their superior, and that was how he made them feel in his presence. He detested the *sedia gestatoria.* He had learned equality with the humble farmers of the dusty fields of Sotto il Monte. He imbibed solidarity around the table at which his poor family ate. He never abandoned those attitudes as he accumulated honor upon honor. John's humanness helps account for the universal love and respect he generated as a leader. Beneath the pomp of his office everyone from Charles De Gaulle to the tribesman of New Guinea perceived a human being who wanted nothing other than to be their brother. That they could accept, and with it they accepted much else he shared with them.

Besides being humble, the Roncalli household in Sotto il Monte was devout. Pope John's quest for holiness started there. The Roncallis esteemed Christian living and sought Christian perfection. They planted high expectations in young spirits and subsequently nurtured them into substantial lives of Christian virtue. After John's death, his older brother Zaverio Roncalli was asked what he thought Pope John had done. He replied, "He was a Christian. He was a Catholic." That sufficed to explain the spirit, the intent and the accomplishment of one of the 20th century's great religious leaders.

To be holy is to commune with God, to live in the divine presence, to radiate the divine. Holiness is the goal of the Christian's lifelong struggle to allow God's grace to penetrate every facet of one's character and every dimension of one's life. Pope John's *Journal of a Soul* is his diary of that pilgrimage. He was a man of prayer and devotion. He rose early in the morning, usually at three or four. His family rose then to till the fields; Pope John did so to till his spirit. As pope, he spent the hours from rising until about eight in the morning in reading, prayer, and study. He maintained many devotions and prayed with an army of saints throughout his life. He read lives of the saints, the Fathers of the Church and the scriptures. He drank deeply of these sources and used them spontaneously to interpret his own life and events in the world.

Most importantly, Pope John lived, moved and acted in God's presence. He had an acute sense of providence — of God's guiding hand in his life and in the course of history. He read the "signs of the times," as he called them, and humbly but confidently made judgments about what was going on and what therefore he must do.[12]

John's habitual way of maintaining communion with God in the midst of tumultuous events is most impressive. A few hours after becoming pope and the preliminary ceremonies and announcements had been made, Capovilla approached him with many things demanding immediate attention. Pope John replied that they should first pray Vespers together, the Church's evening prayer. In September 1962 he made a special retreat to prepare for the October opening of the Vatican Council. He made a pilgrimage to Loreto and Assisi one week before the

Council began. He frequently left the Vatican just to pray at some special church or sanctuary in Rome. Maintaining communion with God in the midst of a busy life was John's chief concern.

The night before he delivered important speeches — such as those of January 25, 1959 and October 11, 1962 — John would place the text on the altar of his private chapel and leave it there, commending it to God. He spent two and a half hours in prayer before he journeyed to the Quirinal Palace to receive the Balzan Peace Prize on May 11, 1963.[13] He was already in the last stages of cancer. He died three weeks later. John prayed while aides worked on such statements as the one that helped resolve the October 1962 Cuban missile crisis. God was thoroughly integrated into John's routine.

Two other episodes summarize John's holiness and communion with God. Near the end of his life he spent a great deal of time reviewing drafts of conciliar documents with Bishop Alfredo Cavagna, his confessor and special representative to the Central Committee of the Ecumenical Council. As one of these sessions began, Cavagna suggested that they call on the Holy Spirit to be with them. John responded, "But Monsignor, I am always in communion with the Holy Spirit." Similarly he once said to a friend, "They say that the Pope is assisted by the Holy Spirit. But I must say in truth, the Holy Spirit does not help me. I help him! He's the one who does everything."[14] John lived what he is reported to have said the night before his election, "I am like an empty sack which the grace of God fills up."[15]

John sought to be holy, and he was perceived as holy. Individuals who saw the opening of the Council only on television remembered years later the image of a man totally concentrated in prayer. Surrounded by his brother bishops, initiating a collaboration which the pope hoped would be a great leap forward for the faith, John knew that only God could grant success. So he prayed. He entrusted his opening speech to the Lord on the altar of his chapel the night before. That speech was one of the most significant in papal history It was the keynote of the four years of work done by the Council, most of it after John died. It was a mighty gust of the fresh air which John wanted to fill his too musty Church.[16]

John's holiness was nowhere more apparent than in the way he died. He received the doctors' final verdict with calm, resolved to die a good death as a good bishop, offered his life for the success of the Council, and bade farewell to those he loved. People everywhere joined his vigil. The pope who prayed for a new Pentecost left this world on the day after Pentecost. He embraced the whole human family during his life. When he died that family felt bereft. A holy man, a holy brother, a holy father had departed.

John's third characteristic spiritual quality was his goodness. "Good" is perhaps the single best term to describe him and the adjective most frequently used. It captures the unique combination of humanness and holiness in Roncalli. He was human, but he was something more than simply a good human being or even a great humanist. He was a saint in the refreshingly human way John himself once described. He noted that certain lives of the saints portray them as being "taken by the hair and carried out of the society in which they lived, even out of themselves." Such accounts turn saints into demigods. They

> blur the concept of a saint among us.... To know how to constantly make nothing of oneself, destroying within and without anything which others would seek to use as a basis of praise in the eyes of the world; to keep alive in one's heart the flame of a most pure love of God, over and above the sluggish loves of this world; to give everything, to sacrifice oneself for the good of one's brothers, and when humiliated, out of love for God and neighbor to faithfully follow the way pointed out by providence, which leads elect souls to the fulfillment of their personal mission, which each person has — this is what sanctity is all about.[17]

Indeed goodness such as Pope John's is what humanness becomes when thoroughly transfused by God's Spirit. When the human personality is penetrated and transformed by God's grace and the two are thoroughly integrated, one is not only good but godly. John's goodness symbolizes the integration of his person and his priesthood, of his own dispositions with the values of the Church. Goodness was the face of his integrity.

John was conscious of the importance of spiritual integrity for his success as a leader in and of the Church.[18] When he became Patriarch of Venice in 1953 he told the people that he wanted to be nothing more than their brother:

> I have made a firm resolution to remain faithful to what has always been the source of my self-respect. This characteristic was probably responsible for my appointment to Venice among noble people who are generous in their manifestations and especially sensitive to sincerity, to simple manners, words, and deeds, to those qualities that mark the man of integrity.[19]

John consciously strove to maintain this integrity, this fidelity to what he had become, this union of his person with the values he represented, this authenticity and simplicity. A year after becoming pope he wrote:

> The welcome immediately accorded to my unworthy person and the affection still shown by all who approach me are always a source of surprise to me. The maxim "Know thyself" suffices for my spiritual serenity and keeps me on the alert. The secret of my success must lie there: in not "searching into things which are above my ability" and in being content to be "meek and humble of heart." Meekness and humbleness of heart give graciousness in receiving, speaking and dealing with people, and the patience to bear, to pity, to keep silent and to encourage.[20]

Spirituality and Leadership

One's spirituality inevitably impacts one's leadership. We are who we are. Our spirituality is the deepest layer of our being. From here, in the end, we live, act, manage, and lead. John's spirituality was the key to who he was and what he did as a manager and leader.

John's spirituality had two major effects on his leadership. First, because he had integrated the essential values of the Church in his person, he represented it in a very natural and personal way. The Church claims to be a unique blend of the human and the divine, an instrument through which God is made present in human life and affairs. John was that, spontaneously stood for it, and easily communicated it.

Second, John's spirituality made the Church believable. His integrity meant that he never just played a role. He really believed and lived what he represented. He was credible. With him and through him the Church too became more credible.

John's spirituality carried some liabilities as well. His insistence on being himself and his spontaneous humanness sometimes led him to act in a way which some felt demeaned the papacy. In their eyes John lacked class. Similarly his insistence on being good sometimes led him to consider persons so much that the well-being of even the Church may have suffered. To John's critics, this weakness was especially apparent in his uncritical manner of making certain appointments and in his failure to gain control of the Vatican bureaucracy. Occasional failures to make hard decisions (as in the case of the Biblicum crisis) led some supporters to wonder just how serious he was about the direction he proposed. These qualities ate away at John's credibility during his lifetime.

A few further observations regarding John's spirit and style will suffice to complete the present portrait of this man who serves as a model and mentor for managers and leaders in all sorts of organizations and situations. Roncalli was born and raised in a farming family. This gave him a sense of growth and a balanced time perspective. He knew that there were times to sow and times to reap and times to patiently wait. This held whether one was concerned about seeds in the ground, in men's souls, or in organizations.

In the seminary, Roncalli took a particular liking to history. This strengthened his time perspective. Just as a farmer watches for critical turning points during the year and learns to recognize their signs, so did Roncalli become especially well read in crucial turning points of Church history. He developed his own interpretations of key events (such as the Council of Trent). He learned to feel history's slow evolutions and the profound, often unnoticed interior transformations that finally determine events.

For a period Roncalli taught history and wrote several short accounts of the Diocese of Bergamo. In 1909 he undertook a major work on the 1575 pastoral visitation of St. Charles Borromeo to his diocese. It took fifty years for him to complete the five-volume project, a scholarly contribution which displays a broad scope and vision within which many details find their place. The work had a lasting impact on Roncalli. Through it he learned that St. Charles' way of being pastoral was to apply the doctrines and disciplines of the Council of Trent to the real life situations he found in Bergamo. The pragmatic St. Charles became one of John's heroes alongside John's model and mentor, Bishop Radini Tedeschi. From Charles Borromeo John learned to interpret the Council of Trent as a predominantly pastoral event and councils in general as powerful instruments for accomplishing the pastoral mission of the Church. All this later blossomed during his pontificate. His historical studies also gave him a sense of the mutability of human institutions within their continuity.

Pope John's large and poor family allowed itself no airs but always maintained its dignity. His seminary training nurtured in him a sense of reverence and respect. Both atmospheres fostered a psychic life rooted in dispositions of faith, hope, and love. The result in the mature Roncalli was a decided esteem for humility and gentleness and a determination to embody basic Christian virtues. He wanted to be a humble, gentle pope and a model for his flock.

John's career combined organizational and diplomatic experiences with assignments as a diocesan priest, a missionary worker, and a bishop. He integrated these around the ideal of being a pastor, a leader devoted to the well-being of persons, both spiritual and temporal. His pastoral spirituality permeated all that he did, even his bureaucratic postings, giving them worth. As John put it, "Oh how poor the life of the bishop or the priest who is reduced to being only a diplomat or a bureaucrat."[21] Again, "the pope… [spends] himself in all that is a service of faith, grace, and pastoral spirituality."[22]

Pope John was markedly traditional in his manners, his devotions, his reading, his customs. He did not advocate novelty for novelty's sake. He maintained a reserve about seriously undertaken innovations, such as France's worker-priests and "new theology." His attitude is reflected in the report that he once wondered aloud why the provocative Jesuit thinker, Teilhard de Chardin, did not stick to the catechism.

Yet John was open-minded. He felt that narrow ideas could entrap people and set them against one another. He remembered with pain the fanaticism of closed minds during the anti-modernist purge at the beginning of the century. Pope John had an active curiosity and he indulged it, often delighting in the unexpected things he found. He enjoyed talking with persons of other persuasions. He wanted to hear their ideas even as he shared his own. He was open-minded too in the special sense of being willing to act upon ideas and inspirations that appeared to him worthwhile. Many of John's innovations were due to an open-minded responsiveness more than to a preset grand design. Thus his conversation with Cardinal Tardini on January 20, 1959 about calling a Council resulted in a threefold program of Synod, Council, Updating of the Code.

John was both realist and optimist. Suspicious of ideologies and closed thought systems, he was free to see things as they were. He saw the discouraging and distressing aspects of modern life. He knew history's sobering lessons well. Yet for all this John chose to be an optimist. This disposition stems from many sources — his faith in God, his confidence in people, his own ebullient spirit. In any case, the combination of realism and optimism enabled John to assess situations frankly and then propose courses of action likely to make the best of them.

Pope John was both a pragmatist and a visionary. Being mostly free of preconceived ideas, he was willing to try something, observe its effect, and then adjust his course in terms of the results. At the same time, he undertook everything in the light of his encompassing vision of what the Church needed at the time. His ability to see much and to organize it according to simple lines is seen in his five-volume work on St. Charles Borromeo, in his threefold program, and in the neat pentecostal pattern of his pontificate. Both pragmatism and a persevering spirit are evident in the fifty years it took for him to bring the St. Charles project to completion and in the three years it took him to get the Council under way.

Pope John labored with a good sense of tactics. His pragmatic behavior exemplified the tactical principles articulated in the last chapter. Early in his career he observed that many administrators seemed determined to "Break but never to bend!" That made no sense to him, so he reversed it and lived by the motto "Bend, but don't break." This transformation was typical of Pope John's prudence. He had both common sense and idealism. He blended mind and heart. John's mind was incisive in an intuitive way. He grasped things as in a glance. His thinking was not ponderous, moving slowly from premise to conclusion. When John saw truth he affirmed it, held firmly to it, and acted upon it. He trusted his intuitions and worked them. They made a difference in both the style and substance of his leadership.

If John did not personally see the truth of a proposal, he inclined to respect the judgment of others he trusted. His own intuitions frequently sprang from reactions to the proposals of others. His insights developed through interaction. He read widely and consulted broadly. He accepted ideas and suggestions from others but not blindly. He thought about it himself and often came up with alterations and new ideas that made the proposals different and in some important instances very successful.

John had a collaborative spirit. He was not a loner. He enjoyed working with others, respected their abilities and happily allowed them to do things on their own responsibility in the realm of their competence. He delegated well and provided others with the encouragement they needed. He relied on persuasion rather than authority to influence events. Since his mind sometimes saw distinctions and concerns others did not, he often judged that a different course of action should be pursued. Yet he did not forcefully overrule others. He bided his time, slowly convincing others to consider alternatives.

A final aspect of John's spirituality is that he was outgoing and communicative. He was not secretive. Nor did he engage in intrigue. If he thought something, he was inclined to say it. If he could not convince others directly, he would often share his thoughts with a larger public that, in turn, might convince those John could not.

The critical aspect of all these qualities was the profound unity they assumed in John's spirit under the consciously sought influence of the Holy Spirit. Pope John was not an either/or person; he was both/and. He was a "union of opposites," a phenomenon the mystics find to be characteristic of the divine. That is not surprising since John lived his life in constant union with God.

John's spirituality was profound. His intriguing personality puzzled others but never seemed dishonest. His actions and/or words were at times disconcerting, even infuriating, but they always came across as straightforward, sincere, simple, good, and holy. They were like the words of a prophet. John was a spokesman for God.

Finally John's spirituality was integrated around his desire to be a pastor patterned on Jesus. He announced that intention on the day of his coronation, and throughout his pontificate that was what he did, that was what he was.

In the end, the secret of John's person and a key to his success as a leader was his pastoral spirituality. In the end his accomplishments were not his own but God's. That dimension of his leadership also provides a model for all managers and leaders, today or any day.

This book has presented Blessed Pope John XXIII as a mentor for managers in the wisdom of leading which he so skillfully modeled. Hopefully its readers will judge that John merits being *their* model and mentor, perhaps even the patron saint of all managers and executive leaders, from pastors to presidents.

Questions for You from John's Model

1. Do you cultivate the spiritual dimension of your life?
2. Do you bring your experience as a manager to bear on your spiritual life, and vice-versa, your spirituality to bear on your role as a leader?
3. Do you write down, log, or capture in some way the lessons you learn as you live and lead?
4. What opposite qualities do you embody? How do you evaluate their balance? How do others experience the balance of these forces in your way of leading and managing? Are you divided or integrated?
5. Do you bring your role into your prayer and your prayer into your role?
6. What have you learned from Pope John XXIII? In what ways can you follow him as model and mentor?
7. Can you look at Pope John as your patron saint in managing your role as a leader?

Notes

Prologue

[1] For background on this chapter cf. works by Abbot (*Twelve Council Fathers*), Algisi, Capovilla, Elliott, Falconi (*The Popes*), Johnson, Lai, Tanzella, Trevor and Zizola. For convenience I shall refer to these works by the author's last name only. For full titles of author's works, see the Selected Bibliography at the end of this volume.

[2] Four powerful members of the Curia — Cardinals Canali, Pizzardo, Ottaviani and Micara — constituted the strength of this group. They had sympathizers within the Curia (such as Cardinals Mimmi, Fumasoni, Biondi, Ciriaci and Cicognani) and in larger dioceses in Italy (such as Cardinals Siri of Genoa and Ruffini of Palermo). Cardinal Aloisi Masella, who was elected Camerlengo (Chamberlain) shortly after Pius XII's death and so was entrusted with administering the Church during the interregnum, also tended to be conservative in his thinking.

[3] This group included Cardinals Valeri, Costantini and perhaps Tisserant, the French dean of the College of Cardinals.

[4] Cardinals Lercaro of Bologna, Roncalli of Venice and Della Costa of Florence constituted this group. Their center and guiding light, however, was Archbishop Montini of Milan, a former aide of Pius XII who was famous for his brilliant and progressive views. He succeeded John XXIII as Paul VI.

[5] Cited from Balducci, pp. 38-39.

[6] *Ibid.*

[7] Capovilla, *Giovanni XXIII,* pp. 121-131.

[8] Cf. Roncalli, *My Bishop.*

[9] Cited by Giancarlo Zizola, *Risposte a Papa Giovanni* (Roma: Coines Edizioni, 1973), p. 54 (author's translation).

[10] *Ibid.*

[11] Cited by Capovilla, *Giovanni XXIII,* p. 305 (author's translation).

[12] Several lists of the Roman Pontiffs exist due to conflicting claims at certain points in history. Hence Roncalli is sometimes called the 259th, sometimes the 261st pope. Here we follow the count which makes him the 262nd.

[13] For background, cf. Falconi, *The Popes;* Hales, *The Catholic Church* and *Pope John;* Nichols, Purdy and Wall.

[14] Tardini, *Memories of Pius XII,* p. 75.

[15] *Ibid.*

[16] Nichols, p.105.

[17] *Acta Apostolicae Sedis,* 50 (1958): pp. 855-861.

[18] *Ibid.*

[19] John XXIII, *Journal of a Soul,* p. 303.

[20] Cf. Zsolt Aradi, Michael Derrick and Douglas Woodruff, *John XXIII: Pope of the Council* (London: Burns and Oates, 1961), p. 181. Also cf. Zizola, p. 463.

[21] Nazareno Fabbretti, *Papa Giovanni* (Roma: Edizioni Arteditorial, 1966), p. 214 (author's translation).

[22] Elliott, pp. 232-233

[23] Tanzella, p. 237.
[24] Abbot, ed., *The Documents of Vatican II*, p. 43, A.22.
[25] Cf. works by Falconi, especially *Il Pentagone Vaticano*.
[26] Purdy, pp. 8-9.

Part I

Chapter 1

[1] DMC 1:3-5. DMC will be used throughout to refer to *Discorsi, Messagi, Coloqui del Santo Padre Giovanni XXIII*, five vols. and index. This is the official collection of Pope John's speeches and writings. Unless otherwise indicated, all translations are by the author.
[2] Trevor, p. 247.
[3] John XXIII, *Journal*, p. 229, entry from late November, 1959.
[4] Interview with Cardinal Koenig of Vienna in Chicago, November 12, 1974.
[5] Cf. Alfredo Bonazzi, *Quel giorno di uve rosse* (Assisi: Cittadella Editrice, 1973). Cf. "Il Vescovo di Roma," *Osservatore Romano*, 17-18 June, 1963.
[6] Capovilla, *Heart and Mind*, p. 52.

Chapter 2

[1] DMC 1:123-133.
[2] *Ibid.*
[3] Cf. Capovilla, *Giovanni XXIII*, pp. 260-268 and 275 ff., and Gorresio, pp. 231-234.
[4] Nichols, p. 118.
[5] Argued eloquently and with an abundance of evidence by Emilio Fogliasso in a documentary entitled *The Second Vatican Ecumenical Council in the Life of the Holy Father John XXIII*. Cf. also Capovilla, *Giovanni XXIII*, pp. 135-170.
[6] Gontard, p. 569.
[7] Capovilla, *Giovanni XXIII*, p. 746; cf. also Felici, p. 58 footnote.
[8] Zizola, pp. 317-318.
[9] Gorresio, p. 232.
[10] Capovilla, *Giovanni XXIII*, p. 352; cf. also p. 192.
[11] Zizola, pp. 317-318.
[12] Interview with Cardinal Koenig of Vienna in Chicago, November 12, 1974.
[13] Gorresio, p. 232 and Capovilla, *Giovanni XXIII*, pp. 265-266.
[14] Capovilla, *Giovanni XXIII*, pp. 265-268.
[15] Reported by Zizola, p. 320 (author's translation).
[16] Capovilla, *Giovanni XXIII*, p. 265.
[17] Zizola, pp. 331-332, citing Pericle Felici, "Il primo incontro con Papa Giovanni," *Osservatore Romano*, 3 June, 1973. Felici was the General Secretary of the Council and a central person in all connected with the undertaking.
[18] Cf. DMC 4:254-260.
[19] *Ibid.*, 4:258-259.
[20] John XXIII, *Journal*, p. 326.
[21] Cf. *Superno Dei nutu*, June 5, 1960, in Anderson, 1, p. 4.
[22] Gorresio, p. 232.
[23] DMC 4:259.

[24] Cf. e.g. Gorresio, p. 234 and Zizola, p. 331ff.

[25] Caprile, I, Pt. 2, 687-689: also cf. Giovanni Caprile, S.J., "Pio XII e un nuovo progetto di Concilio Ecumenico," *La Civiltà Cattolica*, 3 (1966), 209-227: and Gorresio, pp. 234-247.

[26] Zizola, pp. 325-326, and Svidercoschi, pp. 38-43.

[27] DMC 1, 805-838. English translation is taken from *Truth, Unity, Peace* (Washington DC: National Catholic Welfare Conference, 1959).

[28] *Ibid.*

Chapter 3

[1] Trevor, p. 246.

[2] Cf. Congar, *Le Concile Au Jour Le Jour*, pp. 15-18. Also, the name assumed by Popes John Paul I and II suggests that with Pope John something new started.

[3] John XXIII, *Journal*, from retreat of August, 1961, p. 303.

[4] *Ibid.*, p. 317.

[5] *Ibid.*, pp. 313, 314.

Chapter 4

[1] Capovilla, *Giovanni XXIII*, pp. 357-358.

[2] *Ibid.*, p. 487

[3] *Ibid.*

[4] Granzotto, *op. cit.*, pp. 22-25.

[5] Nichols, p. 176. Also, cf. Lai, passim.

[6] *Ibid.*, p. 127.

[7] Unpublished typescript of Curtis Bill Pepper, then chief of *Newsweek's* Rome bureau.

[8] Nichols, p. 176.

[9] DMC 3:818.

[10] Pallenberg, p. 95; Nichols, pp. 176-177.

[11] Nichols, p. 110.

[12] Lai, pp. 127-130.

[13] *Ibid.*, p. 266.

[14] *Ibid.*, p. 159 and Neuvecelle, p. 375.

[15] *Ibid.*

[16] Picker, p. 80, and Elliott, p. 274.

[17] Nichols, p. 110.

[18] John XXIII, *Journal*, p. 299.

[19] Nichols, p. 110.

[20] Felici, p. 119.

[21] Neuvecelle, p. 338.

Chapter 5

[1] For background cf. Elliot, pp. 281 ff.

[2] Roncalli, *Letters*, pp. 823-824 to his brother Zaverio and p. 825 to Enrica.

[3] Capovilla, *Pensieri*, p. 12.

[4] DMC 4:164-165.

[5] Capovilla, *Giovanni XXIII*, p. 174.

[6] Giovanni Caprile, "Un apporto decisivo alla Conoscenza del Concilio." *Osservatore Romano*, 20-21 January, 1975, p. 6.

[7] John XXIII, *Journal*, November 30-December 6, 1958, p. 296.

[8] Capovilla, *Giovanni XXIII*, p. 472.

[9] DMC 4:934.

[10] Purdy, pp. 166, 179.

[11] Interviews with Capovilla and Luigi Ligutti.

[12] Cf. *Pacem in terris*, art. 162.

[13] John XXIII, *Journal*, p. 313.

[14] The description is that of John Tracy Ellis.

[15] Fabretti, pp. 167-168.

[16] Pallenberg, *Inside the Vatican*, p. 213.

[17] Purdy, p. 197.

Chapter 6

[1] DMC 3:568.

[2] DMC 4:845.

[3] DMC 4:37.

[4] DMC 5:128.

[5] Translation of National Catholic Welfare Conference pamphlet, pp. 7-8. Repeated by John word for word on December 23, 1962 in an address to the College of Cardinals.

[6] Häring, pp. 39, 42, 69-78.

[7] Cf. Luigi Cevordi, "Insegnamento di un pontificato. La dignità della persona umana," *Osservatore Romano*, 12 June, 1963, p. 3.

[8] Trevor, p. 278.

[9] John XXIII, *Journal*, November 29-December 5, 1959, pp. 298-299. Also cf. DMC 1:40.

[10] DMC 4:207-208.

[11] Fogliasso, *Il Concilio*, p. 142.

[12] *Ibid.*, pp. 140-146, Pentecost Sunday, 1962.

[13] *Ibid.*, pp. 144-145.

[14] DMC 1:129.

[15] DMC 1:131-132. Cf. also DMC 3:24.

[16] DMC 4:588.

[17] Capovilla, *Giovanni XXIII*, p. 363.

[18] Fogliasso, *Il Concilio*, p. 67.

[19] DMC 1:132.

[20] *Ibid.*, 3:574-575.

[21] Consider Felici, pp. 125-126: "A word of John XXIII's which has been fortunate but not rarely has been misunderstood is "*aggiornamento*" of the Church.... The Church "aggiornaments" itself by nourishing itself on the true doctrine of Christ, enflaming itself with his love, respecting and obeying Christ's will and that of those who in the Church exercise authority in his name. Every concession to unstable human passions, to doctrines which "tickle men's ears," to the needs of a present situation which are not in keeping with the divine plan of salvation are not *aggiornamento* nor invigoration. Such rather make people old spiritually and are the ruin of the Church." (author's translation). Cf. also 284-285, 382-386.

[22] Cf. John W. O'Malley, "Reform, Historical Consciousness, and Vatican II's *Aggiornamento*," *Theological Studies,* 32 (December, 1971): 573-601.

[23] For theologian Bernard Lonergan, *aggiornamento* came to mean "a disengagement from a culture that no longer exists and an involvement in a distinct culture that has replaced it. Christians have been depicted as utterly otherworldly.... If the modern Church has stood aloof from the modern world, the fact is not too hard to explain. On the one hand, the Church's involvement in classicist culture was an involvement in a very limited view that totally underestimated the possibilities of cultural change and so precluded advertence to the need for adaptation and zeal to effect it. On the other hand, modern culture with its many excellences and its unprecedented achievements nonetheless is not just a realm of sweetness and light.... *Aggiornamento* is not desertion of the past but only a discerning and discriminating disengagement from its limitations. *Aggiornamento* is not just acceptance of the present: it is acknowledgment of its evils as well as of its good; and as acknowledgment alone is not enough, it also is, by the power of the cross, that meeting of evil with good which transforms evil into good." *A Second Collection* (Philadelphia: The Westminster Press, 1975), p. 113.

[24] Anderson, *Council Daybook,* vol. 1, p. 26.

[25] *Pacem in terris,* aa. 156 and 163.

[26] From *Humanae salutis* (translation from Anderson), vol. 1, pp. 7-8.

Chapter 7

[1] DMC 1:541-542 and 545.

[2] Fabbretti, p. 264.

[3] Capovilla, *Decennio....,* p. 7 and *XI Anniversario....,* p. 28 and *Giovanni XXIII,* p. 152.

[4] Fogliasso, *Il Concilio,* p. 234.

[5] DMC 1:740.

[6] DMC 5:241.

[7] Cf. Heston.

[8] Herder, p. 29.

[9] DMC 1:82.

[10] National Catholic Welfare Conference, translation (1959), p. 4.

[11] Yzermans, p. 97.

[12] Yves Congar, *Le Concile....,* *Deuxieme Session,* p. 44 and Gaul and Moosbrugger, p. 24.

[13] Capovilla, *Giovanni XXIII,* p. 193.

[14] John XXIII, *Journal,* entry for August 13, 1961, p. 309.

[15] Cf. Rouquette, pp. 169 ff.; Trevor, pp. 276-277; and Wenger, pp. 86-87.

[16] DMC 4:147.

[17] DMC 4:161-172. Cf. DMC 4:877-885.

[18] *Ibid.,* 5:5-6.

[19] Bolté, vol. 1, p. 7.

[20] Some listings number eight, including in the count John's 1959 Encyclical Epistle on the Rosary and his 1960 Apostolic Epistle on the Precious Blood devotion.

[21] Bolté, vol. 1, p. xii.

[22] DMC 3:295-296.

[23] Zizola, pp. 27-28.

[24] DMC 3:342.

Chapter 8

1   Cf. Desmond O'Grady, *Amleto Cardinal Cicognani* in Novak, ed., *The Men Who Made the Council,* 1964. The following is also based on information gathered in several interviews. Cf. also *Informacion Catholique Internationale,* August-September, 1961.

2   Nichols, pp. 117-118, and Gorresio, pp. 165-166.

3   Cf. Nichols, pp. 117-118, and Gorresio, pp. 165-166.

4   Lai, p. 395.

5   John XXIII, *Journal,* pp. 302-19. All of the citations on the following pages are taken from this section of Pope John's *Journal* unless otherwise noted.

6   *Ibid.,* p. 303.

7   *Ibid.,* p. 306.

8   *Ibid.,* p. 318, note 2.

9   *Ibid.,* p. 304.

10 *Ibid.,* p. 307.

11 *Ibid.,* p. 311.

12 *Ibid.,* p. 312.

13 *Ibid.*

14 *Ibid.,* p. 313.

15 *Ibid.*

16 *Ibid.,* p. 315.

17 *Ibid.,* p. 305.

18 *Ibid.*

19 *Ibid.,* p. 308.

20 *Ibid.,* p. 310.

21 *Ibid.,* pp. 307-309.

22 *Ibid.,* p. 309.

23 *Ibid.,* pp. 309-310.

24 Gorresio, pp. 168-169.

25 DMC 3:818-820.

26 John XXIII, *Journal,* p. 317.

27 Bergerre, p. 80.

28 "A questo scemo, tutto gli va bene!" and "Questo non capisce, ma tutto gli va bene!" were phrases frequently muttered by Cardinal Tardini in the halls of the Secretariat of State according to a confidential source within the Vatican.

29 John XXIII, *Journal,* p. 317.

Part II

Chapter 1

1   For background, cf. Svidercoschi, pp. 38-43, and Caprile, I, Pt. 1:39-103.

2   DMC 1:132-133. The quotation here follows what Pope John said — which, as noted, differs from what was published.

3   Svidercoschi, p. 39.

4   Cf. Svidercoschi, pp. 39-40, and Caprile, I, Pt. 1:107-108. note 1.

5   Bea, *Ecumenism in Focus,* p. 24.

6   Cited by Bea, *ibid.,* p. 26.

7   *Ibid.,* p. 25.

8   Bea, *The Unity of Christians,* pp. 157-174 and *Ecumenism in Focus,* pp. 28-30.

9   Cf. Stefan Schmidt, "Il cardinale Agostino Bea," *La Civiltà Cattolica,* 1 (1969): 8-20 and Novak, no. 1 (by Bernard Leeming).

10 Anderson, 1:15.

11 Interview with Stefan Schmidt, S.J.

12 Bea, *Unity in Freedom,* p. 158.

13 *Ibid.,* pp. 36-37.

14 *Ibid.,* pp. 98-99.

15 *Ibid.,* p. 36.

16 Rynne, p. 575 note.

17 Bea, *Unity in Freedom,* p. 71.

18 Falconi, *The Popes,* p. 333.

19 Bea, *Unity in Freedom,* p. 158.

20 Caprile, I, Pt. 1:176.

21 Interview with Fr. John Long, Secretariat for Christian Unity, Rome, February 5, 1975. Cf. Tanzella, p. 375.

22 Cf. Anderson, vol. 1, p. 8.

23 Bea, *Ecumenism in Focus,* pp. 40-41.

24 *Pacem in terris,* a. 162.

Chapter 2

1   Cf. Caprile, I, Pt. 2:343 ff., Rouquette, pp. 73-78 and Algisi, p. 273.

2   Caprile, I, Pt. 2:339, and Gorresio, p. 138.

3   Capovilla, *Pensieri,* p. 12.

4   *Ibid.*

5   John XXIII, *Journal,* p. 299.

6   Kaiser, p. 69.

7   DMC 2:392.

8   Caprile, I, Pt. 2:164.

9   DMC 1:335.

10 Zizola, p. 332.

11 Caprile, I, Pt. 2:164.

12 Cf. *Osservatore della domenica,* p. 21, cited by Caprile 1, Pt. 1:166, note 3; Caprile 1, Pt. 1:164-165; and Lai, p. 86.

13 *Ibid.,* p. 173.

14 Rouquette, pp. 95-96.

15 Lawrence Purcell, "The Priest as Builder of Christian Community" (Rome: Pontifical Gregorian University, 1974), pp. 72-75 (typewritten), and Giovanni Caprile, "Un apporto decisivo alla conoscenza del concilio," *Osservatore Romano,* 20-21 January, 1975, p. 6.

16 Rouquette, p. 94.

17 Caprile, I, Pt. 1:181.

18 *Ibid.*

19 *Ibid.*

20 Anderson, 1:4.

21 *Ibid.*

22 *Ibid.,* p. 5.

23 *Ibid.*

24 MacEoin, p. 29.

25 *Ibid.,* pp. 393-394.

26 *Ibid.,* p. 395.

27 DMC 2:390-402.

28 *Ibid.*

29 Cf. Caprile, I, Pt. 1:192.

30 Caprile, I, Pt. 1:174.

31 Falconi, *The Popes,* p. 329.

32 Felici, pp. 19, 27.

33 DMC 3:18-19.

34 DMC 3:21.

35 DMC 3:24.

36 Cf. DMC 3:322-325.

37 Cf. DMC 3:328-332.

38 Cf. William Manchester, *The Glory and the Dream,* 2 vols. (Boston: Little, Brown & Co., 1974), vol. 2, pp. 1118-1119.

39 DMC 3:408.

40 *Ibid.*

41 Manchester, *op. cit.,* p. 119.

42 Zizola, pp. 65-66.

43 DMC 4:384-390.

44 *Ibid.,* p. 323.

45 *Ibid.,* p. 325.

46 *Ibid.,* pp. 325-326.

47 *Ibid.*

48 DMC 4:555 ff.

49 DMC 4:302-303.

50 DMC 4:302-305.

51 Personal interview (Todi, Italy, February 27-28, 1975) with Curtis Bill Pepper, *Newsweek's* Roman correspondent at the time of the Council.

52 Antoine Wenger, *Vatican II Premiere Session* (Paris: Editions du Cerf, 1963), p. 32.

53 Galli and Moosbrugger, p. 63.

54 Karl Rahner, *The Church after the Council* (New York: Herder & Herder, 1966), pp. 16-17, and Bull, p. 78.

55 Goresssio, p. 282.

56 *Ibid.*

57 Falconi, *Pope John,* pp. 164, 168-169.

58 Falconi, *The Popes,* pp. 330-331.

59 Bea, *Unity in Freedom,* pp. 59-61.

60 *Ibid.*

61 Cf. articles by Indro Montonelli in *Corriere della Sera,* November 24, 25, 26, 1962.

62 Zizola, p. 239.

63 Bea, *Unity in Freedom,* p. 55.

64 Cf. Roquette, pp. 472-475; Falconi, *Pope John,* pp. 245-253, 280-288; Rynne, pp. 34-38.

[65] Rynne, p. 34.

[66] *Ibid.*, pp. 36-37.

[67] Purdy, p. 302.

[68] Zizola, pp. 343-344.

[69] Cf. DMC 4:519-528, and Anderson, 1:18-21.

[70] Cf. DMC 4:574-590, and Anderson, 1:25-30.

[71] Herder, p. 198.

[72] Anderson, 1:25.

[73] *Ibid.*, p. 26.

[74] *Ibid.*, p. 27.

[75] *Ibid.*, p. 28.

[76] *Ibid.*, p. 28.

[77] Capovilla, *Heart and Mind,* p. 133.

[78] Cf. Capovilla, *Giovanni XXIII*, pp. 149-151.

[79] Purdy, p. 303.

[80] Cf. Charles Reymondon and Luc A. Richard, *Vatican II au Travail* (France: Maison Mame, 1965), pp. 1-111 passim.

[81] Cited by Wenger, *Vatican II Premiere Session,* p. 49.

[82] Caprile, II, Pt. 1:179.

[83] Yzermans, pp. 147-149.

[84] Bea, *Unity in Freedom*, p. 55.

[85] Cf. Capovilla, *Giovanni XXIII,* pp. 446-485 passim.

Chapter 3

[1] John XXIII, *Journal,* pp. 283-284.

[2] Balducci, p. 237.

[3] Others count 26 state visits to Pius XII and 34 to Pope John.

[4] John XXIII, *Journal,* p. 308.

[5] Zizola, pp. 165-167.

[6] John XXIII, *Journal,* p. 308 (notes from retreat in August, 1961).

[7] The author was a student in Washington at the time and remembers being instructed to purchase supplies of canned goods and to learn evacuation routes.

[8] Zizola, pp. 210-211.

[9] *Pacem in terris,* art. 158. Translation from *Seven Great Encyclicals* (Glen Rock, NJ: Paulist Press, 1963), pp. 322-323.

[10] *Ibid.*, p. 323.

[11] Herder, p. 30.

[12] Cousins, pp. 122-126.

[13] The Balzan Prizes may be compared to the Nobel Prizes in their international scope but are obviously less prestigious than the Nobel awards. The 1978 Balzan Prize for human kindness, peace and brotherhood was awarded to Mother Teresa of Calcutta. The prize, worth about $300,000, is awarded by a committee of Western Europeans.

[14] Capovilla, *Giovanni XXIII,* p. 475.

Conclusion

1   Novak, p. 20.

2   Giuseppe DeLuca, *Giovanni XXIII in alcuni scritti di Don Giuseppe DeLuca* (Brescia: Casa Editrice Marcelliana, n.d.), p. 9 (author's translation).

3   Cf. Lercaro and De Rosa, p. 25.

4   John XXIII, *Journal,* notes for August 10, 1961, p. 303.

5   *Ibid.,* notes of December, 1947, p. 268. Cf. also Capovilla, *Giovanni XXIII,* p. 370.

6   John XXIII, *Journal,* pp. 278-279, notes of April, 1952. The theme of simplicity is a frequent one throughout this section of the *Journal.*

7   DMC 1:545.

8   Capovilla, *Giovanni XXIII,* p. 181.

9   Unpublished reports of Curtis Bill Pepper and interview with same: Todi, Italy, February 27-28, 1975.

10   Anderson, 1:34-35; cf. Yzermans, p. 95, and Trevor, p. 281.

11   Zizola, *L'Utopia,* pp. 217-219.

12   Cf. Capovilla, *Giovanni XXIII,* p. 227.

13   *Ibid.,* p. 241.

14   L'Arco, p. 8.

15   Capovilla, *Giovanni XXIII,* p. 418.

16   Author's interview with Fr. Edward Malatesta, February, 1975, Rome.

17   John P. Donnelly, ed., *Breviarii Papa Giovanni* (Italy: Adlo Garzcorti Editore, 1966), p. 53, translation.

18   Capovilla, *X Anniversario,* p. 32.

19   Cf. Capovilla, *The Heart and Mind,* p. 29.

20   John XXIII, *Journal,* p. 299.

21   Fesquet, *Wit and Wisdom,* p. 166.

22   John XXIII, *Journal,* p. 321.

Selected Bibliography

Documents

Abbott, Walter M., ed. *The Documents of Vatican II.* New York: Guild Press, 1966.

Acta Apostolicae Sedis. Vatican: Vatican Polyglot Press, yearly.

Acta et Documenta Concilio Oecumenico Vaticano II Apparando. Series I, II. 7 vols. 23 tomes. Vatican: Vatican Polyglot Press, 1960-64.

Acta Synodalia Sacrosancti Concilii Oecumenici Vaticani II. 12 vols. Vatican: Typis Polyglottis Vaticanis, 1970.

Discorsi, Messagi, Colloqui del Santo Padre Giovanni XXIII. 6 vols. Vatican: Vatican Polyglot Press, 1958-1963.

Books

Abbott, Walter M. *Twelve Council Fathers:* New York: Macmillan Co., 1963.

Alberigo, Giuseppe, et al, eds. *The Reception of Vatican II.* Washington, DC: Catholic University of America Press, 1988.

Alberigo, Giuseppe, and Komonchak, Joseph A., eds. *The History of Vatican II,* Vols. I & II. Maryknoll, NY: Orbis Books, 1996, 1997.

Algisi, Leone. *John XXIII.* Westminster, MD: Newman Press, 1963.

Anderson, Floyd, ed. *Council Daybook: Vatican II.* 3 vols. Washington, DC: National Catholic Welfare Conference, 1965.

Balducci, Ernesto. *John "The Transitional Pope."* New York: McGraw-Hill, 1964.

Bea, Augustin. *Ecumenism in Focus.* London: Geoffrey Chapman, 1969.

_____. *The Unity of Christians.* New York: Herder & Herder, 1963.

_____. *The Way to Unity after the Council.* New York: Herder & Herder, 1963.

_____. *Unity in Freedom.* New York: Harper and Row, 1964.

Benigni, Mario, and Zanchi, Goffredo. *John XXIII: The Official Biography.* Boston: Pauline Books & Media, 2001.

Bolté, Paul-Emile. *Mater et Magistra: Texte, Commentaire.* 4 vols. Montreal: University of Montreal, 1964.

Bonnot, Bernard R. *Pope John XXIII: An Astute, Pastoral Leader.* Staten Island, NY: Alba House, 1979.

Bull, George. *Vatican Politics.* London: Oxford University Press, 1966.

Cahill, Thomas. *Pope John XXIII.* New York: Viking Penguin, 2002.

Capovilla, Loris C. *Giovanni XXIII: Quindici Letture.* Roma: Edizioni di Storia e Letteratura, 1970.

_____. *The Heart and Mind of John XXIII.* New York: Hawthorn, 1964.

Caprile, Giovanni, S.J. *Il Concilio Vaticano II.* 5 vols. Roma: Edizioni "La Civiltà Cattolica," 1966.

Congar, Yves M.J. *Le Concile Au Jour Le Jour.* Paris: Editions du Cerf, 1963.

_____. *Le Concile Au Jour, Deuxieme Session.* Paris: Editions du Cerf, 1964.

Cousins, Norman. *The Improbable Triumvirate.* New York: W.W. Norton & Co., 1972.

Elliott, Lawrence. *I Will Be Called John.* New York: Berkley Medallion Books, 1973.

Fabretti, Nazareno. *Giovanni XXIII e il Concilio.* Vicenza: La Locusta, 1963.

Falconi, Carlo. *Il Pentagono Vaticano.* Bari: Editori Laterza, 1958.

_____. *Pope John and the Ecumenical Council.* Cleveland: World Publishing, 1964.

_____. *The Popes in the Twentieth Century.* London: Weidenfeld & Nicolson, 1967.

Feldman, Christian. *Pope John XXIII: A Spiritual Biography.* New York, Crossroad, 2002.

Felici, Pericle. *Il Lungo Cammino del Concilio.* Milano: Editore Ancora, 1967.

Fesquet, Henri. *The Drama of Vatican II.* New York: Random House, 1967.

_____. *Wit and Wisdom of Good Pope John.* New York: P.J. Kenedy & Sons, 1964.

Fogliasso, Emilio. *Il Concilio Ecumenico Vatican II nella Vita del Santo Padre Giovanni XXIII.* Roma: Pontificio Ateneo Salesiano, 1962.

_____. *L'Enciclical "Mater et Magistra" nella mente e nel cuore di Giovanni XXIII.* Roma: Pontificio Ateneo Salesiano, 1961.

_____. *Papa Giovanni: spiega come giunse alla "Pacem in terris."* Roma: Pontificio Ateneo Salesiano, 1964.

Galli, Mario von, and Moosbrugger, Bernard. *The Council and the Future.* New York: McGraw-Hill, 1966.

Gontard, Friedrich. *The Chair of Peter: A History of the Papacy.* New York: Holt, Rinehart and Winston, 1964.

Gorresio, Vittorio. *The New Mission of Pope John XXIII.* New York: Funk & Wagnalls, 1970.

Hales, E.E.Y. *The Catholic Church in the Modern World.* New York: Doubleday Image Books, 1960.

_____. *Pope John and His Revolution,* New York: Doubleday Image Books, 1965.

Häring, Bernard. *The Joannine Council.* New York: Herder & Herder, 1963.

Hatch, Alden. *A Man Named John.* New York: Hawthorn, 1963.

Hebblethwaite, Peter. *John XXIII: Pope of the Century.* Revised by Margaret Hebblethwaite. London and New York: Continuum, 2000.

Herder Correspondence Editors. *John XXIII.* New York: Herder & Herder, 1965.

_____. *John XXIII in World Opinion.* Rome: Herder & Herder, 1963.

Heston, Edward L. *Notes on Vatican II.* Notre Dame: Ave Maria Press, 1966.

_____. *The Press and Vatican II.* Notre Dame: University of Notre Dame Press, 1967.

Hughes, Philip. *The Church in Crisis: A History of the General Councils, 325-1870.* New York: Hanover House, 1960.

Johnson, Paul. *Pope John XXIII.* Boston: Little, Brown & Co., 1974.

John XXIII, Pope. *Journal of a Soul.* New York: McGraw-Hill Book Co., 1965.

Küng, Hans. *The Council in Action.* New York: Sheed & Ward, 1963.

Lai, Benny. *Vaticano aperto.* Milano: Longanesi & Co., 1968.

Lercaro, Giacomo, and DeRosa, Gabriele. *John XXIII: Simpleton or Saint?* Chicago: Franciscan Herald Press, 1967.

LoBello, Nino. *The Vatican Empire.* New York: Trident Press, 1968.

MacEoin, Gary. *What Happened at Rome?* New York: Holt, Reinhart & Winston, 1966.

Martin, Malachi. *Three Popes and the Cardinal.* New York: Farrar, Strauss & Giroux, 1972.

Neuvecelle, Jean. *Giovanni XXIII.* Milano: Valentino Bonipiani, 1970.

Nichols, Peter. *The Politics of the Vatican.* New York: Fredrick A. Praeger, 1968.

Novak, Michael, ed. *Men Who Made the Council.* 12 booklets. Notre Dame: University of Notre Dame Press, 1964.

O'Dea, Thomas F. *The Catholic Crisis.* Boston: Beacon Press, 1968.

Pallenberg, Corrado. *Inside the Vatican.* New York: Hawthorn, 1960.

Purdy, W.A. *The Church on the Move.* London: Hollis & Carter, 1966.

Rynne, Xavier. *Vatican Council II.* New York: Farrar, Strauss & Giroux, 1968.

Roncalli, Angelo Giuseppe. *Letters to His Family.* New York: McGraw-Hill, 1970.

_____. *My Bishop: A Portrait of Msgr. Giacomo Maria Radini Tedeschi.* London: Geoffrey Chapman, 1965.

Rouquette, Robert. *La fin d'une Chretienté.* 2 vols. Paris: Les Editions du Cerf, 1968.

Svidercoschi, Gian Franco. *Storia del Concilio.* Milano: Editrice Ancora, 1967.

Tanzella, Paolo. *Papa Giovanni.* Andria, Italy: Edizioni Dehoniane, 1973.

Tardini, Domenico. *Memories of Pius XII.* Westminster, MD: Newman Press, 1961.

Trevor, Meriol. *Pope John.* New York: Doubleday & Co., 1967.

Wall, Bernard. *Report on the Vatican.* London: Weidenfeld & Nicolson, 1956.

Wenger, Antoine. *Vatican II: The First Session.* Westminster, MD: Newman Press, 1966.

_____. *Vatican II: Premiere Session.* Paris: Editions du Cerf, 1963.

Wiltgen, Ralph W. *The Rhine Flows into the Tiber.* New York: Hawthorn, 1967.

Yzermans, Vincent A. *A New Pentecost.* Westminster, MD: Newman Press, 1963.

Zizzola, Giancarlo. *L'Utopia di Papa Giovanni.* Rev. 2d ed. Assisi: Cittadella Editrice, 1974.

Articles and Periodicals

Aubert, Roger. "Jean XXIII, un 'pape de transition' qui marquera dans l'histoire." *La Revue Nouvelle,* July-August, 1963, pp. 3-33.

Bea, Augustin. "Il Segratariato per l'unione dei Cristiani." *La Rivista del Clero Italiano,* 46 (November, 1965), pp. 3-12.

Caprile, Giovanni. "Aspetti positivi della terza sessione del Concilio." *La Civiltà Cattolica,* 1 (1965), pp. 317-24.

_____. "In Memoria di Giovanni XXIII: Richezza di un breve pontificato." *La Civiltà Cattolica,* 1 (1963).

Schmidt, Stefan. "Il Cardinale Agostino Bea." *La Civiltà Cattolica,* 1 (1964), pp. 8-20.

INDEX

ST PAULS

This book was produced by St. Pauls/Alba House, the Society of St. Paul, an international religious congregation of priests and brothers dedicated to serving the Church through the communications media.

For information regarding this and associated ministries of the Pauline Family of Congregations, write to the Vocation Director, Society of St. Paul, P.O. Box 189, 9531 Akron-Canfield Road, Canfield, Ohio 44406-0189. Phone (330) 702-0359; or E-mail: spvocationoffice@aol.com or check our internet site, WWW.ALBAHOUSE.ORG